ALASTAIR SAWDAY'S
SPECIAL PLACES TO STAY

MOROCCO

Design: Caroline King

Maps & Mapping: Bartholomew Mapping, a division of HarperCollins, Glasgow

Printing: Canale, Italy

UK Distribution: Portfolio, Greenford, Middlesex

US Distribution: The Globe Pequot Press, Guilford, Connecticut

Published in November 2003

Alastair Sawday Publishing Co. Ltd
The Home Farm Stables, Barrow Gurney, Bristol BS48 3RW
Tel: +44 (0)1275 464891 Fax: +44 (0)1275 464887
E-mail: info@specialplacestostay.com Web: www.specialplacestostay.com

The Globe Pequot Press
P. O. Box 480, Guilford, Connecticut 06437, USA
Tel: +1 203 458 4500 Fax: +1 203 458 4601
E-mail: info@globe-pequot.com Web: www.GlobePequot.com

First edition

Copyright © 2003 Alastair Sawday Publishing Co. Ltd

ISBN 1-901970-35-3 in the UK
ISBN 0-7627-2859-0 in the US

Printed in Italy

A WORD FROM
ALASTAIR SAWDAY

'Events' have kept some of us away from Morocco for two years – understandably if irrationally. In her delightful introduction, Ann Cooke-Yarborough quotes her own and Barnaby Rogerson's experience and writes of the unique religious tolerance of the Moroccans, encouraging the pursuit of the many different paths to God. It is a reminder, perhaps, of the great civilisation that flowered in southern Spain under the Moors for so many hundreds of years. Indeed, there is much in Morocco to remind you of those connections.

Now that we have created this irresistible book, there is no excuse to stay away – for Morocco has more colour, light, warmth, interest and unparalleled beauty than we can grasp in a lifetime. You will be welcomed, cosseted, inspired and moved – for the people of Morocco have learned over centuries how to co-exist with foreigners and to make them part, even, of their own culture. We may know of the cultured European gentlemen who took root in Tangier and Marrakech in recent centuries; we will certainly know of the French and their cultured, if colonial, fascination with Morocco. They stayed, and learned, and grew wiser. You will too.

For your first visit you might try taking the ferry from Algeciras in southern Spain to Tangier and its region for a few days. It would, apart from anything else, be a fine way of connecting the two cultures after seeing so much of North Africa in Andalucia. I would urge you, too, to follow Ann's advice and spend time elsewhere, for Morocco must be allowed to seduce you.

Alastair Sawday

ACKNOWLEDGEMENTS

Working on a guide to a new country and a new culture is a new challenge for us. This is only our second foray beyond Europe (after India) but is has been richly rewarding – not least because we found a team of two in Marrakech with the knowledge of the territory, people and customs that we lacked: Alain Bonnassieux and his assistant Ismaïl Nadm.

Without them, this book would not be what it is, would not include so many places to stay as yet unknown to other guides, would not have the benefit of local insight. They battled against dilatory humans and hostile heatwaves, not to mention serious illness, to bring us the meat for this sandwich – I thank them.

However, the guiding spirit behind this enterprise has been the indefatigable, the deeply talented and inexhaustibly patient Ann Cooke-Yarborough. She has nursed her Moroccan crew through the vicissitudes of their voyage and has calmly steered this little ship into harbour. (Her husband, Brendan, has expertly puffed a little wind into the sails at crucial moments, I know.) The administration – and it was daunting – was hers and so is the writing. For this we give thanks, for to have Ann writing is to guarantee a vivid, sensitively crafted book that will be a pleasure for all to read and use.

Alastair Sawday

Series Editor:	Alastair Sawday
Editor:	Ann Cooke-Yarborough
Co-editor:	Alain Bonnassieux
Editorial Director:	Annie Shillito
Production Manager:	Julia Richardson
Web & IT:	Russell Wilkinson, Matt Kenefick
Copy Editor:	Jo Boissevain
Editorial:	Roanne Finch, Toby Sawday
Production Assistants:	Rachel Coe, Paul Groom, Beth Thomas
Accounts:	Jenny Purdy
Sales, Marketing & PR:	Siobhan Flynn, Paula Brown, Sarah Bolton
Writing:	Ann Cooke-Yarborough
Inspections & photographs:	Ann Cooke-Yarborough, Alain Bonnassieux, James Boyd, Annie & Quentin Craven, Guy Hunter-Watts, Ismaïl Nadm
Histories of Morocco & Islam:	Barnaby Rogerson
Watercolours:	Miloudi Nouiga
Photographs:	Jacques Paul, Pierre-Alain Renfer
Arabic scripts:	Ali M Reza

ACKNOWLEDGEMENTS

Launching into a guide to places to stay in this unknown land with only my 35 years in France, the non-Arab country that must be closest to Morocco, and an enduring love of Andalucia and its Moorish legacies was brave – or foolhardy – to a degree. It has been an amazing journey of discovery and delight along the smooth bits with some tense moments in the potholes. This book would not have seen the day in its present form without Alain Bonnassieux, his intimate knowledge of the terrain and his constant enthusiasm, or Ismaïl Nadm, his able and tireless assistant – I know the trouble they took and am deeply grateful to them both.

I must also thank Brendan Flanagan for his love and unflagging support, help and advice through thick and thin. This book owes more to him that I can say.

Lastly, a special word for Julia Richardson: her forbearance and unfailing good humour at all times made the last weeks possible.

Jacques Paul provided many of the photographs. After painting in monochrome for 15 years he was converted to photography by the light and colours of Morocco; then, after 15,000 pictures taken in rural markets, he decided to specialise in interiors. (Tel: +212 (0)61 10 52 20)

Miloudi Nouiga, whose watercolours capture some of the essential atmospheres of Morocco, kindly let us use a selection. Others hang in his gallery in the Kasbah des Oudayas in Rabat. (2 rue Jamaa. Tel: +212 (0)37 70 1763)

Our thanks for their help in researching and compiling this guide:
Pascale and Alain Robinot, Riad Al Zahia, Essaouira
Jalil El Hayar, Riad Zyriab, Fès
Michel Trezzy, Riad Mabrouka, Fès
Jean-Luc Lemée, Riad Malika, Marrakech
Naïma Kamal, Casablanca
MC Voyages, Marrakech

For advice and recommendations:
Vincent Fauveau, Elena Posa and Ferran Grau, Rosalind Grimshaw, Gary Martin,

Ann Cooke-Yarborough

WHAT'S IN THE BOOK?

CONTENTS

INTRODUCTION

Differences

"The distance from the bustle of the city was welcome, although the initial drive there was mildly alarming as we swooped off the road onto a mile of rutted mud... not helped by the driver himself getting lost and stopping to ask various hooded figures the way. All doubts were eliminated as we finally arrived at the small door in the mud wall, were welcomed into a beautiful maze of small courtyards and let into our room strewn with rose petals." **Colin Cameron, BBC**

Be prepared for contrasts of all sorts, look forward to the unexpected and learn to trust those hooded figures – not sinister, just well protected against the contrasted and unpredictable elements. Marshal Lyautey, first French Resident General in 1912, defined Morocco as *"un pays froid au soleil brulant"* (a cold country with a burning hot sun).

And decide from the start to take time. Morocco cannot be rushed. The country and the people are open to those who adapt to their rhythms and don't dash headlong from sightseeing to bracelet-buying to eating 'fast Moroccan'. If this is your first visit, the initial culture shock will probably last a while – it is very different. If you find yourself recoiling from the gaudy cacophany and thronging smells of the city, slow down instead of running away, take the time to stand aside and watch. Look for patterns, gestures and expressions that reveal how things work, how people interact. You need to connect into a new set of behaviours. Once you begin to sense the order in this apparent chaos, you will relax, others will notice that you have opened up and your senses of humanity and humour will take you inside the picture. Then you may fall for ever under the enchantment.

History, culture and religion

Because Morocco is North African and Islamic, both of which many of our readers probably know less well than they know Europe or North America, Christianity or Judaism, we have included a brief history of the country and an introduction to Islam by Morocco expert Barnaby Rogerson. You will find them at the back of the book. Meanwhile, here is what he says about contemporary Moroccan attitudes to the other two 'Mediterranean' religions.

INTRODUCTION

Morocco is a determinedly Muslim nation. It is also an example
to the rest of the Muslim world in the tolerance and hospitality
offered to other religions and cultures. There are still as many
church spires as minarets on the Tangier skyline to baffle a
traveller on that first approach into this famous port-city.
Just above the main square, among tombs and trees, stands
an elegant Anglican church built in the Moorish style with
the Lord's Prayer carved in Arabic script on the chancel arch.
On my last visit the linen-suited expatriate congregation was
completely swamped by Nigerians who, working their way up
the continent (planning to enter Europe illegally), had stopped
off in this home from home.

Away from the grand boulevards of Rabat and Casablanca, it is
still possible to attend mass in a Roman Catholic cathedral as
the call of the muezzin echoes through the whitewashed naves.
Many thousands of Moroccan Jews continue to worship in their
venerable synagogues, maintaining the old Hebrew cemeteries
found in every ancient city as well as the shrine-tombs of saintly
rabbis scattered over the most inaccessible mountain valleys.
Every year – especially during the 'Jewish festival' months of
March and October – more thousands of Jews of Moroccan
descent are welcomed back as pilgrim-tourists. They have an
easy time at the immigration desk for even though they might
now live in Tel Aviv or New York, the Kingdom of Morocco has
never withdrawn their passports, believing that some time they
will return 'home'.

This tolerance is a testament to the Muslim faith of Morocco
and in strict conformity to the Prophet's injunction to honour
the "peoples of the Book", the Jews and Christians who, like
Muslims, believe in one God, in honouring the scriptures,
obeying the laws of the prophets and leading an ethical life.

There was a wise old sheikh from northern Morocco who,
much to the scandal of his followers, had married an Englishwoman
and never attempted to persuade her to convert to Islam. To
explain his actions he would leave a cone of sugar in the centre
of the room and bid his followers to watch silently. Soon the
ants would discover this nectar and orderly columns would
start marching towards the white rock. The sheikh would
explain that just so are the peoples of the Book, dutifully
following their own paths, blissfully unaware of each other
as they ascend the mountain of sweetness.

INTRODUCTION

All Moroccans are expected to fast during Ramadan unless
too old, too young, pregnant or sick. The rule, if you are a
practising Muslim is no food, no drink, no smoking, no sex
between sunrise and sunset for one month. Families gather for
a 'break-fast' meal every evening and another before dawn.
This means less sleep – a lot less if Ramadan, a movable feast,
falls in summer – and considerable hardship as the day wears
on. But they soldier on, keep smiling and looking forward to
the traditional harira soup. Most cafés, bars and licensed grocers
close for the month and sensitive non-Muslims will refrain from
smoking, eating or drinking in public.

We have divided the country into the four essential areas of
Moroccan geography and culture, then into 14 sub-sections based
on a logic for touring.

The Atlantic Region

Despite our Euro-centric conceptions, Morocco is an Atlantic
rather than a Mediterranean country with a seaboard that runs for
over 2,000km and land that produces most of the country's food.

Marrakech & its region

A cultural rather than a geographical area that drains over half
Morocco's tourist traffic and has the highest density of places to
stay; the ultimate must, it alone occupies 40 per cent of this book.

The Atlas Ranges

The great central mountain mass, the second geographical area
of Morocco, has played a major part in her history.

The South

Lastly, the desert and the oases, the harsh and the gentle that
have forged the character and wealth of the region's inhabitants,
as well as the history of the whole country.

What to expect

Staying in this country of extremes can take you from the
luxuriously sublime to the ridiculously simple, from the
grand hotel of legend for that near-celebrity experience to the
roadside inn with the most human warmth and the least
facilities. 'Special' does not mean perfect, it means that
something makes a place stand out – it may be its architecture,
position, people, interior design or history. In our wide
selection of places, most of them classified as guest houses of

INTRODUCTION

varying sizes and degrees of luxury, we hope to have made the
differences clear in the descriptions so that you will not choose a
place that doesn't suit you.

Contact and bookings

Most bookings can be made by e-mail, telephone or fax direct
to Morocco but read the entry carefully: some owners only
accept fax or on-line bookings, others give a French, Spanish or
British telephone number (codes +33, +34, +44 respectively)
alongside the local number. Telephones are not always reliable
so some owners have more than one line and a mobile number.
The national code is 212; all Moroccan numbers start with 0
(for inland calls, not to be used when calling from abroad.)
followed by eight digits. Mobile numbers start with 06.
Numbers given here follow on without repeating identical
elements. e.g.:

+212 (0)44 44 55 55/77 77/66 55 55 66

+ : your international code} for use when calling from outside Morocco

212 code for Morocco   }

(0) dial only if calling from within Morocco

44 44 55 55   the owner's first land-line which reads in full
(0)44 44 55 55

/77 77   the owner's second land-line which reads in full
(0)44 44 77 77

/66 55 55 66 the owner's mobile number which reads in full
(0)66 55 55 66

Rooms and bathrooms

We tell you the types of rooms available (doubles, twins, suites,
etc). Unless otherwise stated, they have their own bath or shower
with wc, and suites are for two people. Given the country's
limited water supply, showers are the rule, baths the exception.
It may be possible to add beds for children; ask when booking.

Prices

The basic price listed is for a room for two for one night with
breakfast, unless otherwise stated. If breakfast is not included,
its price will appear under Meals. Prices are often negotiable,
especially outside the spring and Christmas/New Year peaks.
Many places offer terms for children, half or full board, long
stays, etc., or package deals with desert treks, spa treatments,

INTRODUCTION

golf. Ask when booking. Some prices are quoted with local *taxe de séjour* included, others not. This small amount levied per guest per night by the town council might be added to your bill. The same goes for VAT. Published at the end of 2003, the prices printed here are liable to be altered at any time and most will be changed for autumn 2004.

Breakfast

Generally included in the price, it varies from basic continental to a feast that will have delicious little Moroccan pancakes, eggs and cheese and could set you up for the day.

Other meals in guest houses

Most guest houses employ a permanent cook and do dinner if you book in advance. The commonest menu is delicious mixed Moroccan salads followed by tagine or couscous then a pastry or fruit, but some houses pride themselves on real gourmet food. They will often do light lunches too, or pack a picnic. Small hotels in towns generally leave the provision of meals to their restaurant neighbours.

Meals in hotels

Tourism in Morocco is still very group-based and, in the south, mostly open-air. As a result, apparently small hotels may have intimate interiors for their residents but feeding space for coachloads in their gardens, so the bower where you had settled down for a quiet lunch beneath the acacia tree can suddenly be invaded by bevvies of excited tourists just in from the carpet bazaar who will have a quick lunch and be shepherded off to the next delight.

Alcoholic drinks

Some places sell wine (🦩), others allow you to bring you own (BYO); some say neither but this does not always mean no wine. In this constitutionally Islamic country, the situation is delicate. Some places will neither sell alcohol nor accept that guests bring it in. However, many guest houses and small hotels sell wine with meals but do not have a licence so cannot announce the fact. On the other hand, they want you to drink their wine – probably good and interesting Moroccan – rather than bring in something from the local supermarket. So please understand this before arriving with bags of clanking bottles and asking for a corkscrew.

INTRODUCTION

Directions

We have been as clear as possible but always check the itinerary when booking. Guest houses in the medinas can be hard to find for the first time and will arrange for someone to meet you at an agreed spot and escort you in. Thereafter, you will quickly learn the route – it's a great way of taming one corner of an inscrutable medina.

Out in the country, when we say, for example, 'from Marrakech for Amizmiz 24km...' this generally means that at or very near the 24km 'milestone' there will be a sign or a turning, so no need to worry about the exact distance from some undefined spot in Marrakech.

Disabled and limited mobility

Morocco is behind Europe and America in providing for the disabled but if rooms and especially bathrooms lack the specific equipment, the traditional architecture is in your favour: many places have a ground-floor bedroom and communal life is lived around the patio so once you have negotiated the two or three steps from the front door, it should be plain sailing.

Types of places to stay

Guest house: *Maisons d'hôtes* or B&B Moroccan style

The Moroccan breed of *maison d'hôtes* is comparable to no other I know and the English is an inadequate translation. They all employ permanent staff, the minimum being a handyman, a chambermaid and a cook. Remember, this is the country where the guest palace – *palais d'hôtes* – was invented.

In 2002, 93 per cent of guest houses in Morocco were owned by non-Moroccans. The owners may live elsewhere in the town, or even in another country, in which case they employ a good manager. This is still a new phenomenon, new houses are opening and old houses are changing hands fast, so some of our addresses are bound to have different owners and managers before the next edition is out (2005); others will have been sold to people who are not continuing the B&B activity. We have tried to include guest houses where the owners are present at least for the essential moments: arrival (when tea or a cool drink will probably be offered), aperitif time and possibly dinner if you are dining in, then breakfast the next day. Where the owners are more often absent than present, the atmosphere

INTRODUCTION

will be less immediately 'family' but managers and housekeepers, be they Moroccan or European, are generally friendly, knowledgeable and helpful – "smiling to break your heart".

The traditional architecture of a house with blank outside walls and welcoming courtyard inside usually means that bedrooms give onto the patio only. This makes the smaller riads and dars feel pretty intimate. It's always cooler on the ground floor than up under the roof. In big houses, rooms may be different sizes as the women's quarters were narrower and more secret than the men's quarters, where people from outside were received and a grander display was required.

Country inn – trekking place: travellers' resting place with a few rooms and a good family restaurant open to non-residents; or a relatively remote hostel/base camp for excursions and organised adventures into the desert or the mountains, possibly with an overnight bivouac; or the two combined.

Small hotel or *hôtel de charme*: place with presence and character; can have up to 50 rooms and widely differing levels of comfort and price.

Landmark hotel: a handful of palace hotels have become legends, places which have romantic images or high fashion status, places where you may meet Beautiful People from the world of film and design or the ghosts of long-dead literary giants. They are often very big.

Catered house: either a B&B guest house that can be rented exclusively by one group or family by the day or the week, or a flat or house that is only offered for sole occupancy. As the terms generally include breakfast and staff remain to do the cleaning and provide meals if you want, this doesn't really count as 'self-catering'. We give rental prices where available.

The advantage of having someone who asks you what you want to eat and then does the shopping needs no emphasising; you can even ask to go with her and see how it's done. If you reckon your catering for the week would come to 150, you will probably find that you can spend a little less here and have the work done for you. This could be a novel way of doing your annual family gathering.

INTRODUCTION

Even houses and flats let on a 'self-catering' basis will come with cleaning and laundry included, though the staff will be less present.

Staff

The men and women who staff the Moroccan places to stay are, almost without exception, charming, smiling, friendly and helpful without being obsequious. They hope guests will treat them with the same degree of respect and friendliness. Certain guest-house owners like them to wear the traditional jellabah, others are happy for them to work in civvies, though many women wear headscarves with their tee-shirt and trousers.

Bargaining, hassle and carpet sellers

Bargaining is part of the Moroccan way of life: you are expected to take time doing important things like spending your money. It is a sign of respect, not a nationwide tourist-fleecing plan, a way of civilised relating human to human, not a battle to the death. So relax, smile, enjoy it and aim to reduce most prices by about one third. And if you don't want an object, don't begin the process, however pressing your merchant may be. Use all your acting skills and be properly appreciative of his.

In towns other than Marrakech and Fès, where local police enforce the law against pestering people with offers of goods and services, you may be bothered by sellers of minerals, fossils, brasses, etc and by unofficial guides demanding to show you the sights. If it's your first visit, you may need an official guide. You can find one at the Tourist Office and he will 'protect' you against the others. Or you can choose the most honest-looking chap on the square – at your own risk. Any guide has commission agreements with merchants in the bazaars – but he does know his way around when you don't.

Carpet selling is not confined to shops or bazaars. We were asked by a 'hotel worker' in the Todra Gorge to drive him back to town for his three-weekly visit to his mother. On arrival, he offered us money which we naturally refused. This created a debt: he was obliged to return our generosity with tea at home, "just to meet my family and say goodbye". At 'home', we met his 'brother and sister'. They took us up to a big empty room with six looms round the walls – each with a work in progress – and the tea tray. Our hitch-hiker had vanished. Two hours, six cups of tea and dozens of carpets later, we left with two of the latter and minus a substantial cheque in euros.

Begging

Moroccans are generous with their beggar population – the Koran encourages believers to give money or at least a smile. We found it proper to follow their example. 1Dh is more than fair but smaller change is hard to come by. When you are guiltily and silently cursing the little children grabbing at your garments, their mothers sitting in corners with babes in their arms, their grandfathers chanting religious homilies to the rattle of a begging tin, it's worth remembering that the official minimum monthly wage is between 1,150Dh and 1,850Dh, (roughly 100-160 euros or dollars; no, I haven't dropped any noughts), that very many workers are not even paid this much and that unemployment is high. But don't give money to children.

Under the guidance of the Moroccan-European team at the Kasbah du Toubkal, the villagers of Imlil are teaching their children not to ask tourists for coins or pens or sweets and a neat little message is handed to guests reminding them that children who beg money or biros from foreigners are not in school. If you withhold the easy gift and contribute to the local school books fund instead, you will be helping those children learn their way to prosperity rather than beg their way to a lifetime of poverty.

The section on Conservation and Development at the end of this book gives ideas for useful contributions that should reach their proper destinations.

Women's dress

It is perhaps understandable that, as western women coming from decades of "if you've got it, flaunt it", we should initially feel uncomfortable, even rejected by being looked at askance in our normal clothes and hailed with *"gazelle! bonjour gazelle!"*. From the other side, some people rise in feminist fury at veiled women, though I have never heard anyone remark that the man in the jellabah is downtrodden and needs a defence society to save him from oppression.

Vive la différence! Our cultures, traditions and unwritten rules are different, neither better nor worse, just different, and if we want to reach into the very real cultural, aesthetic and human

INTRODUCTION

pleasures that Morocco offers us, including its simpler way of
life and lack of consumer frenzy, then we must be tolerant of
the ground rules of that simplicity. When I hear that rooftop
swimming pools are, in fact, only allowed if bathers in bikinis
cannot be seen from neighbouring roofs, I feel it is perfectly
reasonable: the Moroccan sense of decency is similar to ours
some 50 years ago. When I am told that bare midriffs, miniskirts
and shorts shock the inhabitants of the old Arab towns, I feel
that is reason enough for not wearing them in public.

In Moroccan towns, one sees women wearing a whole range
of dress, from smart hairdo and lipstick over trendy denim
trousers and jacket to tidy white scarf over designer suit to full
flowing robe, veil and black lace face mask (often competing
with a pair of glasses for space on the nose). Then I remember
that my grandmother would never have worn trousers but
found it perfectly all right that her daughter did and that her
grand-daughters wore skimpy bikinis in front of her friends. In
Morocco today, women are less hassled when soberly dressed
without too much skin showing.

Food and drink

Water People living here drink the water from their wells or
from their taps when they know it is safe but it is advisable to
stick to bottled water until you are acclimatised. Flat spring
water is *eau pure*, fizzy water is *eau gazeuse*. Waiters will
automatically bring you a big bottle unless you specify small.

Alcohol Consumption of alcohol, specifically wine, is forbidden
by the Koran. Morocco is an Islamic monarchy, the King is
a direct descendant of the Prophet Mohammed with the title
of Commander of the Faithful, and Moroccan Muslims are
theoretically forbidden to buy alcoholic drinks. In fact, only
hotels and guest houses may serve alcohol in the medinas but
bars, cafés and restaurants in other parts of town are often
licensed, though drinking alcohol out of doors is still prohibited.
A bottle of drinkable Moroccan table wine should cost about
100Dh in a restaurant.

Non-alcoholic specialities Mint tea, the national drink, is
offered as "Moroccan whisky" by gently-smiling half-apologetic
waiters; it comes with excessive amounts of sugar – you can ask
for *sucre à part* (sugar separate) and dose your own – and it can

INTRODUCTION

turn out to be an unexpected pep-up. They may offer many other drinks with healing properties. Try their herbal infusions, especially *romarin* or *thym* (rosemary or thyme) for an upset stomach. Alternatively, if you choose *thé noir* it will most probably be that familiar yellow-labelled echo of tea.

The freshly-squeezed juice of several oranges is a recurring delight – you should get it for breakfast and find it at market stalls or in any café when you collapse from sights-overload.

Food Moroccan food can be remarkable – memorable mixes of ultra-fresh vegetables, meat and fish in subtle sauces. Most meat is mutton or chicken as the climate is not good for bovines. Unfortunately, the tourist menus found all over the country tend to be repetitive and bland. One tip is to eat cheaply – vegetable couscous, salads – for two or three days and save up for a good restaurant at the end. It's really worth it, the contrast is so striking.

Vegetarians Moroccan cooking uses a lot of vegetables but, paradoxically, it isn't an easy place for pure vegetarians. Lovely vegetables are generally cooked with meat, or at least steamed over the top. So flexibility is needed. You can always get vegetables only, you can't often avoid all traces of meat.

Organic produce It is quite difficult to give a true organic label to food grown in Morocco because a lot of the water used to irrigate crops is polluted and the land tends to be used and used until it is exhausted and another piece brought into exploitation. However, crops are subjected to far fewer pesticides and chemical fertilizers than in the west and in this sense are 'cleaner'. The budding Moroccan organic industry is mostly for export at this early stage.

Language: Arabic or Berber, French or Spanish

Arabic is the official language but this is a multi-lingual country, its history illustrated by the languages its people speak. The presence of the original Berber inhabitants from early pre-history is proven. In the eighth century, the Arabs invaded, brought Islam in their wake, and continued into Spain. For seven centuries, Morocco and Andalucia were interwoven by dynastic currents and cross-cultural influences until the Andalucian Moors were expelled from rechristianised Spain in the 15th century. In the 19th century, various European countries tried

INTRODUCTION

to gain a foothold until, eventually, Spain and France were allowed to share the task of 'protecting' Morocco.

Half the population are of Berber (properly Amazigh) descent and speak one of three Amazigh languages and Arabic. In towns, almost everyone also speaks French but in the north many people are more comfortable with Spanish. Moroccans are excellent linguists and you will find great willingness to try and speak English but remember that this is, from a traveller's point of view, a francophone country. Children in the street want to practise the French they are learning at school. It is a joyous hubbub of sense-making, not a tower of Babel.

Modernities

When you stay in a medina and stand on one of those wonderful roofs, you will be astounded by the forest of satellite dishes growing there. The effects are not always visible on the ground but world television is entering every Moroccan home.

Photography, rural exodus and urban poverty

The culture of modesty, in women and girls especially, is part of traditional Amazigh upbringing, where women are to be respected and not looked at – a woman is always tied to someone else, first her family then her husband. Coachloads of loud tourists brandishing cameras make them retreat even further into their haïks (veils) and they are reluctant to be photographed. In other families things are more relaxed and it's not a problem. Always ask before taking a picture of a Moroccan; asking for an address to send them the printed picture (only if you really intend to do this, of course) is much appreciated.

Do not give money for photographs, particularly to children. 10Dh, a minute sum for us, represents one third of a farm worker's daily wage. Children, quickly learning to skip school for the sake of these coins, just as quickly come to despise their parents' way of earning a living and take off as early as possible for the 'city paved with gold'. There, the hideous truth of slums and shanty towns forces them into begging, drug-dealing and prostitution. Yet again, don't give money to children.

Speaking the social and body language of Morocco

Moroccans appear to spend half their lives out in public and are naturally friendly and helpful – if you share a language. From

INTRODUCTION

another point of view, they are very secret people, draping their bodies in coveralls, living in houses that face inwards, denying any but the faithful a look into their places of worship. They live quite differently inside their own homes among their own clan.

Practical tips

Packing reminder

Bring a rubber bung plug, a torch, ear plugs, a corkscrew and a remedy for diarrhoea.

Baths and basins

Take a flat rubber bung plug as even in the best houses plugs disappear and it's especially upsetting to waste water here (see Conservation and Development at the back of this book).

Driving

Avoid driving after dark. Roads may be pot-holed, lorries drive determinedly down the middle, cars and bicycles cannot be relied on to carry decent lights, pedestrians and donkey carts disappear into the night.

Electricity

The current is 220 volts and Moroccan sockets are two-pin style, like French ones, so you will need an adaptor for your plugs and a transformer for 110-volt appliances.

Lighting seems to be planned for its capacity to create atmosphere rather than to make things visible and dinner is very often served by candlelight. Take a good torch for reading in bed! Also, power cuts are not infrequent, particularly outside the cities, and some country places only have electricity from 6pm to 10.30pm. The rest of the time it's candles and lanterns.

Health

Though not inevitable, it is likely that you will suffer a bout of *la turista* during your first visit. Take a reliable diarrhoea remedy.

Maps

Our general maps are not for use as road maps and if you are planning to drive, get a good map such as the Michelin: clear and accurate, it even shows the types of trees that grow in different areas. For really detailed walking maps, consult a specialist bookshop. The Éditions Gauthey city maps are useful for detailed exploration of Tangier, Essaouira, Marrakech or Fès.

INTRODUCTION

Money

The national currency, the dirham, is divided into 100 centimes. It is illegal to take dirhams out of Morocco or bring them in so you need to change money at your point of arrival (or at a French airport). You may be asked when leaving to change any dirhams you have left into hard currency – at a relatively unfavourable rate, so aim to have as few as possible in your pocket when you get to the airport.

Cash dispensers are found in the most out-of-the-way places and your hosts are usually happy to be paid in cash – some only take cash. Unless they have the 🌑 symbol, owners accept payment by credit card, (often excepting American Express or Diner's). However, the card machines in guest houses, hotels and petrol stations do not always work, in which case you have to go to the nearest cash dispenser.

Should you ever find you need to write a cheque, be prepared to be asked to do it in blue ink, not black. There is a belief that black ink does not make legal tender.

Small change is rare – you may begin to wonder what 50 centimes look like. There appears to be a dirham economy and a centime economy: foreigners join the former and are seldom given centimes in change so if you want change for tips or alms or you are simply curious, buying individual stamps should bring in the little ones. And you quickly learn to hoard small coins like a miser gathering gold.

Noise

Not all hotels are protected from street noise so take your ear plugs.

Taxis

They come in two sizes, big and little. *Petits taxis* are restricted to inner city areas. They are numerous, battered, quick and cheap – this is the best way to get around, even over short distances such as inside the medinas. *Grands taxis* are indeed, bigger, and more 'luxurious' for the longer distances. Always either make sure the driver turns the meter on (it is illegal not to) or, in a *grand taxi*, agree on the total charge before driving off. It is normal for visitors to tip about 10% over the meter charge.

INTRODUCTION

Your silent reaction when you get your very first taxi may be "I'll choose better next time", it looks and sounds so worn and patched-up. But you soon realise that they are all like that, as hard-working and enduring as the donkeys. Moroccan taxi drivers are highly skilled and you will learn to trust them as they weave and hustle through alleyways already filled to the brim with pedestrians, animals and pavement stalls.

Telephoning

Telephone connections are pretty good and everyone has a mobile but using your own mobile can be very expensive. Some old hands buy the cheapest Moroccan mobile on offer when they arrive plus a card – after the initial outlay, it costs very little. Otherwise, the *téléboutiques*, found in the remotest spots, are brilliant. Quieter and easier than outdoor call boxes, they are like old post office boxes where you can stand and talk for hours, sheltered from sun and rain, feeding coins into the slot. It's 2Dh for any local call, more for long distance; the manager has a bottomless stock of coins.

Tipping

It is normal to tip waiters, taxi drivers, porters, petrol pump attendants etc. something like 10 per cent. When you park your car, look for the *gardien* to make sure he has taken you in charge. A picturesque ancient or a young boy, he will ward off all marauders. The normal rate is about 2Dh an hour.

Trekking and adventure – at your own risk

Many hotels and guest houses offer to organise excursions and treks, often with their own guides. There are also dozens of little shopfronts, especially in the desert-edge south, proclaiming their guiding skills on desert and mountain treks and bivouacs on foot, mule or dromedary or in 4x4 vehicles. You should know that few of these 'organisations' are registered or insured and you join their expeditions at your own risk. To be totally insured, choose a travel agent who displays his *Numéro de Patente*.

We have found the Moroccans to be among the gentlest and most tolerant of people. They are easy with foreigners and, as long as you don't appear to be aiming to offend their sensibilities, they are helpful and hospitable and sharing. However, it's useful to know that permits of all sorts, including driving licences and mountain guide certificates, appear to be obtained as often by

INTRODUCTION

connections as by practical test. Thus, one young Parisian Moroccan visiting her family in Casablanca was offered a driving licence as a birthday present; one competent, knowledgeable and committed young Berber was unable to pass his mountain guide exams because he could not afford the 'personal fee' charged by the examiner.

And beware of 'false guides' in the desert who are said to lay false trails, then leap to your succour when you get stuck in order to earn a goodly sum for your salvation.

Environment

We try to reduce our impact on the environment by:

- publishing our books on recycled paper
- planting trees. We are officially Carbon Neutral®. The emissions directly related to our office, paper production and printing of this book have been 'neutralised' through the planting of indigenous woodlands with Future Forests
- re-using paper, recycling stationery, tins, bottles, etc
- encouraging staff use of bicycles (they're loaned free) and car sharing
- celebrating the use of organic, home-grown and locally-produced food
- publishing books that support, in however small a way, the rural economy and small-scale businesses
- publishing *The Little Earth Book*, a collection of essays on environmental issues and *The Little Food Book*, a hard-hitting analysis of the food industry. *The Little Money Book* has also just been published. See our web site www.fragile-earth.com for more information on any of these titles.

Subscriptions

Owners pay to appear in this guide; their fee goes towards the high production costs of an all-colour book. We do only include places and owners that we find special. It is not possible for anyone to bribe their way in.

Internet

Our web site www.specialplacestostay.com has online pages for all the places featured here and from all our other books – around 3,500 Special Places in Britain, Ireland, France, Italy, Spain, Portugal and India. There's a searchable database, full details, a taster of the write-ups and colour photos.

For more details see the back of the book.

INTRODUCTION

Disclaimer   We make no claims to pure objectivity in choosing our
Special Places to Stay. They are here because we like them.
Our opinions and tastes are ours alone and this book is a
statement of them; we hope that you will share them.

We have done our utmost to get our facts right but apologise
unreservedly for any mistakes that may have crept in. Feedback
from you is invaluable and we always act upon comments.
With your help and our own inspections we can maintain our
reputation for dependability.

You should know that we do not check such things as fire
alarms, swimming pool security or any other regulation with
which owners of properties receiving paying guests should
comply. This is the responsibility of the owners.

And finally   We are hugely grateful to those of you who write to us about
your experiences – good and bad – or to recommend new
places. We love your letters and your comments make a real
contribution to our books, be they on our report form, by
letter or by e-mail to info@sawdays.co.uk. Or you can
visit our web site and write to us from there.

Ann Cooke-Yarborough

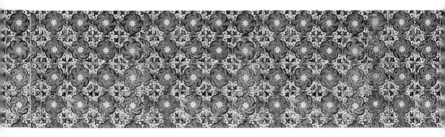

A guide to our map page numbers

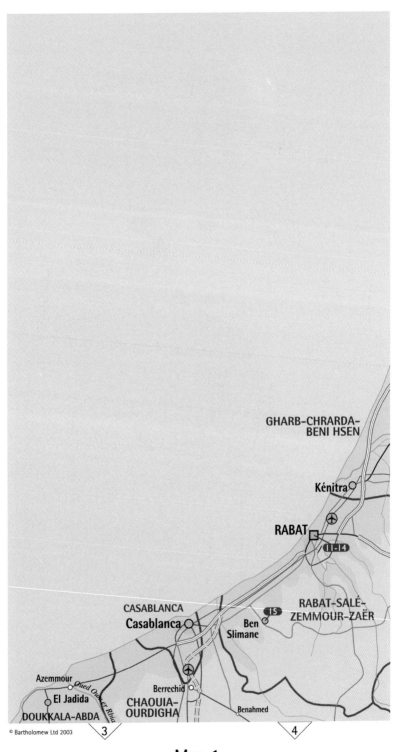

GHARB–CHRARDA–
BENI HSEN

Kénitra

RABAT
11-14

RABAT-SALÉ-
ZEMMOUR-ZAËR

CASABLANCA
Casablanca
Ben
Slimane
15

Azemmour
Oued Oum er Rbia
El Jadida
Berrechid
DOUKKALA-ABDA
CHAOUIA-
OURDIGHA
Benahmed

3

4

Map 1

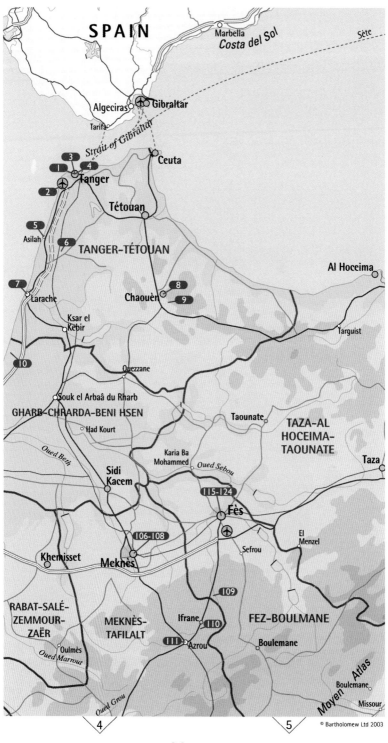

SPAIN

Marbella

Costa del Sol

Sète

Algeciras Gibraltar

Tarifa

Strait of Gibraltar

Ceuta

Tanger

Tétouan

Asilah

TANGER-TÉTOUAN

Al Hoceima

Larache

Chaouèn

Targuist

Ksar el Kebir

Ouezzane

Souk el Arbaâ du Rharb

GHARB-CHRARDA-BENI HSEN

Taounate

TAZA-AL HOCEIMA-TAOUNATE

Had Kourt

Oued Beth

Karia Ba Mohammed

Oued Sebou

Taza

Sidi Kacem

115-124

Fès

106-108

El Menzel

Khemisset

Meknès

Sefrou

109

RABAT-SALÉ-ZEMMOUR-ZAËR

MEKNÈS-TAFILALT

Ifrane

110

FEZ-BOULMANE

Oulmès

Oued Marrout

111 Azrou

Boulemane

Oued Grou

Moyen Atlas

Boulemane

Missour

4

5

© Bartholomew Ltd 2003

Map 2

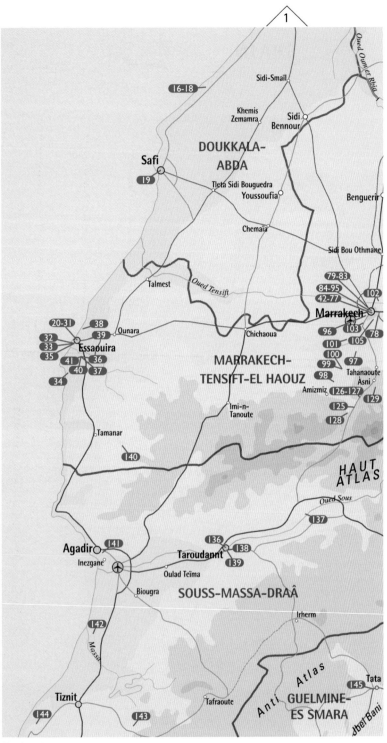

© Bartholomew Ltd 2003

Map 3

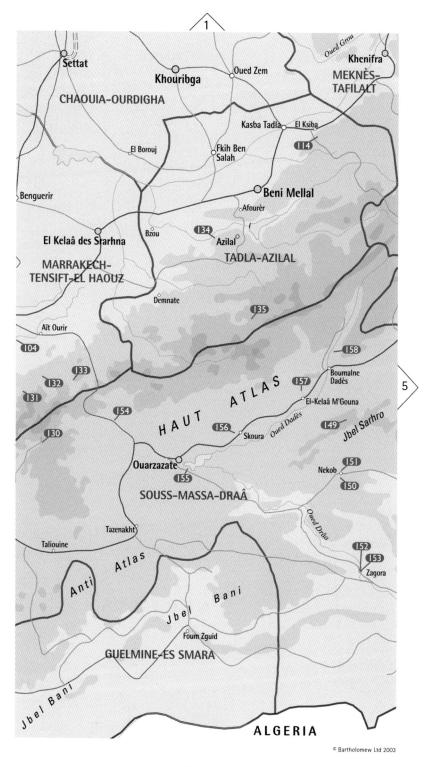

Map 4

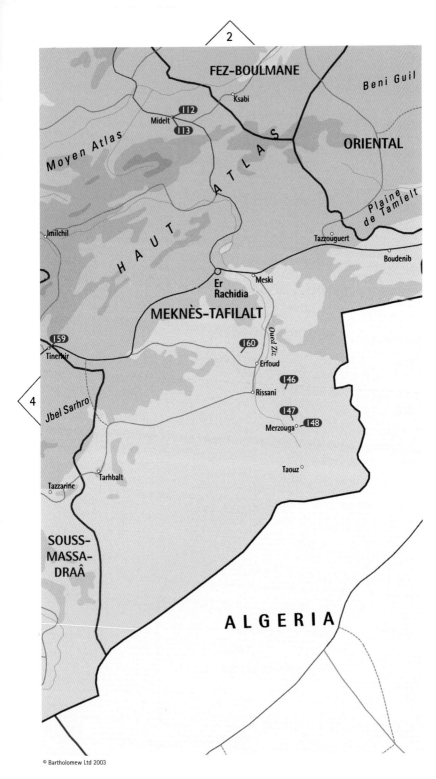

Map 5

HOW TO USE THIS BOOK

explanations

1 rooms

Assume all rooms are 'en suite' unless we say otherwise.

If a room is not 'en suite' we say **with separate,** or **with shared bath**: the former you will have to yourself, the latter may be shared with other guests or family members.

2 room price

The price shown is for one night for two sharing a room. A price range incorporates room/seasonal differences.

3 meals

Prices are per person. BYO: you may bring your own wine.

4 closed

When given in months, this means for the whole of the named months and the time in between.

5 directions

Use as a guide; the owner can give more details.

6 map & entry numbers

Map page number; entry number.

7 symbols

See inside back cover for fuller explanation.

sample entry

MARRAKECH–MEDINA

Ryad El Borj
63 Derb Moulay Abdelkader, Derb Dabachi, Marrakech-Medina

*B*orj means tower. 150 years ago, when Pasha Glaoui owned the whole quarter, one of the liveliest in Marrakech, he built a lookout here to oversee the area. Still the highest view of the whole city, it is magic at any hour, sublime at sunset. The typical dark entrance takes you down five steps then on to the blue patio, whence up to the green first floor then the red terrace – all properly dramatic. When renovating the ryad three years ago, your host was careful to preserve the original décor and almost all the very comfortably furnished rooms have painted or carved ceilings while the great glass-vaulted suite is remarkable value with its big bedroom, sitting room, excellent bathroom and an extra salon that gives onto the patio via a superb moucharabieh screen. Colours are pale and sober, materials are noble cedarwood and finely wrought ironwork, doors are antique, floors are strewn with carpets and leather cushions from the Saharaoui south giving the wonderful exotic feel of being in a *khaima*, a nomad tent; breakfast is superbly generous. Pool, drinks and meals available just 20 metres away.

rooms	5: 4 doubles, 1 suite.
price	600Dh–1,200Dh. Sole occupancy for 8: 17,0000Dh–23,000Dh per week.
meals	Lunch or dinner by arrangement. BYO.
closed	Never.
directions	From Place Jemaâ El Fna take Derb Dabachi (behind Café de France); pass mosque on right then first left; house 30m along on right.

	Daniel Ghio
tel	+212 (0)44 39 12 23/61 67 59 42
fax	+212 (0)44 39 12 23
e-mail	ryadelborj@wanadoo.net.ma
web	www.ryadelborj.com

Guest house & catered house

entry 68   map 3

$\angle$ 🏠 👤 🐾

المنطقة الاطلسية

the atlantic region

One does not tend to think seaside resorts when conjuring up visions of Morocco but there are hundreds of miles of gorgeous beaches along the Atlantic coast and once you are more than a dozen miles or so from any major town you'll meet few other people. It is a beautiful and varied coast, the ocean beats the shore relentlessly, be it rock or sand, the fish and seafood are superb, the swimming is exhilirating but can be dangerous: there is a strong and constant undertow.

This has been a cosmopolitan trading area since the Phoenicians, a meeting point for merchants and marauders, pirates and power-seekers from far and wide who have left a great variety of historic cities, architecture and rich craftsmanship. There are a few rare pearls, jealously protected by heavy ramparts and needing time if you want to penetrate their subtleties: the medinas of Asilah, El Jadida, Essaouira. The throbbing coastal cities of Tangier, Rabat, Casablanca and Agadir are interesting places to visit and the delightful hinterland, with some simple, authentic places to stay, must not be neglected.

Economically, most of the phosphates mined here, the country's primary resource, are exported from Safi. Almost all fishing - another major resource - takes place off the Atlantic coast, from the ports of Tan-Tan, Agadir, Essaouira, El Jadida and Casablanca. The climate is subject to the capriciousness of the Azores anti-cyclone and a lot of Morocco's agricultural wealth is fed by Atlantic-driven clouds that are stopped by the Atlas mountains.

The southernmost part of the Moroccan Atlantic coast is where the Sahara Desert meets the Atlantic Ocean - a fearsome, hostile land of outstanding wild beauty.

Photography by Guy Hunter-Watts

Minzah Hotel & Spa

85 rue de la Liberté, Tangier

High above the Straits of Gibraltar, the Minzah is a place of legend walked by the ghosts of writers and adventurers who squeezed the muse in its cool Moorish patio (stupendous breakfasts served here), plotted in its fabulous gardens, imbibed in its oh-so-British mahogany bar; a place to dream of celebrity and stardom. Built by Lord Bute in 1930, its vastness is hidden in proper oriental style by plain walls and a great studded door, the glorious patio has all the right arcading, plaster embroidery and blue mosaics, the grandeur of the salons is touchingly old-fashioned, the lift is an Art Deco marvel while the antique Caïd Bar drips with intriguing fusty old photographs. This timelessness lessens the impact of an ultra-modern spa and modernised bedrooms: they are impeccable, five-star comfortable (ask for a renovated room with sea view) but lack that nostalgia. Friendly, efficient and multilingual, the staff are delightfully attached to the Minzah's weighty history and the new management is applying green ideas on water and energy conservation – we salute them. Three restaurants with a superb choice of fine food, too.

rooms	140: 124 doubles & twins, 15 suites for 2, 1 suite for 4.
price	1,500Dh-2,200Dh; suites 2,700Dh-9,000Dh.
meals	Lunch or dinner: vast choice à la carte.
closed	Never.
directions	From port, south on Ave des F.A.R.; fork right along ramparts Rue de Portugal, over Rue Salah Eddine El Ayoubi 200m, left Rue de la Liberté.

Yves de Boisgency

tel	+212 (0)39 93 58 85
fax	+212 (0)39 93 45 46
e-mail	infos@elminzah.com
web	www.elminzah.com

Landmark hotel

Le Mirage

Grottes d'Hercule, Route de Cap Spartel, Tangier

They call it a club: the words 'exclusive' and 'out-of-this-world' do come to mind. Hunkered down on an Atlantic-battered headland, the Mirage's brilliantly flowered, manicured garden, and above it the superb plum-coloured restaurant, look south to sweeping golden sands – incomparable, no beach hotel could be better sited. Sheltered in salons of classic European comfort from the unfettered elements, you have a sense of intimacy and secret magic up here fed by original paintings and prints, some of remarkable quality, an excellent piano bar, world-renowned cuisine. White steps hurry down the cliff to the vast empty beach where the Caves of Hercules and the ancient Roman site of Cotta lie waiting. Each hidden in its own ground-hugging villa, the sumptuous suites come in several sizes of big, done in rich-coloured fabrics, smelling of traditional carved cedarwood, with luxuries of cushions, marble bathrooms and private terraces onto palms and pool. Opulent, chic and nurturing, the Mirage is a place to be cocooned in exclusive peace (celebrities love it) and staff are appropriately top-class.

rooms	27 bungalows with salon: 15 doubles, 5 superior doubles, 7 suites with 2 bedrooms.
price	1,400Dh-6,000Dh.
meals	Lunch or dinner 100Dh-500Dh.
closed	Never.
directions	From Tangier for Rabat & airport 9km; right for Grottes d'Hercule. Hotel on left at 1st r'bout.

	Ahmed Chakkour & Roger Schwarzberg
tel	+212 (0)39 33 33 32/34 91
fax	+212 (0)39 33 34 92/34 34 92
e-mail	mirage@iam.net.ma
web	www.lemirage-tanger.com

Small hotel

map 2   entry 2

Hôtel Continental

36 Dar Baroud, Tangier

Oh! the friendly nostalgia and fun of the place – Tangier's first hotel, built in 1865 for the cosmopolitan élite, used by spies on both sides in wartime, the Continental has seen many incarnations and never lost its charm or its heavenly marble staircase. Imaginatively renovated by the present owner and a young Fassi designer, the bedrooms are stylish and bold with rough-painted wide-striped wall finishes, thoughtful colour schemes, hangings and paintings old and new, decent bathrooms. The writer/poet/painter atmosphere, the whiffs of Graham Greene, are part of the fabric, in there among the keyhole arches and geometric tiles of the grand hall, on the vastly beautiful terrace whence Spain can be seen on fine days, in the dining room with its dripping chandeliers. The people here are relaxed and friendly, happy to swim in such rich streams and share their luck with fortunate guests. Right on the port, this is the place to be in summer when the city's windows are open east and west every hot afternoon and the draught cools it so blissfully. Staying at the Continental means living, however briefly, inside a legend.

rooms	60: 28 doubles, 21 twins, 6 triples, 3 quadruples, 2 suites.
price	365Dh–420Dh.
meals	Lunch or dinner 50Dh–100Dh.
closed	Never.
directions	Visible from port entrance but ask taxi to guide you in.

Mohamed Soussi

tel	+212 (0)39 93 10 24/37 58 51
fax	+212 (0)39 93 11 43
e-mail	hcontinental@iam.net.ma

Small hotel

Dar Nour

20 rue Gourna, Kasbah, Tangier-Medina

Follow your escort ever deeper and higher into the medina, wonder at the mysterious journey – then rejoice in the civilised hospitable house at the end of it. Not only is it beautiful, it is unusual, brilliantly positioned and serves totally memorable breakfasts. Pure Tangier white outside, the 'house of light' is utterly personal inside, the home of an intellectual that exudes the energy of rich culture: books everywhere, a desk in every room, eye-catching pictures and sculpture, antiques and hangings against white walls, yet nothing overdone. With Louis, a relaxed, sensitive, nature-loving convert to Morocco, and his willing aides Khadija and Abdellatif you will be well and intelligently cared for. Rooms are as vertical as the house with level changes, the odd duplex and two staircases, two ground-floor windowless womb-like salons – so restful – and two kitchens. The owner's suite is the most striking with the bed under a splendid light well. Then up you climb to the flowering terraces to contemplate the evening light over the panorama and dine on superb food. Everything here is seeking the light – you may join in.

rooms	7: 2 doubles, 1 single, 4 suites.
price	300Dh-1,000Dh.
meals	Dinner 120Dh-200Dh. By arrangement.
closed	Never.
directions	From Kasbah car park take 1st right to fountain on little square, immed. right 30m, lime green door.

**Philippe Guiguet Bologne
& Louis Soubrier**
tel   +212 (0)62 11 27 24
e-mail   pgb.tanger@caramail.com
web   www.darnour.com

Guest house

 map 2   entry 4

Hôtel Patio de la Luna
12 Place Zellaka, Asilah

Plumb in the middle of lovely old Asilah, next to the mystery of its medina and a hundred yards from the port, the small solid door opens onto a simple, welcoming place with much good humour and no pretensions – also two big friendly dogs, cooing doves and a very vocal cockerel. Juan Antonio or Hassan will welcome you to this typically whitewashed and indigo-tinted house with smiles and help in many languages and show you to your room across the patio where the moon (*luna*) may be shining through the two looming rubber plants. Here and there, things may be a bit worn but there's nothing synthetic, the rough-plaster walls and earth-coloured floors are warm and sensuous, mattresses are wool, furniture is blue wicker, the feel is a good, appealingly spartan mix of Spanish and Moroccan and six of the rooms look out over fields of grazing sheep; our favourites are the two at the top with a terrace whence you can also catch a glimpse of the sea. There are dozens of tempting little seafood restaurants beneath the massive ramparts, a summer arts festival, an all-pervading smell of the sea and adventure.

rooms	8: 3 doubles, 3 twins, 2 triples.
price	350Dh–450Dh.
meals	Café next door for breakfast. Choice of restaurants in town.
closed	Part of Ramadan - check.
directions	Entering Asilah, follow signs for medina. Hotel just outside medina on north side next to well-known Casa Pepe.

Juan Antonio González Ortega
tel +212 (0)39 41 60 74
e-mail patiodelaluna@caramail.com

Small hotel

Berbari

Dchar Ghanem, Cercle de Tnine Sidi El Yamani, Asilah

The gift of Berbari? gentle but real contact with local customs. The house? two old buildings, one with three hefty pillars bending under the weight of the years, the other grander with an upper floor. And storks on their tangled nests, the widest starriest skies in the north (only candles or dim bulbs so as not to compete), a splendidly light-hearted approach to décor – every item is resuscitated, recycled, full of experience and soul. Beamed, lime-washed rooms have the simplicity of bright local fabrics, the uncluttered Moroccan salon has comfort in its benches and your private space, salon or patch of garden behind its rustling hedge, is a delight. The atmosphere? slow time flows over the animal kingdom and their occasional concerts, the house and its people. This is a place of tradition and universals so relax, stop dashing around, take time to discover the neolithic village, the beaches, the countryside. The owners? wonderful hosts, deeply committed to life and the land they love – take time to get to know them. In summer, you can rent one of their beach huts (berbaris) and sleep in splendid isolation.

rooms	7: 4 doubles, 3 suites, each with private salon or garden.
price	250Dh–700Dh. Summer beach huts 200Dh. Book ahead.
meals	Snacks 60Dh. Lunch or dinner 120Dh–200Dh. By arrangement.
closed	Never.
directions	If you have no 4x4 vehicle, essential to ring from Asilah for escort last 4km.

	Louis Soubrier & Rachida Youdra
tel	+212 (0)62 58 80 13 (lunchtime)
e-mail	louis.soubrier@caramail.com
web	www.berbari.com

Guest house

map 2   entry 6

La Maison Haute

6 Derb Ben Thami, Larache

As you pass under the great old arch from colonial Hispania into eternal Arabia, this jewel of a medina house promises exoticism, with its ground floor of centuries-old souk shops, and gentle rest. Rising tall above that friendly bustle of an unsmartened medina, so far from the sophisticated frenzy of our cities, it is no deluxe tourist trap but a place to make contact with other people's reality and possibly your own. The owners have kept their renovation of the old house discreet and simple, respecting its original shapes and atmosphere. Sea light caresses the vibrant colour-washed walls until the sun dips and tinges the world with fire – you'll want to climb the four floors to the incredible terrace every day for this. Rooms are furnished with taste, rich Moroccan rugs and old colonial furniture, the fruit of many *brocante* hunts, in an attractive personal mix of red velvet armchairs, dark old Spanish trunks, big iron candlesticks. On the two bedroom floors, the central patio/landing is the place for cool-weather breakfasts and the terrace, of course, a must for dinner, all served with smiles and intelligence.

rooms	7: 5 doubles, 1 triple, 1 suite.
price	400Dh–800Dh.
meals	Lunch or dinner. By arrangement. BYO.
closed	Never but advance booking essential October to May.
directions	From Place de la Libération enter medina by Bab El Khemis: house is opposite.

Bertrand Capet & Marc Louis
tel +33 (0)1 43 66 26 94
e-mail info@lamaisonhaute.com
web www.lamaisonhaute.com

Guest house

Pension Casa Hassan

22 rue Targhi, Chefchaouen

Hassan was born here, in one of the loveliest little towns in Morocco, once forbidden to non-Muslims. Fifteen years ago he turned one of its old houses into this colourful, romantic little hotel. Bedrooms and restaurant are wrapped around the cobbled courtyard, light seeps in through its stained-glass canopy, a great arch opens onto the kitchen and veiled figures squeezing oranges for you. This central sitting space is the hub of a well-loved house where charming, dynamic Hassan has established a delightful team who will look after you with natural friendliness and good Spanish. His décor is in well-balanced Moroccan idiom: brass lanterns and tiled tables, interesting niches and lots of modern art (he also has an art gallery), a fine collection of antique doors and central heating – though half the rooms have open fireplaces, wonderful on those cold winter nights. Bedrooms can be exotic with draperies and niches, a painted ceiling here, a four-poster there; one has a double staircase leading to two double beds on a starry mezzanine. To crown it all, the roof terrace is a glorious spot for breakfast or a good book.

rooms	7: 3 doubles, 4 triples.
price	Half-board 600Dh for two.
meals	Lunch or dinner included. Other meals 60Dh. By arrangement.
closed	Never.
directions	In Chefchaouen follow for Medina; park at Parador Hotel. Casa Hassan about 150m away in narrow street above kasbah.

	Hassan Benhamda
tel	+212 (0)39 98 61 53
fax	+212 (0)39 98 81 96
e-mail	lacasahassan1987@yahoo.fr

Guest house

map 2   entry 8

Auberge Dardara
Route Nationale 2, Chefchaouen, Al Hoceima

The Rif mountains are little known, so why not become one of the privileged few who do know? With the El Hababi family (four brothers are involved here), come and discover the glories of the northern Rif, its remote valleys, cedar (and hash)-clad hillsides and little Berber settlements where local crafts are sold. From the Dardara, you can take a well-tended Berber Arab pony or walk out into the hills with one of their excellent guides or join a local sports monitor in water activities. The inn is built in local stone, brick and timber, the reception area doubles as a woodwork and craft shop (the carpenter brother makes all their furniture – and more for you, if you like) where you might find some handsome rustic utensils of unclear use but full of history. They are fabulous cooks, too: their varied family recipes – local game, home-grown meat and veg – are prized by the county who descend in droves on the simple, convivial restaurant. Colour is another delight here: traditional painted doors, rooms in harmonies of yellow and blue, pink and red with fireplaces and neatly tiled bathrooms. A super, generous place.

rooms	12: 3 doubles, 6 twins, 1 triple, 1 suite for 4, 1 suite for 8-10.
price	Half-board 590Dh for two.
meals	Lunch 70Dh; children 45Dh.
closed	Never.
directions	Leaving Chefchaouen for Al Hoceima on N2, left just outside town.

Yassine & Jaber El Hababi

tel	+212 (0)39 88 33 25/39 19
fax	+212 (0)39 88 33 25
e-mail	elhababi@dardara.com
web	www.dardara.com

Inn – Bivouac

La Maison des Oiseaux

Moulay Bousselham

In the limpid air, flamingoes wing their pink way across the lagoon, past Gentiane's clear white house where it stands in thriving shrubbiness, all organic simplicity and taste. The antithesis of the chain hotel, it is relaxed and homespun, a place where everything seems to work without the need for rules. Rooms, white, blue and ochre, are gently harmonious in their mix of antique doors, painted or carved furniture, particularly lovely Moroccan tiles, bird posters (naturally), Gentiane's paintings, sculptures and glass, bits of driftwood… disposed with love and an eye for what works. She is a deeply creative person, has travelled widely and is very good company. Washing arrangements are various and flexible, the bedding is excellent, food is good home cooking, the freshest possible. Take your time, read the books, use the field glasses, consult your wonderful hostess on the rarer feathered friends, then possibly take a boat trip and get up close: this little settlement with its pure white holy man's tomb is on one of the main migration routes between Europe and Africa. Gentle and very special.

rooms	7: 1 double with basin & wc, 2 triples & 1 family sharing 2 showers, basins & wcs; 1 triple with shower; 1 triple with kitchenette; 1 room for 5 with shower & wc.
price	Half-board 300Dh p.p.
meals	Dinner included. BYO.
closed	Rarely.
directions	From Tangier P2 & m'way for Rabat 125km; exit for M'y Bousselham; at Total garage, left on track 500m.

Gentiane Dartigue

tel	+212 (0)37 43 25 43/61 30 10 67
fax	+212 (0)37 43 25 43
e-mail	gentiane.dartigue@caramail.com
web	www.multimania.fr/moulaybousselham

Guest house

map 2   entry 10

Villa Mandarine

19 rue Ouled Bousbaa, Souissi, Rabat

Some sort of miracle operates here: there may be 36 rooms yet you feel you are a personal guest of a delightful, lively, cultured family. Art historian and lover of all Islamic arts, Claudy Imbert, dreaming her own architectural dreams, decided to transform her family's holiday mansion, with a Moroccan architect's valuable advice, into a very special hotel. Set in five acres of delirious gardens, it has enough private corners for everyone – *Eden au Maroc* – and three daughters to help run it. In great-grandfather's original house are the glorious ochre-washed, Marrakech-red communal spaces – blue-tiled bougainvillea patio, 'African' bar, serene library, wide-open restaurant where the garden rushes in through great panels of glass. Round the generous new blue-edged patio are the sophisticatedly simple rooms, each with its own balcony-terrace, its own warm colours, its own pretty rugs and lamps, its own share of Claudy Imbert's personal and rewarding gallery of Morocco-linked pictures, from Michelangelo to local landscape to modern abstract. Sheer delight. And moreover – a famous restaurant, a fitness centre, modem slots...

rooms	36: 31 doubles, 5 suites.
price	1,800Dh-2,800Dh. Ask about special terms.
meals	Lunch or dinner 260Dh.
closed	Never.
directions	From west-bound ring-road, right Ave Mehdi Ben-Barka; pass two sets traffic lights; right Rue Ouled Saïd; 2nd right Rue Ouled Bousbaa; hotel on left (sign).

Claudy Imbert

tel	+212 (0)37 75 20 77
fax	+212 (0)37 63 23 09
e-mail	reservation@villamandarine.com
web	www.villamandarine.com

Small hotel

entry 11   map 1

Riad Oudaya

46 rue Sidi Fateh, Rabat-Medina

Old Morocco, rich and fascinating: with a rare 14th-century mosque with octagonal minarets next door, the 19th-century Andalucian Riad Oudaya melds the Spanish and Moroccan sources of Moorish style. Your hosts, people of taste, culture and a great sense of hospitality, came from La Rochelle, fell for Rabat and live here half the year; theirs is a house of simplicity and deep comfort, generosity, good humour and soothing freshness. Carved stone door surrounds, wrought-iron railings, green-tiled eaves seem to kneel before the beautiful fountain while greenery and bougainvillea bow down from the roof – the patio is superb. Inside, cedar doors and ceilings, carved furniture, zellige and stone arches build on that sense of enduring class, a painted ceiling, a Bill Willis fireplace and a beige tadelakt salon with antique benches speak of refinement without snobbery. Suites are big, each with a real sitting room; bedrooms are luminous; all have individuality and lovely old pieces. Good beds too. Latifa and Beadia will make you feel instantly at home and Aïcha will cook unforgettably.

rooms	4: 2 doubles, 2 suites for 3.
price	1,170Dh–1,650Dh.
meals	Lunch from 190Dh.
	Dinner from 250Dh.
closed	Never.
directions	Park at Bab Lalou phone for escort.

Pierre & Mireille Duclos

tel	+212 (0)37 70 23 92
fax	+33 (0)5 46 41 32 17
e-mail	reservation@riadoudaya.com
web	www.riadoudaya.com

Guest house

map 1 entry 12

Dar Al Batoul

7 Derb Jirari, Rabat-Medina

The clean white alley and the simple but beautiful front door give little idea of the wealth that lies behind. With its slim white columns and original tiled floor, the patio announces the calm elegance of this 18th-century mansion – and brings birdsung peace, so precious after the chaos of the city outside. Here is a house of taste and culture with a library (cum-video room, of course), good Moroccan antiques and rugs and a riot of plates, teapots, mirrors and lamps. Real Morocco it is, but never overdone or gaudy. Each bedroom is different, walls are pale wash with strong paintwork or traditional tiles, beds are often four-posters, fabrics always in harmony and bathrooms – with bath or shower and more mosaic tiling – pretty and well-lit. A clever design idea is the large cupboard alcove behind each bed. The suite is sumptuously furnished with carved and painted pieces, richly shimmering many-coloured fabrics and even more zellige. The friendly, efficient owners are delighted with their faithful restoration of this old medina house and welcome their guests with pride – and good food.

rooms	9: 8 doubles, 1 suite.
price	1,100Dh–1,600Dh.
meals	Lunch or dinner 100Dh–300Dh. By arrangement.
closed	Never.
directions	From town centre, west for medina central market; left on Avenue Hassan II, right Avenue d'Egypte, right Chari Laalou, right Derb Jirari.

Alexandra & Nabila Ventolini

tel	+212 (0)37 72 72 50/61 40 11 81
fax	+212 (0)37 72 73 16
e-mail	albatoul@menara.ma
web	www.riadbatoul.com

Guest house

Dar Baraka

26 rue Jamaâ, Kasbah des Oudaïas, Rabat-Medina

Dar Baraka (divine blessing) stands deep inside the pretty white medina that has grown within the austere fortress built on this cliff by the great Sultan Al Mansour as a centre for launching soldier monks against the heretics. From the fabulous terrace, protected by billows of bougainvillea, you gaze down on the peaceful cemetery, out to the Atlantic, and feel you are master of the world. The lady owner has taken immense care over the restoration of her magical house, light pours in from all sides onto the gentle colourless colours of the walls and hangings – ivory, beige, ecru and white – and the contrasting richnesses of carpets and cushions, the antique mirrors and 1920s inlaid furniture, the books and music of the great living room. Fine big bedrooms too, where you get a sense of colonial times, and matching bathrooms full of old-style chrome fittings. Jean Vassort, a refined, cultured and fascinating old Moroccan resident, suits the house perfectly and Hamza, his righthand man, as friendly and helpful as you could wish, will take you shopping or show you the astounding double vaulted cellar dug into the cliffside.

rooms	2: 1 double, 1 twin.
price	800Dh-1,100Dh B&B; 1,900Dh sole occupancy for 1-5 persons, including breakfast.
meals	French dinner 330Dh, Moroccan dinner 260Dh. By arrangement.
closed	Never.
directions	Enter Kasbah des Oudaïas at main gate Bab Al Qasha into Rue Jamaâ; last house in street.

	Jean Vassort
tel	+212 (0)37 73 03 62
fax	+212 (0)37 26 34 71
e-mail	jvassort@iam.net.ma

Catered house & guest house

map 1   entry 14

Centre La Forêt

Ain Tizgha - km13, Ben Slimane, Casablanca

Walking among the cork oaks one day, Jilali El Karama, a busy Casablanca caterer, had a revelation: he must build a health and relaxation centre here, in this pure air. And a tremendous place it is – organic and alternative and friendly and delicious – a dream come true. He and his wife, a glowing energetic couple, are here at weekends; on weekdays you are warmly received by charming village folk who are also fiercely committed. The project involves this partnership with the local people and the environment, you can ride, walk, do yoga or take aromatherapy, a little library cabin stands solitary down by the lake, tables are set up for dinner beneath trees shining with health and when the lanterns are lit in the garden the whole forest looks like fairyland beneath the stars. The five little cottages for guests are built round the main building which houses the indoor pool, the yoga and meditation rooms, the sauna and the common rooms. Each cottage has its own private terrace onto the garden and comfortable space for a family of four. Serenity of place, generosity of staff, food and nature, complete rest.

rooms	5: 4 cottages, 1 suite.
price	Half-board from 350Dh p.p.
meals	Lunch or dinner à la carte.
closed	Never.
directions	From Ben Slimane P3331 for coast 13km; centre on left.

	Jilali El Karama
tel	+212 (0)22 25 89 06/61 17 76 46
fax	+212 (0)22 25 89 06
e-mail	laforet@menara.ma
web	www.centrelaforet.com

Guest house

L'Hippocampe
Oualidia Plage

Good food, delightful, unaffected rooms in a beautiful spot giving straight onto the beach of the lovely lagoon, the Hippocampe has been revamped since Abdellatif Illame took it over. He and his charming Lebanese wife care a lot about this pretty resort against the hill used by the royal family (he remembers making sandcastles with princesses when he was a child) and their hotel thrives in a green paradise of age-old trees, bougainvillea, mimosa and roses where the little bedroom bungalows, each with its green and pleasant patch, climb the terraces of these sublime gardens. Doubles are light, comfortable and good-sized, the suites with their private terraces are more showily done – canopied beds in alcoves, a Moroccan salon corner, pastel zellige bathrooms – and much sought after by honeymooners and celebrities. In the fine chalet-like dining room warmed by beams and log fires, the attentive, discreet and relaxed staff will serve you delicious Moroccan and international family cooking – their seafood really stands out – that entirely justifies the half-board arrangement.

rooms	25: 14 doubles, 7 twins, 2 triples, 2 suites.
price	Half-board 1,176Dh–2,500Dh for two.
meals	Lunch à la carte.
closed	Never.
directions	From centre town for lagoon, 1st right.

Abdellatif & Martine Illane

tel	+212 (0)23 36 61 08
fax	+212 (0)23 36 64 61
e-mail	hotelhippocampe@hotmail.com

Small hotel

map 3   entry 16

Maison de l'Ostréa II

Parc à Huitres et Coquillages No7, Oualidia

Fancy sleeping over the oyster beds! Every room in this delightful inn fills with sunset glory over the most beautiful lagoon in Morocco where the Phoenicians once fished and Jacques Pinscloux's beds grow most of the country's oysters. The place is always full at lunchtime for the freshest shellfish imaginable prepared by a brilliant fish chef. Manager Adbelhadi knows all there is to know about oysters, their lives and times and always has a helpful suggestion. Then book a lagoon tour on the Ostréa's own barge. The bedrooms, in a row above the restaurant, are classically simple, each has one wide double and one single bed, soft colouring, a walk-in cupboard and a plain white bathroom with all the necessary bits and excellent towels. You can fling the big square windows wide and breathe in the invigorating sea air or close their double-glazing against wind and wave – this is a peaceful place to sleep then wake to the morning activity of fishermen and gulls in that limpid view across calm water and gleaming sands. Divine food in a sublime spot served by friendly, first-class staff – highly unusual and definitely special.

rooms	5 doubles.
price	600Dh.
meals	In-house restaurant 80Dh-250Dh.
closed	Never.
directions	From Casablanca, on right as you enter Oualidia. Signposted.

**Jacques Pinscloux
& Adbelhadi Mounadi**

tel	+212 (0)23 36 64 51/63 24/64 49 12 76
fax	+212 (0)23 36 64 53
e-mail	ostrea007@yahoo.fr
web	www.ilove-casablanca.com/ostrea

Guest house

Hôtel-Restaurant l'Initiale
Oualidia Plage

A new and friendly place down by the lagoon near the fishing port, the Initiale stands like a blue and white picture framed against sand and sea – and is said to be one of the best restaurants in town. Designed in modern Mediterranean style, it only has its arched windows to give in a Moroccan something but, like the rest of Oualidia, it is very popular with Marrakchi families in summer. The terracotta-coloured dining room has seascapes on the walls, simple wooden tables and chairs, pretty tablecloths, good music and ocean light to give it a relaxing atmosphere. Or you can eat on any one of the terraces – the roof has spectacular views of both Atlantic and village sides. The good-sized bedrooms, some over the restaurant, some in a separate building, are in the same mood, light and airy, white-painted with marbled floors, all the essential fittings and furniture, basic but adequate, snug little functional shower rooms. Bedding is new, of course, and several rooms have balconies facing either the sea or the street. A clean and welcoming place to stay for a few tranquil days and enjoy some good seafood.

rooms	6: 2 doubles, 4 quadruples.
price	300DhDh. Half-board 500Dh for two.
meals	Lunch or dinner from 850h.
closed	During Ramadan.
directions	From Oualidia for Oualidia Plage right down to beach: l'Initiale is one of the last buildings.

	Ahmed Joubaer
tel	+212 (0)22 36 62 46
fax	+212 (0)23 36 62 46

Small hotel

map 3   entry 18

Hôtel Atlantide
Rue Chawki, Safi

The palm-lined avenue, the magnificent gardens, the pool area with its green lattice screening and perfectly extraordinary view of the bay of Safi are all worthy of four full stars; built in 1919 at the beginning of the French Protectorate, the very fine building has all the right Art Deco features plus cupola, columns and a monumental Bauhaus-style staircase; the prices and the plastic garden furniture reflect the simpler truth and, with impeccable cleanliness, the combination of all this makes the Atlantide a great-value place to stay. Don't expect luxury upstairs: rooms are simple and old-fashioned but with the endearing charm of a world gone by, especially in the period furniture (some bathrooms definitely need renewing but all have bathrobes...). A dozen have been redone with wallpaper, carpet and air conditioning, beds are good — and coming down each morning to breakfast with that ocean view through the 1930s glass is a treat indeed. Add staff who are exceptionally kind, helpful and, when appropriate, amusing and you have a definitely special place.

rooms	34: 32 doubles, 2 suites.
price	340Dh.
meals	Breakfast 36Dh. Lunch or dinner 130Dh.
closed	Never.
directions	From port, Ave Moulay Youssef along south side of medina 800m; right Rue Ibnou Badis; left Ave Aerktouni; right Rue Chawki.

	Abdelaziz Alaoui
tel	+212 (0)44 46 21 60/61
fax	+212 (0)44 46 45 95

Small hotel

Hôtel-Restaurant-Hammam Lalla Mira

14 rue d'Algérie, Essaouira-Medina

Morocco's very first organic hotel! Felicitas stopped growing organic veg in Germany to build her dream in Morocco because she loved the country, the people and the quality of the food. Princess Lalla Mira gave her name to Essaouira's oldest bathhouse, now restored as a magnificent traditional green and yellow two-roomed hammam for 30 so that the locals could still use it for just 7Dh. Above it she built a house in natural, untreated materials and opened the sweetest, most colourful organic restaurant where locally-grown ingredients and spices are transformed with northern know-how. House and hammam are solar heated (another first), mattresses, blankets and linen are non-allergic kapok or organic cotton. So, virtuous and prettily anchored in Moroccan style: carved keyhole-arch doors, lots of wrought iron in the soft yellow patio, fine four-posters in the double rooms, good use of one strong colour on white – blue, purple, red, green or terracotta – for bedcovers and cushions. Elegantly light-hearted atmosphere, charming helpful staff under excellent Khalid, greenery growing apace.

rooms	13: 6 doubles, 6 triples, 1 suite for 2-4.
price	412Dh-752Dh including hammam.
meals	Lunch or dinner menu 70Dh, full buffet 120Dh. Organic vegetarian menus and meat dishes à la carte.
closed	Never.
directions	From Bab Marrakech into Rue Mohamed El Qorry; second left Rue d'Algérie.

Felicitas Christ

tel	+212 (0)44 47 50 46/61 14 50 87
fax	+212 (0)44 47 68 50
e-mail	lallamira@lallamira.ma
web	www.lallamira.ma

Small hotel

map 3   entry 20

Jacques Paul

Émeraude Hôtel

228 rue Chbanate, Petite Porte Bab Marrakech, Essaouira-Medina

The little street is scruffy, the green sign garish – the outside belies the deeply attractive house inside where light bounces off the white walls onto the deep blues, soft yellows and pale peace of the furnishings. The rooms are not big in this small-scale 'dar' with its cool fountainless patio, but it's never claustrophobic, there are outside windows and the air is intimate and peaceful. Frédérique has a sunny carefree manner, her easy friendliness filling the three floors of tiled, rope-banistered stairs out onto the terrace where glass-topped tables and wicker chairs lie around under the slatted canopy. Here you discover a delightful shambles of white walls, angled roofs and distant medina while the sea pounds ever on beyond. Little bedrooms are pale and tempting with excellent mattresses and linen, no decorative excesses, the odd alcove, drawers under beds, Moroccan lamps and framed posters, knotted scarves and other fun young touches – and really miniature bathrooms. Remarkable value and a delightful welcome from the owners or their kind, smiling staff. Mohamed V once slept next door!

rooms	12: 9 doubles, 3 rooms with bunks.
price	390Dh.
meals	Lunch or dinner 80Dh-120Dh. By arrangement.
closed	Never.
directions	Park at Petite Porte Bab Marrakech; hotel 30m up on right. Ring for escort first time.

Frédérique Berger & Stéphan Boeri

tel	+212 (0)44 47 34 94
fax	+212 (0)44 47 34 94
e-mail	contact@essaouirahotel.com
web	www.essaouirahotel.com

Small hotel

Hôtel Riad Dar El Qdima

4 rue Malek Ben Rahal, Avenue de l'Istiqlal, Essaouira-Medina

Built in the 19th-century on the dry side of the medina, the 'old' house (qdima) is indeed one of the oldest in Essaouira and its stone columns and arches, low, round, solid, give it an unusual look. It is very simply done, all Moroccan, without frills or pretensions. The long red-benched Moroccan salon reaches darkly down to its fireplace; there are pretty wrought-iron tables and chairs for sitting out in the patio; walls are done in a very pleasing earth-coloured lime wash, woodwork in a harmonious soft green and you can see down from stairs and corridors through the original little spyholes. Bedrooms, all fairly small, give onto the patio so the higher you are the lighter it is and the more flourishing the potted plants; the terrace rooms are flooded with that ocean light. The sober rooms have 'gothic' windows and coloured glass, brand new beds and typical lamps, sitting spaces are mostly out on the galleries, tadelakt shower rooms are delightful. Dr Sayegh, a charming, intelligent local dentist, and manager Jalil are eager for ideas to improve their house, Madame Sayegh oversees daily life, their staff are young and willing.

rooms	14: 6 doubles, 5 triples, 3 singles.
price	450Dh.
meals	Lunch 60Dh. Dinner 110Dh. Picnic possible. By arrangement.
closed	Never.
directions	From Bab El Minzeh up Avenue Oqba Ben Nafia, through Bab My Youssef into Avenue de l'Istiqlal, 2nd right.

Dr Mohammed Hassan Jaafar Sayegh & Jalil Jassim

tel	+212 (0)44 47 38 58/61 53 38 71
fax	+212 (0)44 47 41 54
e-mail	contact@darqdima.com
web	www.darqdima.com

Small hotel

map 3　entry 22

Jacques Paul

Dar Al Bahar

1 rue Touahen, Essaouira-Medina

From some windows you dive into a dramatic, unbroken view of the Atlantic crashing onto the rocks; set in well-known San Dion area, this is indeed the 'house by the sea'. And from the magnificent black and white tiled roof terrace you can see across the medina. Blue is naturally one of the colours here, but there are green and purple and orange as well. The Parisios recently-finished renovation is lovely indeed: stylish yet not over-designed, classy yet never cold, coordinated yet never banal. So forget the dirty street, open the door and discover the joyful hand-painted shutters that make pictures of the windows (four frame that seascape), the smart tiled floors holding simple white plaster beds, brand new mattresses and cuddly, colourful wool blankets, the pretty tiled and rustic-rough bathrooms that are just right, the good modern Moroccan art on the walls. You can learn a lot about the area, well cushioned on a wrought-iron chair, possibly by the patio fire, while the owners or their staff direct you to their favourite craftsmen, tell you about local activities, history and design. Deeply inviting.

rooms	10: 6 doubles, 3 triples; 1 apartment (4 with sea view).
price	400Dh–550Dh.
meals	Dinner 150Dh. Picnic possible. By arrangement.
closed	Never.
directions	House in San Dion quarter; on arriving at Parking du Port, telephone for assistance. Map on web site.

	Jean-Claude & Lise Parisio
tel	+212 (0)44 47 68 31
fax	+212 (0)44 47 68 31
e-mail	daralbahar@yahoo.fr
web	www.daralbahar.com

Small hotel

Madada Mogador
5 rue Youssef El Fassi, Essaouira-Medina

The newly-renovated upper floor of this rich old Souiri merchant's house brings you right to the top of the old ramparts, into lovely big rooms that are high enough for sleeping platforms: you'll wake into eyefuls of plunging sea. The breathtaking terraces are even higher. The design is by well-reputed Jonathan Amar, as is this sketch, the light is the ineffable Atlantic reflection – his skill in leaving space for its subtlety is admirable. Pale pale colours, fabulous finishes in matt and gloss, just enough of the right furniture and a few Grecian urns so that the evening light is even more fascinating than the broad day. Bedrooms are sober, soft and quiet with books and music and a gentle pastel touch to lift the natural background. The perfect hostess, Chris is beautiful, refined and produces fabulous breakfasts. Add a dazzling smile, a brilliant sense of presentation – lights, scents, music, as well as food – and a fine sense of humour: you feel deeply privileged to be eating at her table. Essaouira's latest guest house, Madada is a cocoon of enormous class. *Genuine, inventive vegetarian cooking.*

rooms	6: 3 doubles, 3 twins; 4 with own terrace.
price	1,000Dh–1,200Dh.
meals	Lunch or dinner 150Dh. Picnic 75Dh. By arrangement. BYO.
closed	Never.
directions	Just inside ramparts opposite Orson Welles Garden.

	Christine Dadda
tel	+212 (0)44 47 55 12
fax	+212 (0)44 47 55 12
e-mail	info@madada.com
web	www.madada.com

Guest house

map 3   entry 24

Jacques Paul

Dar Loulema

2 rue Souss, Essaouira-Medina

This house is a cocoon of superb design and comfort. The 18th-century mansion was on the damp side of the medina so the last owners simply dismantled it entirely, dug a damp-proof pit, put every stone back in place – and moved to the country. They have just sold the house to Nathalie but she is keeping their whole team of polished and highly attentive staff under Ismaël's guidance. The little white patio carries the house up to the sky, past galleries and light-filtered sitting spaces to the fabulous furnished terrace with its wraparound view. A rare, soberly perfect staircase of unglazed tiles, wood and zellige will take you up to a festival of bedroom décors: *Marrakech* is rich red, of course, with a superb orientalist picture over the vaulted bed, *Todra* has the shapes and colours of the southern kasbahs, *Majorelle* celebrates the artist, then there's *Mogador, Zagora,...* all with soft sensuous bathrooms. Every rug, lamp, chair and fabric is thought through and put in just the right place and Nathalie is bringing her refreshing and happy presence to make it all a form of perfection.

rooms	7: 3 doubles, 1 twin, 3 mini-suites (1 double, 2 twins).
price	750Dh–1,300Dh.
meals	Lunch or dinner by arrangement. Choice in town.
closed	Never.
directions	From Place Moulay Hassan, Rue Scala, 1st right Rue Souss.

	Nathalie Burnet & Ismaël Fathi
tel	+212 (0)44 47 53 46/61 24 76 61
fax	+212 (0)44 47 53 46
e-mail	info@darloulema.com
web	www.darloulema.com

Guest house

Jacques Paul

Dar Liouba

26-28 impasse Moulay Ismaïl, Essaouira-Medina

Maria is a Russian thoroughbred, brimming with exuberance, high spirits and the desire to please; she's also a designer, and her house reflects her talent. First, the dressed stone façade is beautiful; then the broad main room is sheer seduction with its little indoor garden under the octagonal light that caresses the cedarwood moucharabieh balustrades and infinitely subtle colouring. The octagon is sacred to Muslims and this was an imam's house with the mosque just over the way. From here, the salon entices you into its clean-cut elegance of white, sand and warm flame until you succumb to the sweep of the superb staircase and move on up. Bedrooms, on two floors, are worth the climb – full of light that dances over lustrous rich cottons, beautiful objects, carved alcoves, all celebrating Maria's delight in form and texture. Her shower rooms are little gems in tadelakt and zellige, her linen, of course, is a pleasure to see and touch, her terrace is pretty and comfortable. If possible, dine with this fascinating, eccentric, voluble artist who receives so brilliantly. When it's his turn, Peter is the perfect cultured host.

rooms	6: 4 doubles, 2 twins.
price	550Dh-750Dh.
meals	Dinner 150Dh. By arrangement.
closed	5-20 January.
directions	Enter medina at Bab Marrakech into Rue Mohamed El Qorry; 3rd right Rue Ibn Khaldoun; 1st right Rue Moulay Ismaïl; 2nd impasse on right.

	Maria Pergay & Peter Cheung
tel	+212 (0)44 47 62 97/63 18 29 60
fax	+212 (0)44 47 64 13
e-mail	lallaliouba@menara.ma
web	www.darliouba.com

Guest house

map 3   entry 26

Jacques Paul

Riad Al Zahia

4 rue Mohamed Diouri, Essaouira-Medina

Riad Al Zahia is a genuine *maison d'hôtes* whose relaxed and charming owners always greet their guests with tea and pastries, smiles and interest, as generous as their beautifully furnished, miraculously sheltered 360° terrace. Art lovers and collectors, they show the best local painters in their salon while media folk occupy the house every year for the G'naoua music festival. It's a privilege to know Pascale, fine and elegant with her deep knowledge of many subjects, Alain the former racing driver with his sunny humour and easy contact, not forgetting Attila the Pasha tomcat; to watch the water of the tiled fountain flicker in the lantern light; to sit by the fire in the ochre-red salon and feel the quality of old furniture and modern art. Bedrooms, with sublime kaftans as wall hangings, wear Moroccan rugs, blankets and fabrics, all their colours and patterns, to perfection; muslin shimmers over beds, fresh flowers welcome, colourful tadelakt bathrooms have all the latest equipment. Finally, essentially, the nicest possible staff will look after you with intelligent smiles and delicious breakfasts.

rooms	8: 4 doubles, 2 twins, 2 suites for 4.
price	650Dh.
meals	Plenty of choice nearby.
closed	10 November-20 December.
directions	From Avenue de l'Istiqlal take Rue Attarine; 4th left Rue Mohamed Diouri.

Pascale Robinot & Alain Crozet

tel	+212 (0)44 47 35 81/61 34 71 31
fax	+212 (0)44 47 61 07
e-mail	zahia@essaouiranet.com
web	www.riadalzahia.com

Guest house

Jacques Paul

Dar Ness
1 rue Khalib Ben Walid, Essaouira-Medina

James and Élisabeth may be new to *maison d'hôtes*, they clearly know how to make guests happy, their house is as full of heartfelt intelligence as their fabulous roof terrace is flooded with ocean light and an incredible view of Place Moulay Hassan, Essaouira's heart. The fine old architecture has pride of place: the patio soars skywards on its stone columns, some bedrooms have super trefoiled Moorish arches, doorways are crowned with stone 'spy' holes. Within this frame, your hosts have created two salons, one Moroccan, one European, furnished with a mix of typical thuya-wood and French country pieces. The bedrooms, on two floors round the patio, are big with good storage space, wide beds and simple yet unconventional old-rose tadelakt bathrooms; some even have their own sitting area. The décor is Berber carpets, cactus-silk blankets of yellow and brown stripes in the right proportions and a very personal feel. With her strong, endearing personality, Élisabeth is the heart and soul of Dar Ness, ever ready to advise or chat to you over a cup of coffee, and very involved with a project to help local street kids.

rooms	9: 6 doubles, 2 twins, 1 single.
price	590Dh-690Dh.
meals	Dinner 120Dh. Picnic possible. By arrangement
closed	Never.
directions	Rue Khalib Ben Walid gives directly into the main square Moulay Hassan.

James Desforges & Élisabeth de la Bourdonnaye

tel	+212 (0)44 47 68 04
fax	+212 (0)44 47 68 04
e-mail	contact@dar-ness.com
web	www.darness-essaouira.com

Guest house

 map 3   entry 28

La Casa del Mar

35 rue d'Oujda, Essaouira-Medina

The sea, the wind: essential Essaouira. You can drink in as much sea view and wind as you like on the roof terrace but once down below you are cosily protected from the blast by the traditional layout of a courtyard house. And cosily welcomed into the bosom of a warm united family from Majorca – three generations, from Tolo and Sanam's baby boy to her mother Isabelle, all involved in the gentle, friendly living here. The imaginatively arranged ground floor has an open-plan kitchen, soft relaxed colouring and a view right up to the sky bringing a great sense of space and airiness. The whole place is delightfully decorated in warm colours and furnished in a simple but thoughtful way, bedrooms are attractive and light, their openness to the courtyard sky easily making up for the lack of outside windows. Two rooms have an open-plan bathroom-bedroom layout. You feel you are sharing something genuine here with these nice, easy, polyglot people. And they will guide you expertly to the many local delights. *Children welcome but small ones need supervision on steps. French, German, Spanish, English spoken. Cash only.*

rooms	4 doubles.
price	600Dh; sole occupancy for 8: 2,400Dh per day.
meals	Lunch or dinner 30Dh–150Dh. By arrangement.
closed	Never.
directions	Park by port, Bab Marrakech, and ring owners who come with handcart for luggage.

Sanam, Tolo & Isabelle

tel	+212 (0)44 47 50 91/68 94 38 39
fax	+212 (0)44 47 50 91
e-mail	info@lacasa-delmar.com
web	www.lacasa-delmar.com

Guest house & catered house

Riad Gyvo

3 rue Mohamed Ben Messaoud, Essaouira-Medina

After 10 years as nomads in a 10m² camper, Guy and Ivo surfed in from Belgium in 1993 to anchor here and learn Essaouira from inside its skin, sharing their 1,000m² house with locals and their animals; now they belong. Belonging includes running a crêche and surfboard lessons for street children, collecting art from Berber Morocco and sub-Saharan Africa, writing two tomes about it and opening one of the finest houses in the medina. In the gracious salon off the superbly sober sea-lit patio, you will breakfast with African carvings, Berber textiles and magnificent pots of joyful plants and, if you're lucky, hear them talk fascinatingly about these cultures. Given the powerful shape and atmosphere of this old house, they deliberately chose clean lines, plain colours and no craftsy clutter: lots of white, good beds, modern paintings that are worth looking at, highly original wall hangings. The two ground-floor rooms are darker and cooler than higher rooms, all are huge, high, simply wicker-furnished; the terrace room shares the eye-stretching view out to the Mogador Isles. Utterly human and extraordinary.

rooms	6: 2 suites, 4 studios; 5 have kitchenettes for self-catering.
price	1,050Dh-1,400Dh. 930Dh-1,280Dh for two per day self-catering.
meals	Only for large groups by arrangement. BYO. Wide choice nearby.
closed	Never.
directions	Enter medina at Bab Sbaa; 1st left Rue Mohamed Ben Messaoud.

Ivo Grammet & Guy Bellinkx

tel	+212 (0)44 47 51 02
fax	+212 (0)44 47 51 02
e-mail	reservat@riadgyvo.com
web	www.riadgyvo.com

Guest house & catered house

map 3   entry 30

Jacques Paul

Jack's Apartments
1 Place Moulay Hassan, Essaouira-Medina

Jack and his family are central actors in the microcosm that is Essaouira, his Kiosk a meeting place for all. His apartments are all higgledy-piggledy in a couple of old houses, side by side on the ramparts facing the sea, the rocks and the Mogador Isles: one of the greatest views in town. In converting them, he respected the original architecture, painted everything white with typical Essaouira blue woodwork, ingenious use of of unusual corners – with utterly charming results. Each flat has a sitting area, one or two bedrooms, a cooking/eating space and an excellent tadelakt or zellige bathroom: Jack's Swiss origins show in the quality of fittings and finishes. Bedding is superb, too. The decoration is simple and delightful: Berber blankets, good divan sofas, Moroccan lamps with loads of character, super rugs on terracotta tiles and pretty wooden furniture – string-back chairs and cushions, glorified deckchairs, bamboo cupboards. The light bounces off the sea and into all the windows, top-floor flats may be a steep climb but the view is worth the effort. Self-catering couldn't be sweeter.

rooms	12: 2 doubles; 10 apartments: 1 studio for 2, 3 studios for 3, 4 apartments for 4, 1 for 6, 1 for 8.
price	300Dh (double room)-1,200Dh (apartment for 8), inc. daily cleaning.
meals	Lunch or dinner from 60Dh. Delivered by arrangement. BYO.
closed	Never.
directions	In Place Moulay Hassan on SW edge of medina, go to Jack's Kiosk for information, keys, books, stamps,...

Jack Oswald
tel	+212 (0)44 47 55 38
fax	+212 (0)44 47 69 01
e-mail	apartment@essaouira.com
web	www.essaouira.com/apartments

Catered house

Villa Flora

7 quartier des Dunes, Essaouira

If you feel that a riad in the medina may be slightly claustrophobic, come to Khalid Rahham's discreet little family-run hotel where all the rooms, each with its own piece of terrace, give onto the pretty rose garden and quiet comfort is guaranteed. The long terrace at the front looks straight out to the beach, the dunes and old Essaouira – an enchantment at sunset. The big white bedrooms are magnificent for the price with good wide beds, lovely thuya furniture and plenty of storage while the odd Moorish arch gives that oriental touch. Bathrooms are big too, and excellently fitted and fixtured. There's a classic dining room full of light that gives onto the back garden so that guests can have breakfast at the little mosaic tables outside if they wish. Khalid, a modest, attentive host, wants this to be a relaxed and memorable feast and is eager that his guests lack nothing. He was born here, knows Essaouira and the area inside out, can tell endless tales and advise on all sorts of visits. Villa Flora, a great base for exploring the region, invites you to settle in among her flowers and stay a while.

rooms	9: 7 doubles, 2 twins.
price	600Dh.
meals	Picnic by arrangement.
closed	Never.
directions	Entering Essaouira, pass sea-front roundabout, 1st right, 1st left.

	Khalid Rahham
tel	+212 (0)44 47 39 46
fax	+212 (0)44 78 47 91
e-mail	villa.flora.souira@caramail.com/
	villaflora@menara.ma
web	marocreservation.com/villaflora

Small hotel

map 3   entry 32

Riad Zahra Mogador

90 Quartier des Dunes, 44100 Essaouira

The family atmosphere at Riad Zahra Mogador will gather you up in easy welcome. Mohamed came home after 20 years in America, bringing his relaxed and dynamic Quebecoise partner Céline. They mustered his family and built the prettiest, friendliest new hotel in Essaouira with mother and sisters in the kitchen making delicious Moroccan crêpes for breakfast and brothers in the dining room serving super Moroccan or international dishes. The local architecture inspired the generous open patio with its sandstone pillars, the big luminous Moroccan salon/dining room, charming in its rosy-red outfit, the giant pots that stand guard everywhere, their leafy green sentries waving at you. Bedrooms wear the red and green of the Moroccan flag, the larger ones have Moroccan cushioned bench-beds for two extra sleepers, all have good shower rooms, top-floor rooms give great views over the pool to the dunes. Laughing and attentive, Mohamed and Céline can't do enough to make your stay memorable – they love their new life and, just 150 metres from beach and dunes, their riad is excellent value. *Surfing courses available.*

rooms	20: 8 doubles, 2 triples, 10 quadruples.
price	350Dh–600Dh.
meals	Lunch or dinner 110Dh. Picnic possible. By arrangement.
closed	Never.
directions	From Marrakech into Essaouira, at sea-front roundabout, right then 1st left.

Céline Bélanger & Mohamed Najid

tel	+212 (0)44 47 48 22/61 70 42 47
fax	+212 (0)44 47 43 12
e-mail	riadzahra@menara.ma

Small hotel

Auberge de la Plage
Sidi Kaouki

A blocky modern building high above Sidi Kaouki, the 'beach inn' has inestimable riches on its terrace: the view of the whole bay, the beach and the wind-driven surfboarders is so extraordinary you could gorge your eyes for hours as the light changes. And when you reach the courtyard and discover the charming little garden and the two fine horses galloping round their paddock you will understand why we like this place. Inside, the welcome from your Italo-German hosts and Halima, the discreet and likeable housekeeper, is smiling and genuine, spaces are wide and luminous with rooms round the covered patio or the terrace and almost all windows look out to sea. Beyond, the warmly atmospheric dining room has instant appeal with books here and there for guests to borrow and lanterns in the evening (no electricity and hot water 8am-10am and 4pm-10pm only). Carina and Gabriel, great horse-lovers both, can organise camel or horseback treks: very much present, they are only too happy to advise and the whole place breathes an air of friendly courtesy. They are active in an Italo-Moroccan local crafts development project.

rooms	10: 5 doubles, 2 twins, 3 triples (5 with baths, 5 sharing 2 baths).
price	260Dh sharing bathroom; 360Dh with bathroom.
meals	Lunch or dinner 120Dh, or à la carte. By arrangement. BYO.
closed	Never.
directions	Entering Sidi Kaouki, take track on left and follow signs.

Gabriel Meletti & Carina Fisher

tel	+212 (0)44 47 66 00/61 61 85 74
fax	+212 (0)44 47 33 83
e-mail	aubplage@iam.net.ma
web	www.kaouki.com

Country Inn – Trekking place

map 3   entry 34

Dar Mimosas
Route d'Agadir, Essaouira

One of the finest luxury guest houses in the kingdom where royalty may come to steal some peace, this walled country estate sprawling among the dense mimosas – planted to fix the dunes – and its sublime gardens has space and privacy in its earth-red arcaded houses; civilisation in its library and music corner; high art in its Syrian-style inlaid thuya furniture and superb orientalist and modern paintings; room for all in salons and dining rooms galore; its own path to beach and bird-thronged river. Vast bedrooms are decorated with refined elegance and embroidered linen, fabulous bathrooms with midnight-blue and white Portuguese tiles and heaps of thick towels. Each has a fireplace and a little garden of its own though the Maison Bleue riad suites are our favourites with their high-flying terraces that look way out across the countryside. As well as a second bedroom and little kitchen, the Royal suites rejoice in the complete traditional patio-and-fountain set. Delicious and sophisticated food, perfectly discreet and efficient staff, a charming and civilised host. Garbo stayed at this place of exceptional class.

rooms	8: 4 Royal suites for 4-5 with kitchenette; 4 Riad suites for 2, each with small private garden.
price	3,200Dh-5,200Dh. Sole occupancy possible.
meals	Light lunch (salad & barbecue) 330Dh. Dinner 440Dh. Picnic possible. By arrangement.
closed	Never.
directions	From Essaouira for Agadir; right at sign 2km after end of town.

Philippe Cachet
tel	+212 (0)44 47 59 34
fax	+212 (0)44 78 52 74
e-mail	mimosas1@iam.net.ma
web	www.darmimosas.com

Guest house

Le Jardin des Douars

Essaouira

This magnificent house could have grown naturally out of its fairytale setting of red cliffs and river bed but in fact, having first planted many wonders on many terraces (Jean is a landscape designer) and dug a dazzling duck-green infinity pool (you could be swimming in the river), Jean and Aurelio finished their mansion in 2003. A splendid gathering of red blocks and towers, it sees for miles from its hilltop and every prospect pleases. The dining room is a vast convivial marvel with central fireplace, circular benches, 15-metre window and some of this couple's fine collection of African woodwork and weaving: set against natural rough walls in shades of Marrakech red to softest orange, their masks, fabulous tribal fabrics and Dogon doors carry strong vibrations. There are spaces galore for reading, relaxing, being private. The generous bedrooms are wonderful, each with a sitting area, rustically 'faded' green wooden furniture and carefully contemporary bedding and linen. Your delightful hosts – Aurelio the glittering, amusing master of ceremonies, Jean the backroom boy – used to be in catering so dinner is a must.

rooms	18: 10 triples, 4 suites for 4, 2 bungalows for 4.
price	800Dh–1,000Dh.
meals	Lunch or dinner 150Dh. Picnic possible. By arrangement.
closed	Never.
directions	From Essaouira take coast road for Agadir 10km; right for Marrakech 3km; on right-hand bend, track on left to house.

Aurelio Bonachera & Jean Secondi
tel   +212 (0)44 47 64 92/64 24 00 05
fax   +212 (0)44 47 40 72/64 92

Small hotel

map 3   entry 36

Baoussala
Douar El Ghazoua, Essaouira

In a green eucalyptus oasis far from the wild windy coast, this amazing womb-like house, all curves and alcoves in earthy reds and ochres, centres on a brilliantly rug-strewn circular patio with a high vaulted recess – your first gasp. Original, organic shapes and spaces are the norm: shimmering fabrics, unusual traditional weaves, warm colours and wood – wicker, oleander, eucalyptus. The vast round salon with a mini-amphitheatre of cushions round the sunken central hearth under leaping white arches is irresistibly attractive – second gasp. The same theatricality carries the marvellous bedrooms: platforms and draped turban cloths, superb Berber blankets and modern art, fireplaces and mosquito nets – you could stay all year and never tire of it or its warm friendly atmosphere. Big bathrooms are naturally lovely in oodles of taste and shot-silk tadelakt. Dominique is the hostess whose flair and personality have created this brilliant place and keep it alive with convivial candlelit dinners, African musical evenings, absolutely delicious food, books and music everywhere, even a tiny pool. Utterly, utterly special.

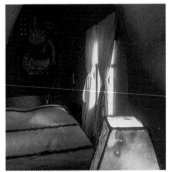

rooms	6: 4 doubles, 1 twin, 1 suite for 4.
price	500Dh–700Dh.
meals	Lunch 70Dh. Dinner 130Dh. Picnic possible. By arrangement. BYO.
closed	Never.
directions	From Essaouira, coast road for Agadir 8km to Douar El Ghazoua; right on track 3km to last telegraph pole.

	Dominique Maté
tel	+212 (0)44 47 43 45
fax	+212 (0)44 47 43 45
e-mail	dchoupin@yahoo.fr
web	www.baoussala.com

Guest house & catered house

Villa Clementina

Route Côtière Essaouira-Safi - km12, Essaouira

It's easy to find this ground-hugging stone house, out in the middle of the countryside. Rachid and Sandrine loved Essaouira life but needed something healthier, more peaceful. Clementina was the answer: it's taking shape fast and with such tender care the garden will be a delight. The water is heated with wood, the house is lit by candles and, within its plain white walls and beamed ceiling, is a picture of soberly relaxing taste, its splashes of warm bright colour always in harmony. Sandrine's succulent meals - she's a passionate cook - are a delicious and varied mix of French and Moroccan. Lying round a patio that opens onto the countryside and the sea, bedrooms are big, comfortable and gently pastel with super soft tadelakt bathrooms. Rachid and Sandrine create an atmosphere of convivial sharing and want you to get to know the area they love. Let them organise camel treks, mountain biking or hikes to the little fishing villages, country bazaars and *marabouts'* tombs in the neighbourhood. The beach is just 15 minutes' walk away and the pretty bungalow is ideal if you want that extra independence.

rooms	7: 5 doubles, 1 triple, 1 bungalow for 3 with kitchenette.
price	450Dh-600Dh.
meals	Lunch or dinner 120Dh. Picnic possible. By arrangement.
closed	Never.
directions	From Marrakech, right before Essaouira on coast road R301 for Safi. House signposted on left.

	Rachid Loukid & Sandrine Fayolle
tel	+212 (0)61 08 87 09
fax	+212 (0)44 47 30 30
e-mail	villaclementina@yahoo.fr

Guest house & catered house

map 3   entry 38

La Maison du Chameau

Douar Jmel, Douar Al Arab, Essaouira

Yes, the camel is king here – not any old camel, the pure white thoroughbred long-distance runner from Mali. You meet him as you arrive (you can learn to ride and go trekking, long or short). In the garden, more beautiful well-tended things grow, including vegetables for Salka's wonderful Berber family cooking – the bougainvillea-flooded inn is renowned for its table. From garden to big Moroccan salon where unadorned white walls reflect the traditional red and blue cushions. The utterly simple, almost monastic lifestyle of the desert people inspires this tiny renovated hamlet of three houses, each with its patio (sleep out and enter stardom), communal washing space with saloon-doored showers and rush-matted rooms with (very firm) floor-level mattresses. There is elegance in such sobriety, softness in the pink and blue washes, romance in the lantern light (no electricity here and a wood-burning stove for hot water). The people are as calm and human and welcoming as the place itself. Beyond the village are dunes, fields, woods and thousands of birds. You could scarcely imagine a more Moroccan experience.

rooms	12: 3 houses each with 4 twins/doubles, 2 showers, 1 washbasin, 2 wcs.
price	240Dh–320Dh.
meals	Lunch or dinner 90Dh. By arrangement. Picnic possible. BYO.
closed	Never.
directions	From Essaouira for Marrakech 5km; right on track 3km; signposted.

Michel Laurent

tel	+212 (0)44 78 50 77
fax	+212 (0)44 78 59 62
e-mail	maisonduchameau@yahoo.fr
web	www.maisonduchameau.com

Guest house

Dar Salsa (Cap Sim Trekking)

Douar El Ghazoua, Essaouira

These two delightful, generous Bretons welcome you in all simplicity to their open and environmentally friendly village home which hums with interest and artistic talent. No designer décor, just the Souiri blue and white, wicker furniture, local pots dotted around. No luxury – all guests share two showers and two loos – but a pretty, sheltered enclosure for deckchairs round the swimming pool and a thoroughly attractive bar and barbecue spot at the back where artists and nature-lovers gather under the rush roofing to share their day's adventures or sing a little song of an evening. Cat (Catherine) and Jipé (Jean-Paul) love their adopted country and work with Mohamed from the village to run discovery treks and alternative excursions in the area: bike it, walk it or take a camel – Mohamed is an excellent guide who can take you to see potters in their workshops, argan-oil makers, little fishing villages. Jipé the professional musician organises traditional music workshops, there are local water-colourists who can take you out into the countryside to paint, wind- and kite-surfing lessons and… Outstanding value.

rooms	6: 2 doubles, 4 triples, sharing 2 showers, 2 wcs. Or 3 rooms let with kitchen as self-catering apartment.
price	180Dh; pool 25Dh p.p. Apartment 4,000Dh–5,200Dh per week.
meals	Breakfast 20Dh. Picnic possible. Use of kitchen 10Dh p.p. By arrangement. 2 restaurants 1km.
closed	Never.
directions	From Essaouira for Agadir 8km; right onto track 1.2km; house on left.

Jean-Paul &
Catherine Gueutier-Le Querré

tel	+212 (0)62 20 18 98/70 01 64 61
fax	+212 (0)44 47 43 23
e-mail	contact@capessaouira.com
web	www.capessaouira.com

Guest house & self-catering

map 3   entry 40

Dar Bouslam

Douar Ghazoua, Route d'Agadir - km8, Essaouira

Kébir is a driftwood artist in love with simplicity and light so his house is full of light, simplicity and driftwood – bits of furniture, ornaments, sculptures, even branches 'growing' out of the walls, it has the most marvellously original atmosphere. Quiet and smiling, he is something of a sage, feels close to the Sufi brotherhoods and adores G'naoua music, so fantastic evenings of music and trance occasionally happen in the great white salon with everyone sitting on the multitudinous carpets and cushions by the round fireplace. Rooms and bathrooms are unassumingly natural, minimalist and spotless; the garden pavilion bedroom has trees growing from the beach-pebble floor and out through the roof... There's a superb garden outside, too, with greenery and flowers luxuriating everywhere, plenty of secret corners, a nomad tent and barbecue; the swimming pool is being dug this year. This is a family guest house: Madame Bouslam runs the functional little kitchen and is very talented with traditional Berber dishes. Remarkable value for both B&B or self-catering, a wonderful place for a quiet retreat.

rooms	6: 3 doubles, 1 apartment for 4 (1 double, 1 twin) with kitchen; 2 family rooms sharing bath.
price	300Dh. Sole occupancy including breakfast for 12: 1,500Dh per day.
meals	Lunch or dinner 50Dh. By arrangement. BYO.
closed	Never.
directions	From Essaouira for Ghazoua 3km; red crenellated house on right.

	Kébir Bouslam
tel	+212 (0)44 47 29 23/63 56 94 50
fax	+212 (0)44 47 29 23
e-mail	kebir_bousslam@yahoo.fr
web	www.capessaouira.com

Guest house & catered house

HOW TO USE THIS BOOK

explanations

❶ rooms

Assume all rooms are 'en suite' unless we say otherwise.

If a room is not 'en suite' we say **with separate,** or **with shared bath**: the former you will have to yourself, the latter may be shared with other guests or family members.

❷ room price

The price shown is for one night for two sharing a room. A price range incorporates room/seasonal differences.

❸ meals

Prices are per person. BYO: you may bring your own wine.

❹ closed

When given in months, this means for the whole of the named months and the time in between.

❺ directions

Use as a guide; the owner can give more details.

❻ map & entry numbers

Map page number; entry number.

❼ symbols

See inside back cover for fuller explanation.

sample entry

MARRAKECH-MEDINA

Ryad El Borj
63 Derb Moulay Abdelkader, Derb Dabachi, Marrakech-Medina

*B*orj means tower. 150 years ago, when Pasha Glaoui owned the whole quarter, one of the liveliest in Marrakech, he built a lookout here to oversee the area. Still the highest view of the whole city, it is magic at any hour, sublime at sunset. The typical dark entrance takes you down five steps then on to the blue patio, whence up to the green first floor then the red terrace – all properly dramatic. When renovating the ryad three years ago, your host was careful to preserve the original décor and almost all the very comfortably furnished rooms have painted or carved ceilings while the great glass-vaulted suite is remarkable value with its big bedroom, sitting room, excellent bathroom and an extra salon that gives onto the patio via a superb moucharabieh screen. Colours are pale and sober, materials are noble cedarwood and finely wrought ironwork, doors are antique, floors are strewn with carpets and leather cushions from the Saharaoui south giving the wonderful exotic feel of being in a *khaima*, a nomad tent; breakfast is superbly generous. Pool, drinks and meals available just 20 metres away.

rooms	5: 4 doubles, 1 suite.
price	600Dh-1,200Dh. Sole occupancy for 8: 17,0000Dh-23,000Dh per week.
meals	Lunch or dinner by arrangement. BYO.
closed	Never.
directions	From Place Jemaâ El Fna take Derb Dabachi (behind Café de France); pass mosque on right then first left; house 30m along on right.

Daniel Ghio
tel	+212 (0)44 39 12 23/61 67 59 42
fax	+212 (0)44 39 12 23
e-mail	ryadelborj@wanadoo.net.ma
web	www.ryadelborj.com

Guest house & catered house

entry 68   map 3   ∠ 🐾 ℗ 🐕

مراكش و المناطق

marrakech
& region

What makes this city the magical place it is, a fashionable magnet for the worldly and the artist? Its position on the frontier between desert nomads and 'civilised' northern tribes, between proud African cultures and Spanish sophistications, give it an inimitable buzz. "Black Africa starts at Marrakech", they say - and Andalucia stops here. Within the dauntingly blank walls of the medina are marvels of Moorish art, gardens imitating Eden, 350 mosques, gastronomic delights and some exceptional people. Non-Muslims may not enter the mosques but they vibrate into the streets with calls to prayer and white robes.

The French Protectorate left the Arab towns and their secrets intact and built their brave new towns outside the ramparts: tree-lined avenues, spreading government offices, big houses in wide gardens.

Old world, new world, world apart, the Palmeraie is full of contrasts. The palms have shaded modest farming villages for centuries. Now, celebrities and designers have dug huge wells and built modern palaces, in total contrast to these dry and humble surroundings yet bringing valuable work for the villagers. Marrakech is the ultimate dream machine, dreams of light and glamour, if only for one night - the Palmeraie is its latest cog.

It has design of extraordinary extravagance, gardens of such lush romance you could lose your heart in their imaginings. And there are places of pure lines and quiet sobriety where heart and eye will rest in peace. Despite doubts about the sustainability of such places in the semi-desert, we know that the Palmeraie is part of Moroccan travel and have included a few of its more approachable houses to give you the chance of living briefly in someones else's dream.

Finally, a short drive from Marrakech are the lovely green and temperate lands at the foothills of the High Atlas and some ideal refuges from the city's blazing summer or simply its year-round hubbub, inns and guest houses that serve good local or organic food, in natural surroundings where a walk is always a voyage of discovery.

Dar Doukkala, entry 58; photography by Ann Cooke-Yarborough

La Mamounia

Avenue Bab El Jdid, Marrakech-Medina

What is the legendary Mamounia? Six hectares of idyllic gardens inside the 12th-century ramparts, acres of sumptuous hotel, two fez-capped porters to hold the doors for you, wafts of Churchill and Myriam Makeba – it is a star-spangled cosmopolitan community with 40 gardeners, a staggering collection of menus (the head chef is world renowned) and enough fun and fitness temptations to keep you here for weeks, including a casino. Designed in 1923, the glorious interior is an apotheosis of clear, sober Moorish Art Deco: colonnades and cupolas, subtle marbles and precious inlaid woods, gleaming vistas of Alhambra-like patios where the discreetly wealthy rub shoulders with the overtly fashionable, people come for lunch and a gossip by the pool or to ride, play golf, have a massage. But take a room and taste the real class of deep-plush rooms, bedding, bathrooms and service. You may have the proud Koutoubia floodlit at your balcony and if you splurge on one of their top-knotch themed suites you can sleep with the memory of Winston or in a 'genuine replica' of an Orient Express carriage. Unbelievable.

rooms	231: 171 doubles & twins, 57 suites, 3 villas for 3.
price	2,000Dh–5,500Dh; enquire about suites and villas.
meals	Choice of five restaurants on site.
closed	Never.
directions	Enter medina by Bab Jdid then first right. Signposted.

	Madame Hanane Baqali
tel	+212 (0)44 44 44 09/38 86 00
fax	+212 (0)44 44 46 60
e-mail	resa@mamounia.com
web	www.mamounia.com

Landmark hotel

La Villa des Orangers
6 rue Sidi Mimoun, Marrakech-Medina

A sublime mix of French refinement and Moroccan authenticity, this true daughter of the medina rubs shoulders with rowdy, crowdy Jemaâ El Fna, preserving soft peace behind her beautiful doors, her roof terrace gazing at the great 12th-century Koutoubia, her heated pool tranquil in its garden. The Beherecs furbished their hotelier arms in Paris – then fell in love with Marrakech. There are brass and bronze, inlay and filigree, shimmering rugs and sumptuous stucco, the song of water at every patio turn. Have featherlight breakfast crêpes beneath the orange trees, soft drinks in the subtly-lit salon where light and shade, indoors and out, play games with each other and the fire leaps in the Luxor-style fireplace on cool evenings. Wonderful big uncluttered bedrooms, some with their own terraces; hyper luxury in the new garden suites; stunning bathrooms, each with bath and shower; superb bedding; and no colour overload, just genuine understated luxury. The beautifully-mannered staff will serve you perfectly, as befits the only *Relais & Châteaux* in Morocco. One per cent of income goes to a Moroccan village project.

rooms	19: 6 twins/doubles, 10 suites, 3 duplex; 10 have private terraces.
price	Half-board 2,900Dh–6,000Dh including light lunch, soft drinks at bar, laundry, airport transfer.
meals	Breakfast & lunch included. Dinner by arrangement.
closed	Mid-July–mid-August.
directions	Enter medina by Bab Jdid; Houmane El Fetouaki 600m; right into Rue Sidi Mimoun.

	Véronique & Pascal Beherec
tel	+212 (0)44 38 46 38
fax	+212 (0)44 38 51 23
e-mail	message@villadesorangers.com
web	www.villadesorangers.com

Small hotel

map 3   entry 43

La Sultana

6-8-9 Derb Agadir, Kasbah – El Mechouar, Marrakech-Medina

After two years' work by the best craftsmen, La Sultana is one of the most dazzling luxury riad hotel in the medina. Four riads steeped in history (one shares a wall with the Saadian Tombs), a wealth of marble (columns, fountains, floors), stucco chiselled into original floral designs, exquisitely carved doors and ceilings, touches of Africana. To each riad a different atmosphere, one a showcase for Moroccan Art Deco; another, *Piscine*, soberly done in brick and antique wood like the old palaces, its pearly pool a perfect mirror for gentle arches and great palms (heated, too); a third, a little gem of finely-worked cedarwood and tadelakt. There are salons for all seasons and activities, including creative gourmet meals; a superb spa and wellbeing centre; vast and beautiful panoramic terraces. Bedrooms are in luxurious keeping, all decorated on a different animal theme with antiques, works of art and, of course, exquisite craftsmanship. The owners, refined aesthetes, share their treasures with you, provide stylishly human service and help with ancient monuments conservation. Also a place for an unforgettable, fairytale party.

rooms	21: 12 doubles, 8 suites, 1 apartment.
price	2,000Dh-5,800Dh including soft drinks. Each riad can be let for sole occupancy.
meals	Lunch 200Dh. Dinner 400Dh. Visitors by arrangement.
closed	Never.
directions	Enter medina at Bab Agnaou, right at mosque, first left after Saadian Tombs.

	Saïda Loutou
tel	+212 (0)44 38 80 08
fax	+212 (0)44 38 77 77
e-mail	contact@lasultanamarrakech.com
web	www.lasultanamarrakech.com

Guest house & catered house

Riyad El Cadi

87 Derb Moulay Abdelkader, Derb Dabachi, Marrakech-Medina

Ancient foundations, antique hangings, eight centuries of art from Morocco and all over the Islamic world: it's an exceptional place. Sadly, their collector, El Cadi's greatest treasure, scholar and diplomat Herwig Bartels, left his collection, his passion, his research for ever in August 2003. His high-class tinker's universe of 'pots, pans and old rags', a hymn to Islamic and Berber cultures, is his epitaph; his daughter succeeds him. Eight old houses round a maze of patios in pure local style, the finest one an exuberance of citrus; quiet, harmonious décor as a perfect backdrop for original painted woodwork, a highly personal mix of furniture – vibrant gifts of human talent from down the centuries – and no clutter. No artificial authenticity either: copper and brass are confined to a budding collection of local Art Nouveau kettles. The 'budget' Blue House – two bedrooms, salon, patio – is a dream retreat for two couples; suites are simply magnificent, all rooms revel in natural gracious taste and soft tadelakt bathrooms. And the staff are a delight with their ready smiles and quick intelligence. A rare privilege for body and spirit.

rooms	12: 1 single, 5 doubles, 6 suites.
price	1,450Dh-2,900Dh.
meals	International cuisine. By arrangement. Lunch 100Dh-150Dh. Dinner 200Dh-350Dh.
closed	Two weeks in July.
directions	From Place Jemaâ El Fna, right Derb Dabachi (beyond Café de France), left Derb Moulay Abdelkader; No 87 is little low door on left.

	Julia Bartels & Ahmed El Amrani
tel	+212 (0)44 37 86 55
fax	+212 (0)44 37 84 78
e-mail	riyadelcadi@iam.net.ma
web	www.riyadelcadi.com

Guest house

map 3   entry 45

Les Jardins de la Médina

21 Derb Chtouka, Quartier de la Kasbah, Marrakech-Medina

After the medina dazzle, the upside-down tree in the dark hall is a brilliant trick: carry your graciously-proferred key out, and gasp at the miracle of the gardens where birds rejoice and a heated infinity pool smiles smoothly. The abandoned palace (celebs was here once: Princess Farah Diba, Egyptian singer Oum Khalsoum), its rich garden turning to jungle, was resuscitated in 2001 by a family of passionate Morocco-lovers. There might be 80 people in the hotel but, apart from summer swimming bustle, you could believe it's empty, so clever has the architect been with leafy private terraces, cosy secret corners and jigsaw layouts. His Moroccan/Tuscan influences inform the clean, uncluttered décor, timeless in its sober fancy and luxurious detail. Every secluded room has careful individuality in rich fabrics against plain walls, well-chosen pictures and carpets, superb Moroccan-finish bathrooms. The many terraces, spray-cooled in summer, include a new beauty centre; below, a brilliant chef conducts a symphony in Moroccan, Mediterranean and Thai; salons and dining rooms are fitting backgrounds for these delights.

rooms	37: doubles, triples, quadruples & 'Privilege' rooms.
price	1,650Dh-2,950Dh.
meals	Lunch 70Dh-150Dh. Dinner 220Dh-350Dh.
closed	Never.
directions	From Bab Agnaou right at mosque into Rue de la Kasbah; pass Saadian tombs, straight on to Derb Chtouka; hotel down on right, white doorway.

	Annie Rigobert & Michel Sautereau
tel	+212 (0)44 38 18 51
fax	+212 (0)44 38 53 85
e-mail	info@lesjardinsdelamedina.com
web	www.lesjardinsdelamedina.com

Small hotel

Riad Mehdi

2 Derb Sedra, Bab Agnaou, Marrakech-Medina

Built recently at the entrance to the kasbah, with part of the rampart in its walls, this small hotel has a big claim to fame: the best oriental spa in Marrakech. Occupying one of the two patios, the spa offers fabulous oriental experiences such as a milk bath, a master shiatsu masseur known throughout Morocco, a magnificent hammam, alongside the classic swimming pool, pressurized water massage and beauty treatments. You can book for an hour, a day or a whole weekend. The intention is to provide calm and relaxation, the rampart gives the riad a protected, historic atmosphere, the enclosing architecture creates plenty of private spaces, the welcome is quietly polite, attentive and friendly – and the rooms are appropriately luxurious. Big, done in lovely tadelakt colours – yellow, plum, chestnut, caramel – with carved furniture, well-chosen rugs and fabrics, fireplaces and some private balconies, superb bedding and embroidered linen, they exude good taste and rest. All for your greater wellbeing. The young owner has chosen to exhibit and sell pieces of pottery made by young handicapped Moroccans – we salute him.

rooms	9: 3 doubles, 1 twin, 5 suites.
price	1,000Dh-2,500Dh.
meals	Picnic lunch 150Dh. Full lunch or dinner 300Dh. By arrangement.
closed	Never.
directions	Directions given on booking. Very easy access.

	Abdelkader Boufraine
tel	+212 (0)44 38 47 13/64 17 21 88
fax	+212 (0)44 38 47 31
e-mail	contact@riadmehdi.net
web	www.riadmehdi.net

Guest house

map 3   entry 47

La Maison Arabe

1 Derb Assehbe, Bab Doukkala, Marrakech-Medina

A small army staffs this legendary restaurant grown into small hotel, yet it has the intimate atmosphere of a guest house – one feels like royalty staying with friends. Pillars and sumptuous antique tables divide the big salons into traditional-feel quiet corners (the buildings are in fact modern) lit by Berber stripes and good pictures; the fabulous painted ceiling of the big new restaurant, its raw marble floor and the gentle patio beyond frame a superb Moroccan food experience. And the 'Arabian Nights' bedrooms are no let-down: the designer owner melds furniture, colours and paintings with thoughtful skill so that antique carpets and mirrors, surfaces of traditional brick, beautiful tiles or smoothly polished tadelakt, rich and varied furnishings and some excellent modern art co-exist in powerful harmony. In its lush oasis setting, the swimming pool is exceptional for Marrakech, birds sing and your dinner vegetables grow in the vast kitchen garden… it's 10 minutes out of town by Maison Arabe shuttle – they have thought of everything. You can even take Moroccan cookery courses out there.

rooms	17: 8 doubles, 9 suites.
price	1,300Dh-2,300Dh; suites 1,300Dh-6,000Dh; including afternoon tea.
meals	Lunch from 120Dh. Dinner from 250Dh.
closed	Never.
directions	From Rue Fatima Zohorn, opposite Bab Doukkala mosque, signposted on Derb Assehbe.

	Fabrizio Ruspoli, Taoufik Ghaffouli, Nabila Dakir
tel	+212 (0)44 38 70 10
fax	+212 (0)44 38 72 21
e-mail	maisonarabe@iam.net.ma
web	www.lamaisonarabe.com

Small hotel

Riad El Ouarda

5 Derb Taht Sour Lakbir, Zaouia El Abbassia, Marrakech-Medina

The magnificence of a noble old mansion echoes in the powerful white verticals that protect the central space and its exceptionally magical brand of civilisation. Rooms are big and high, the restored antique stucco is proudly perfect, bathrooms are well done in tadelakt and copper, suites have a touch of suggested opulence as well as luxuries of space. Thierry and Laurent have decorated their little palace with loving sensitivity, colours rich and soft, nothing busy or overdone; their Mauritanian 'wall mats', for example, are original but don't shout. There are gentle reminders of traditional design in the main house – keyhole-arch wall velvet, glorious stylised Berber patterns over a plain white fireplace – and surprising modernity in the Douiria where the second patio, warmed with log fires in winter, greened with banana plants in summer, leads to a brilliant great grey and white bed-and-bath suite. Split-level terraces offer plenty of private spaces – and 360° medina-to-mountain views. But most important of all is the impeccable, attentive yet friendly service from the owners and all their delightful staff.

rooms	9: 5 doubles, 4 suites.
price	1,100Dh–2,000Dh.
meals	Lunch 100Dh–200Dh. Dinner 320Dh. By arrangement.
closed	Rarely.
directions	In medina, go to Bab Taghzout and telephone for guide to riad.

	Thierry Saint Marc & Laurent Bocca
tel	+212 (0)44 38 57 14
fax	+212 (0)44 38 57 10
e-mail	elouarda@yahoo.fr
web	www.riadelouarda.com

Guest house

map 3   entry 49

Riad Noga

78 Derb Jdid, Douar Graoua, Marrakech-Medina

The radically different treatment of the two halves of Riad Noga is very clever, you feel you've been offered two experiences in one. The first patio wears gentle clothes of faded pink wash and flower-spotted creeper green that open onto a fine vaulted dining room, a zelliged and cushion-strewn salon and two bedrooms where rich-coloured bedcovers, Berber rugs and painted furniture glow against pale plain walls. All shyness vanishes as you step into the second patio and drama strikes: red and yellow arches march round a stunning emerald-green pool, the walls are showcases for fancy brickwork, Kleini the parrot chats quietly. The dining room on this side is red too, with a black fireplace; bedrooms share the brave new look; bathrooms are vaulted – it's both fun and very smart. So is the great three-level horizon-sweeping roof terrace. Contemporary works of art make Gabriele's mix of Moroccan decoration and modern German design yet more pleasing, the staff's quiet, attentive presence is comforting yet efficient and Fatima's superb cooking is rightly renowned.

rooms	7: 2 doubles, 4 twins/doubles, 1 triple.
price	1,400Dh–2,050Dh.
meals	Lunch 80Dh–100Dh. Dinner 175Dh–225Dh.
closed	August.
directions	Map will be sent when booking. Airport transfer arranged.

Gabriele Noack-Späth

tel	+212 (0)44 37 76 70/38 52 46/38 52 47
fax	+212 (0)44 38 90 46
e-mail	riadnoga@iam.net.ma
web	www.riadnoga.com

Guest house

Hôtel Sherazade

3 Derb Djamaa, Riad Zitoun El Kdim, Marrakech-Medina

The studded door looks hefty but beyond the smiles of the little reception hall you discover the cool sweet light of a tiled and tinkling courtyard. This delightful hotel spreads over two old mansions: two courtyards, two histories, joined at the top by a wonderful frondy pot-planted terrace that stretches from one side to the other. The atmosphere up there is delectable: intimate corners with little garden tables, a breakfast tent with its generous buffet and the four simpler, white, light-filled rooms that share washing facilities. The Sherazade, restored by friendly, attentive Sabina who hails from Pakistan and Germany, and her warmly intelligent Moroccan husband, is a simple, attractive place to stay, done in those reds, blues and greens that are so well suited to the Moroccan light, striped fabrics, multi-coloured zellige and brass trays, all with space round the network of galleries and staircases. Every room feels different in shape and décor, most give onto the galleries, beds are good, bathrooms are spotless, some bigger than others, and the staff are exceptionally welcoming. *Day trips to mountains and desert.*

rooms	19: 8 doubles, 4 twins (one with kitchenette), 3 triples; 2 doubles, 2 twins sharing 2 showers & 2 wcs.
price	250Dh-600Dh with bathroom; 200Dh sharing bathroom.
meals	Buffet breakfast 50Dh. Lunch or dinner 60Dh-100Dh. BYO.
closed	Rarely.
directions	From Place Jemaâ El Fna, through archway into Riad Zitoun El Kdim, 3rd turning on left.

	Ahmed & Sabina Benchaira
tel	+212 (0)44 42 93 05
fax	+212 (0)44 42 93 05
e-mail	sharazade@iam.net.ma
web	www.hotelsherazade.com

Small hotel

map 3   entry 51

Jnane Mogador Hôtel

116 Riad Zitoun Kedim, Derb Sidi Bouloukat, Marrakech-Medina

Expectations are high as you step proudly through the great 19th-century doorway in the heart of the old imperial city into a gloriously decorated patio with its smooth pillars, fine floor tiles, marble fountain in the centre and plants all over. You should not be disappointed. The young owner restored the authentic architecture of this magnificent riad mansion with a Marrakech red basis and great attention to the traditional arts of chiselled stucco, sculpted stone and silky tadelakt, all restored or created by the best craftsmen in town. The marble staircase marches hand in foot with antique leather-trimmed urns, doors are hand-painted wood, windows screened with moucharabieh. Deeply, richly attractive. Rooms are in simple contrast with their curly wrought-iron furniture and fixtures and unfussy wide-striped bedcovers. Bedding is excellent and cupboards generous, bathrooms are snug and pretty in their various tadelakt finishes and more storage. There is, of course, a fine terrace for breakfast or mint tea and Moroccan cakes. A friendly, welcoming new place for smaller budgets just yards from Jemaâ El Fna.

rooms	17: 6 doubles, 5 twins, 1 triple, 3 quadruples, 2 singles.
price	348Dh.
meals	Lunch or dinner à la carte about 90Dh.
closed	Never.
directions	From Place Jemaâ El Fna take Riad Zitoun Kedim; hotel 100 metres down on right.

Mohamed Araban

tel	+212 (0)44 42 63 23
fax	+212 (0)44 42 63 23
e-mail	jnanemogador@hotmail.com
web	www.jnanemogador.com

Small hotel

Riad El Arsat

10 Derb Chemaâ, Arset Loughzail, Marrakech-Medina

What is special behind that fine door? The garden, a hundred times the garden. This is the one place in the medina with a true riad garden, 1600m2 of bird-filled orchard and jungly greenery, singing fountains and big pool. Each bedroom has its own little terrace onto this magical space, the colonnade marches proudly past it, joining winter house to summer house – it is palatial. Nicole's collection of old photographs, paintings and drawings adds yet more interest to the grand salon, fit for royalty, where the stupendous carved and painted cedarwood ceiling demands admiration, a flurry of rich carpets softens the natural bejmat-tiled floor and you may use the house music system and CD collection. Bedrooms, shared between the two houses and one little cottage, are appropriately big and exotic with yet more original paintings, fine old brass beds, lots of draperies and regal colours, chiselled stucco friezes and a sitting corner by the fireplace, a very welcome sight on some winter evenings. Bathrooms are, of course, excellent, the terraces are sublime and the staff perfectly discreet and helpful.

rooms	7: 5 doubles, 2 suites.
price	1,700Dh-3,000Dh.
	Sole occcupancy 15,000Dh per day.
meals	Lunch or dinner 250Dh. Picnic
	50Dh. By arrangement. BYO.
closed	Never.
directions	Easy directions given on booking.

Nicole Arbousset

tel	+212 (0)44 38 75 67/61 58 27 49
fax	+212 (0)44 38 75 05
e-mail	nicolearbousset@yahoo.fr
web	www.riad-elarsat-marrakech.com

Guest house & catered house

map 3   entry 53

Riad Kaïss

65 Derb Jdid, Riad Zitoune Kedim, Marrakech-Medina

Christian Ferré's talent has married two riads with the best of France and Morocco. His sense of space and volume is impeccable, his eye for detail unerring, his pool one of the most beautiful ever, pure form, like a hidden abstract painting. Kaïss is red, true Marrakech red, the patio garden bathes you in cool green light and running water which inspire a multitude of birds, the paintwork is that quintessential Majorelle blue. Each bedroom is touched with personality and a few choice hangings and objects so that, again, one feels let into a secret meeting of tradition and modernity, subtle colour, sensual texture... with bathrooms as little jewels. Christian is the discreetest of hosts, there with knowledge and intelligent conversation but only when you want them, happy that you appreciate his work of love. The opulence of the salons, one small and French, the other magnificently oriental, is made of discernment taste and enough original pieces to keep you gazing for a week. The courtyard turns to lantern-lit magic in the evening, the terrace has a colonnaded menzeh for refined dinners, the gym is green marble. Exceptional.

rooms	8: 5 doubles, 2 twins, 1 mini-suite with own terrace; connecting rooms possible.
price	1,465Dh-2,260Dh.
meals	Lunch 150Dh. Dinner 300Dh. By arrangement.
closed	Never.
directions	From Place Jemaâ El Fna, take Riad Zitoun Kedim to Dar el Salaam restaurant; left into little street; house along on right: red building.

Christian Ferré
tel	+212 (0)44 44 01 41
fax	+212 (0)44 44 01 41
e-mail	riad@riadkaiss.com
web	www.riadkaiss.com

Guest house

Riad Les Yeux Bleus

7 Derb El Ferrane, Bab Doukkala, Marrakech-Medina

The owner's deep blue eyes gave this fabulous house its name, her distinction and taste create its very special feel, her passionate knowledge of Moroccan culture and customs make her a most interesting person to meet. A sky-blue pool reflecting the Moorish arcades that grace all four sides of the elegant patio, lovely leafy trees rustling round the fountain, a rich-red salon calling you to admire its magnificently carved doors, stunning African-inspired furniture and excellent library – of such things is refinement made. There's exoticism too, echoes of north and sub-Saharan Africa or classical Arab Andalucia, in the big, serenely beautiful bedrooms, each with embroidered linen and a different scintillating sabra bedcover in harmony with its particular colour scheme. And so up to the glorious split-level terraces where another green paradise spreads over the pergola, past the delightful little hammam into the sun-bathing corner with its deckchairs and parasols. Nothing ugly is to be seen in any corner of this splendid mansion and, under Brick's eagle eye, the staff have as much class and delicacy as the house.

rooms	5: 2 doubles, 3 twins/doubles.
price	1,800Dh.
	Sole occupancy 8,000Dh per night.
meals	Lunch or dinner 300Dh, with wine.
closed	Never.
directions	In Guéliz, just on edge of medina: directions given on booking.

	Jocelyne Despin
tel	+212 (0)44 37 81 61/61 42 26 82
fax	+212 (0)44 37 81 61
e-mail	despin@wanadoo.net.ma

Guest house & catered house

map 3   entry 55

Pe're Planells

Riyad El Mezouar

28 Derb El Hammam, Issebtinne, Marrakech-Medina

Glorious shock! Step from the populous, picturesque old Arab town into serenity. One of the fine mansions once owned by the Alaoui dynasty, Riyad El Mezouar has an angel star that fell into the patio and a sublime emerald-green pool to reflect the magnificent symmetry of its arcades and the rich greenery that lines them: this long and lovely perspective breathes like the Alhambra. Exquisitely renovated by two French interior designers who have Morocco in their bones, it has the unostentatious elegance of pale backgrounds and natural cedar, perfect detailing and occasional flashes – a deep pink curtain, a glowing red vase from China. Bedrooms? space, light and a perfect mix of antiques and Michel's own designs. Bathrooms? marble and gleaming copper, tadelakt and the odd claw foot. But richest of all is their extraordinary collection of oriental paintings, objects and hangings, each one so sensitively positioned. Your charming hosts and their staff adore this pure and lovely house and will do anything to convert you, including superb food served with white-gloved style. Exceptional.

rooms	5: 1 double, 1 twin/double, 3 suites.
price	1,700Dh-1,950Dh including afternoon tea.
meals	Lunch 200Dh. Dinner 400Dh. By arrangement. BYO.
closed	Never.
directions	Directions given on booking. Accessible by car.

	Jérôme Vermelin & Michel Durand-Meyrier
tel	+212 (0)44 38 09 49
fax	+212 (0)44 38 09 43
e-mail	info@mezouar.com
web	www.mezouar.com

Guest house

Dar Hanane

9 Derb Lalla Azzouna, Marrakech-Medina

So much space. So much simple beauty. A century ago, these exceptionally wide, high rooms were the sign of a grand family and Françoise has renovated and decorated the old house with love, respect and absolutely no frills. From the crowded, picturesque streets with their little market and the tanneries nearby, enter the quiet alley, stop before a majestic doorway and prepare to fall in love, as she did in 2000. The monastically white walls, deep-lobed doorways and blue-grey carved woodwork round the perfect little patio say it all: here are peace and grandeur, here you can be yourself. The white and ivory base is warmed by purple divans, mauve pouffes, red cushions and some lovely Berber rugs. Big serene bedrooms have a fine piece of furniture each, a carefully-chosen lamp, a walk-in cupboard and a pale tadelakt bathroom; the wonderful great first-floor suite extends to a latticed mezzanine; the panoramic terrace is one of the highest in Marrakech. Soft, gentle taste: these are the hallmarks of a perfect but unintrusive hostess and her delightful assistants Aïcha and Raja. *Free entry to pool in the Palmeraie.*

rooms	5: 4 doubles, 1 suite for 2-6.
price	850Dh-1,400Dh.
	Sole occupancy 4,300Dh-4,800Dh
	per night; 29,000Dh-43,000Dh
	(New Year) per week.
meals	Lunch 80Dh. Dinner 200Dh.
	Picnic possible. By arrangement.
closed	Never.
directions	Near Medersa Ben Youssef:
	directions given on booking.

	Françoise Lefebvre
tel	+212 (0)44 37 77 37
fax	+212 (0)44 37 70 74
e-mail	contact@dar-hanane.com
web	www.dar-hanane.com

Guest house & catered house

map 3   entry 57

Dar Doukkala

83 Arset Aouzal, Bab Doukkala, Marrakech-Medina

Those lovingly painted front doors, originally a 17th-century Berber ceiling, were freed from their sheet-metal prison by renovator Jean-Luc Lemée. His hand and eye have caressed every inch of this 19th-century palace, returning it to its Glaoui glory (with the help of French/Moroccan craftsmen of the 1930s) plus ancient doors in new frames, the odd reminder of black Africa and his own vastly original fireplaces. Palm trees rise from the patio past shimmering mosaic pillars, stucco marvels and darkly carved galleries; the grand yet inviting salons burst with contrasting antiques. The patio is a foretaste of the leaping landscaped terraces up above, one for the discreet pool and its outdoor salon, one for guests of the grand suite (with double bath…), the largest with masses of cushioned space beneath slatted canopies – and endless views. Each big bedroom has a richly individual feel and one of Jean-Luc's exceptional bathrooms while the new managers Alain and Marie-Noëlle and owner Philippe create a convivial atmosphere that is as stylish and warmly human as the house. An unforgettable place.

rooms	6: 4 twins/doubles, 2 suites.
price	1,600Dh–2,400Dh.
meals	Lunch 150Dh. Dinner 210Dh. By arrangement.
closed	Never.
directions	From Dar El Bacha, Rue Bab Doukkala west; first left (under arch labelled Riad Malika); first left: door at end of short alley.

Philippe Bouyé, Marie-Noëlle
& Alain Schenck

tel	+212 (0)44 38 34 44
fax	+212 (0)44 38 34 45
e-mail	dardoukkala@iam.net.ma
web	www.dardoukkala.com

Guest house

Dar Tchaïkana
25 Derb El Ferane, Azbest, Marrakech-Medina

At 'the house where one drinks tea', a young, vibrant Belgian couple are realising their clear and luminous dream. A dream of simplicity, sobriety, softened Marrakchi light on beige, sand and ochre, gentle blue arcades against pure white walls and a personal, sensitive mixture of furniture: modern black easy chairs and Moroccan basketweave pouffes, tadelakt bathrooms and original batik pictures, some fascinating sub-Saharan pieces which Delphine used to import into Europe bring her beloved nomads indoors: her knowledge is as deep as her passion, the engraved funeral urn on the staircase is a quiet wonder, the bed made of sturdy Berber tent posts, rough-hewn with the marks of their other life, an image of strength. Big rooms, huge suites, where firm, unintrusive decoration makes the shape and atmosphere of the old house palpable and each tiny detail takes its place with pride. Between the white salon and the red salon lies the green-planted, terracotta-tiled patio where water plays and meals are shared at simple black tables with hosts of intelligence and lively humour. This is quiet magic, the purest of the pure.

rooms	4: 2 doubles, 2 suites.
price	800Dh-1,500Dh; sole occupancy for 12: 25,000Dh-28,000Dh per week.
meals	Dinner 150Dh. By arrangement.
closed	Rarely.
directions	Airport transfer (100Dh) or meeting place arranged for escort to house.

Jean-François Claeys
& Delphine Mottet
tel	+212 (0)44 38 51 50
fax	+212 (0)44 38 51 50
e-mail	info@tchaikana.com
web	www.tchaikana.com

Guest house & catered house

map 3   entry 59

Riad Meriem

97 Derb El Cadi, Azbest, Marrakech-Medina

In the old medina, the approaches get narrow, narrower… all the better to flood you with the joyous harmony of François and Myriam's house. A remarkable couple, they came from Belgium, fell in love with the red city, found this riad in the oldest part of the medina, bathed it in that sensual builder's milk called tadelakt – ivory for salons, glowing colours for bedrooms – found the best trio to help them scatter petals on the little pool, make heavenly pastries and be happy here – then opened it to their privileged guests. Zohra, with Fatima's smiling help, will spoil you horribly with her luscious cooking; wonderful Hassan will take you to the bazaar. In cooler weather, the salon is sheer delight in its quiet oriental dress and its steps down to the hearth; or be private in the small patio room; otherwise, the bedouin tent or the parasols on the terrace invite you to laze between sun and shade with your mint tea and home-cured olives. And sleep at last in a generous room with its gentle décor, wide bed, big cupboards and splendiferous bathroom: candles, rose petals, oils, baths big enough for two. A dream house.

rooms	5 twins/doubles.
price	850Dh-1,500Dh. Sole occupancy 3,500Dh-5,000Dh per day.
meals	Lunch or dinner 180Dh-280Dh. By arrangement.
closed	Never.
directions	Directions given on booking.

	Myriam & François Gottignies
tel	+212 (0)44 38 77 31/ +32 47 386 3702
fax	+212 (0)44 37 77 62
e-mail	contact@riadmeriem.com
web	www.riadmeriem.com

Guest house & catered house

Dar Mouassine

148 Derb Snane, Mouassine, Marrakech-Medina

Owned and run by a delightful, impish former television producer and a warmly smiling ex-advertising executive, Dar Mouassine is a place of civilisation and rest. Fleeing the alienation of Parisian life, they discovered this lovely old house with lots of original stucco, woodwork and tiles around which they have arranged draperies and rugs, cushions and pictures – just enough of everything in harmonious colour schemes against simple white walls. A serenely timeless patio garden and a blue pool in a secret ochre corner are their own very talented inspiration and the long bedrooms, one with a fireplace, one with a deep stuccoed sitting alcove, have exciting touches of contrast – rich velvet cushions in vibrant colour matches, old-fashioned and modern fabrics, carved cedar chairs, the odd family antique – to spice up the quiet filtered light. You know that this is their home (although their new baby has meant moving to a larger space next door), especially in the grand salon where lots of French chairs and pictures and 19th-century sofas jostle beneath the original beams. Vital and totally enjoyable.

rooms	6: 3 doubles, 3 suites.
price	650Dh-1,200Dh including afternoon tea. Sole occupancy for 13: 33,600Dh-42,000Dh per week.
meals	Dinner 180Dh. By arrangement.
closed	Rarely.
directions	Airport transfer. In town, at Bab Ksour, opposite Restaurant Diafa, ring for escort.

	Carole Blique & Erick Kolenc
tel	+212 (0)44 44 52 87
fax	+212 (0)44 44 52 87
web	www.terremaroc.com

Guest house & catered house

map 3   entry 61

Riad Zina

38 Derb Assabane, Riad Laârouss, Marrakech-Medina

The architecture of the gently renovated Riad Zina takes centre-stage here against the serenely uncluttered backdrop of white walls and blue shutters. A delightful, strong, intelligent woman, Beate has faithfully adapted the original intentions of her mansion: four symmetrical beds grow surprising spiky cacti among great smooth pebbles; a daily libation of rose petals blesses the octagonal pool; in the simple pale rooms, alcoves and corners play with the light, pools of colour ripple in rich curtains, covers, rugs and wall hangings, contemporary pictures call for real attention, tadelakt bathrooms relax. The Great Moroccan queen of the house is the first-floor suite, a remarkably fine big room with a breathtaking ceiling, said to be 350 years old, surrounded by a delicately excised and gaudily painted frieze of Koranic verses – you sleep in heavenly peace; there are heaps of cushions and a fireplace; through one set of towering double doors is the sitting space. And moreover... Beate was once a professional cook so there are mouth-watering French dishes one day, Malika's Moroccan delicacies the next.

rooms	4: 2 doubles, 1 triple, 1 suite.
price	1,100Dh-2,000Dh including afternoon tea.
meals	Lunch 50Dh-150Dh. Dinner 200Dh. By arrangement.
closed	Never.
directions	Directions given on booking.

	Beate Prinz
tel	+212 (0)44 38 52 42
fax	+212 (0)44 38 52 42
e-mail	beate_prinz@yahoo.fr
web	www.riadzina.ma

Guest house

Riad 72

72 Arset Awzel, Bab Doukkala, Marrakech-Médina

Giovanna, Riad 72's strong-minded Italian owner, worked with an Italian-trained Moroccan architect to do this superbly white renovation of one of the highest mansions in the medina whose lofty terrace looks eye to eye with the Pasha's palace. In the patio, a dream of rest and clear spirit, a breathtaking white cubic fountain overflows beneath giant banana plants – the colours of serenity. In bedrooms and salons, the marriage of Moroccan decorative arts and Italian style and sobriety brings class and originality: quiet greys, shimmering dark velours, subtle sabra stripes set off clean contemporary shapes and strikingly beautiful old carved ceilings. Bedrooms have big tempting beds, some straight from design magazines, occasional bright touches, nothing flashy, masses of presence. And the vast suite raises the roof, right up to a 100-year-old octagonal carved cupola whence the light filters down onto the great red bed and the grey tadelakt floor. Each bathroom is utterly original in shape and finish, every detail attended to… as you will be by Raja, Giovanna's sweet and efficient housekeeper, and her ever-helpful staff.

rooms	4: 2 doubles, 1 twin, 1 suite.
price	900Dh–2,500Dh inc. afternoon tea.
meals	Lunch 30Dh–110Dh. Dinner 250Dh. By arrangement.
closed	Never.
directions	In the medina, telephone from Dar El Bacha for guide to riad.

	Giovanna Cinel
tel	+212 (0)44 38 76 29
fax	+212 (0)44 38 47 18
e-mail	riad.72@wanadoo.net.ma
web	www.riad72.com

Guest house

map 3   entry 63

Riad Malika

29 Arset Aouzal, Bab Doukkala, Marrakech-Medina

Let yourself be swept up in this collector's passion – and deposited luxuriously in a 1930s club sofa or a 1960s leather Saarinen. Your host is larger than life and enchantingly human, his whole wonderful house is living museum of 20th-century design, every piece Moroccan: at the height of their glory, the Glaoui clan took on European ideas and mixed them with tradition behind high palace walls. Malika was one of these, updated in the 1920s with balconies and huge windows over the luxuriant patio. In a labyrinth of stairways and levels (there's a triplex suite flashing with glorious colour) Jean-Luc's designer talents and Martine's quiet presence do the rest. Every one of the multitudinous details deserves attention: six decades of clocks, mirrors, statues, paintings; deep-carved Moroccan doors, intricate lamps, hand-painted pieces from renovated mosques, beautiful zellige walls, stucco above, rugs below. And so much space. Generosity embraces every bedroom, brilliant tiled bathrooms have yet more antiques, meals are sybaritic delights, staff are friendly with buckets of class. It's hard to leave.

rooms	9: 5 doubles, 4 suites.
price	800Dh-1,200Dh.
meals	Light lunch from 100Dh. Dinner 210Dh. By arrangement.
closed	Never.
directions	From Dar El Bacha, Rue Bab Doukkala west; 1st left under arch labelled Riad Malika & follow signs.

Martine Hubert & Jean-Luc Lemée

tel	+212 (0)44 38 54 51
fax	+212 (0)44 38 54 51
e-mail	jean.luc@iam.net.ma
web	www.riadmalika.com

Guest house

Dar Nadir

93 Derb Tizzougarine, Marrakech-Medina

The arrival is dramatic: down a blind alley, through a brass door, a studded wooden door, a dark lamp-lit hall where a brazier glows in winter – and into the patio: on a striking old marble floor, three keyhole arches stand astride a still dark pool that glimmers in the lantern light, your eyes climb to the top of the magnificent old doors then up with the vigorous plants to the roof. Converting Dar Nadir for themselves, the architect-decorator owners, who now live in France, did the bedrooms, big or small, with panache and strong colours, silky white duvets and rich hangings, made each bathroom an original creation to fit its odd space. Details are perfect, nothing is repeated, Moroccan traditional objects do not clutter and local contemporary art provides interesting focus in the darkly atmospheric interior. Houda's sister Amal runs the house with gentle smiles, quiet efficiency and delicious meals, be it grilled sardines and salad or the full gastronomic works, in the little red and white salon off the patio or the superb 'men's quarters' Moroccan dining room upstairs or on the roof terrace. Super breakfasts, too.

rooms	5 twins/doubles.
price	1,380Dh. Sole occupancy 6,000Dh per day including breakfast.
meals	Lunch 60Dh-150Dh. Dinner 150Dh-250Dh.
closed	Never.
directions	From Dar El Bacha Glaoui ring for escort.

Francis & Houda Mabileau

tel	+212 (0)44 42 92 61/+33 (0)1 45 85 34 15
fax	+212 (0)44 42 92 61/+33 (0)1 45 85 34 15
e-mail	darnadir@free.fr
web	www.ryad-nadir.com

Guest house & catered house

map 3   entry 65

Dar Al Kounouz

45 Derb Snane, Mouassine, Marrakech-Medina

Renowned for its exceptional chiselled stucco, the patio at Dar Al Kounouz foams like a wedding veil in its delicate lightness, salon and bedroom walls are subtly friezed, ceilings and arches are frosted with loving care. The restoration took two years, the artist was the best ma'allem in town, the owners finished the job with traditional zellige tiling, tadelakt plaster and painted woodwork. A lovely long hallway leads to the blue mosaics and green palm trees of the refreshing patio; galleries are eggshell white to show off the beautiful carving; the gently ochre terrace has blue trellises, pink-cushioned chairs and views over the treetops of Dar El Bacha where the King's guests stay: Mouassine is one of the oldest parts of the medina. Within this stunning framework, each room is differently, attractively decorated and eminently comfortable; so are the bathrooms (jacuzzi!). Michel and his team are proud of the house, will offer you mint tea and much help on living in the medina and beyond; you can watch the Moroccan cook preparing her delicious local recipes then relax in the marble hammam with a wonderful massage.

rooms	6: 2 doubles, 3 twins, 1 triple.
price	900Dh-1,200Dh.
meals	Lunch or dinner 120Dh. By arrangement. BYO.
closed	Never.
directions	From Koutoubia, Rue Fatima Zohra north to Bab Ksour; right Rue Sidi Yamami to Derb Snane (on left) & follow signs.

Michel Arno & Michel Mongelard

tel	+212 (0)44 39 07 73/62 40 11 28
fax	+212 (0)44 39 07 74
e-mail	info@daralkounouz.com
web	www.daralkounouz.com

Guest house

Riad Magi

79 Derb Moulay Abdul Kader, Derb Dabachi, Marrakech-Medina

Magic? Yes, magic in the oldest quarter of the medina. A magic team under Iliass who carried the restoration through hitch and hindrance to accomplishment. A magic place to stay in colourful simplicity. Maggie Perry designed the interior: she has a painter's feel for colour. There's a small citrus forest and two fountains in the graceful patio where Islamic green, white and yellow make a fresh background to antique painted doors. One of them leads to the refined Moroccan salon where a carved frieze ties white and cream walls and plum-coloured cushions into luscious harmony. Lemonwood tables and silver teapots finish the picture; there are silvery touches in your bedroom too. White and pale blue or green or yellow, it may have a stucco ceiling, it will certainly have an antique chest or two, super fabrics and a pretty little tadelakt shower room. The whole place, from patio to roof terrace (those medina-to-Atlas views), has a gentle-firm personality, modern yet respectful of the fine old architecture. Maggie is often here and Iliass, the welcoming and efficient manager, also speaks fluent English. *Trips organised.*

rooms	6 doubles.
price	800Dh–900Dh.
meals	Lunch or dinner about 150Dh. By arrangement. BYO.
closed	Never.
directions	From Place Jemaâ El Fna, right Derb Dabachi (behind Café de France); pass mosque then first left; down to bottom, right to end, house on right.

Maggie Perry & Iliass Tafroukht

tel	+212 (0)44 42 66 88/
	+44 (0)207 923 9287
fax	+212 (0)44 42 66 88

Guest house

map 3   entry 67

Ryad El Borj

63 Derb Moulay Abdelkader, Derb Dabachi, Marrakech-Medina

*B*orj means tower. 150 years ago, when Pasha Glaoui owned the whole quarter, one of the liveliest in Marrakech, he built a lookout here to oversee the area. Still the highest view of the whole city, it is magic at any hour, sublime at sunset. The typical dark entrance takes you down five steps then on to the blue patio, whence up to the green first floor then the red terrace – all properly dramatic. When renovating the ryad three years ago, your host was careful to preserve the original décor and almost all the very comfortably furnished rooms have painted or carved ceilings while the great glass-vaulted suite is remarkable value with its big bedroom, sitting room, excellent bathroom and an extra salon that gives onto the patio via a superb moucharabieh screen. Colours are pale and sober, materials are noble cedarwood and finely wrought ironwork, doors are antique, floors are strewn with carpets and leather cushions from the Saharaoui south giving the wonderful exotic feel of being in a *khaima*, a nomad tent; breakfast is superbly generous. Pool, drinks and meals available just 20 metres away.

rooms	5: 4 doubles, 1 suite.
price	600Dh-1,200Dh. Sole occupancy for 8: 17,0000Dh-23,000Dh per week.
meals	Lunch or dinner by arrangement. BYO.
closed	Never.
directions	From Place Jemaâ El Fna take Derb Dabachi (behind Café de France); pass mosque on right then first left; house 30m along on right.

	Daniel Ghio
tel	+212 (0)44 39 12 23/61 67 59 42
fax	+212 (0)44 39 12 23
e-mail	ryadelborj@wanadoo.net.ma
web	www.ryadelborj.com

Guest house & catered house

Dar Pangal

132 Derb Chtouka, Kasbah, Marrakech-Medina

As authentic as can be is this typical medina house deep inside the well-guarded 'royal estate' between kasbah, palace and great Agdal Gardens. And one of the best views in town is to be had from its roof terrace, across the palace and the looming Koutoubia minaret to the snowy Atlas beyond. The owner, a Chilean who adopted Morocco many years ago, is a well-reputed designer (he did the famous and fashionable Dar Moha restaurant) whose talents shine forth at Dar Pangal. A gentle eggshell colour is the background for a luxury of orange trees and hanging greenery in the arcaded patio and for his own mix of Latin American, Moroccan and sub-Saharan styles in the delightfully sober salon and bedrooms: fine-looking tables and chairs, very clever storage systems made of woven palm leaves and pale lemonwood, terracotta lanterns and little gourd water pots, ingenious raffia blinds to screen rooms from the patio – all his own designs. You can order yours from his showroom here. You will find pretty yellow and ochre tadelakt shower rooms and quantities of peace and quiet in this gentle house streaked with originality.

rooms	4 doubles.
price	600Dh.
meals	Lunch or dinner 100Dh. Picnic 50Dh. By arrangement. BYO.
closed	Never.
directions	From Bab Agnaou right at mosque into Rue de la Kasbah; pass Saadian tombs, straight on to Derb Chtouka.

	Julio Miranda Thiel
tel	+212 (0)44 38 09 50
fax	+212 (0)44 38 69 98
e-mail	pangal2003@yahoo.fr

Guest house

map 3   entry 69

Dar Soukaina

19 Derb El Ferrane, Riad Laârouss, Marrakech-Medina

Small and peaceful in its plain white robe, Dar Soukaina is a perfect example of a modest medina house where Alain has preserved the traditional, almost monastic atmosphere: simple furniture, light-handed decoration, flashes of colour to remind one of the brilliant sun outside. The little patio sums it up: a small, light square with one humble tree and arches and doorways in the palest of pale mauves. Swathed in contrasting red, orange and crimson, the bed in the ground-floor *Marjoram* room lies proudly in an elaborate alcove, at the windows are curtains of rough natural cotton, built-in storage spaces look as original as the steep staircases, the shower is through a narrow arch. Each room is coloured to fit its spice name with fabrics of superb quality, simple yet stylish. Floors in ecru tadelakt, white walls, the odd gossamer mosquito net, excellent bathrooms, together give a sense of peace and rest. Alain will generally be here for breakfast or evening drinks on the warm ochre terrace and the intelligent attentive staff are ever at your service with gentle smiles and not a scrap of obsequiousness.

rooms	5: 3 doubles, 1 twin, 1 triple.
price	600Dh–750Dh. Sole occupancy (11 max.) 3,000Dh per day.
meals	Dinner 200Dh. By arrangement.
closed	Never.
directions	Directions given on booking.

	Alain Bonnassieux
tel	+212 (0)44 37 60 55
fax	+212 (0)44 37 60 54
e-mail	darsoukaina@hotmail.com
web	www.riadmania.com

Guest house

Dar Limoun

25 Derb Ben Amrane, Riad Zitoun El Qdim, Marrakech-Medina

In one of the medina's liveliest neighbourhoods and hard by the famous 'square', the sudden quiet as you turn into Derb Ben Amrane is striking. Down here is the neatest little Moroccan house you could imagine, its low front door opening onto a Berber rug which points the way to the arcaded patio. Here, the greenery climbs out of great earthenware pots and up towards the sky while others hang over the edge of the roof to shelter the house from the summer sun. The off-white walls and green doors are in complete harmony with these natural elements. In a Moroccan salon off the patio you will find books and music, a fireplace for chilly days, a cool space in summer. Lanterns flicker on the stairs every evening and the paintings of life in early 20th-century Morocco call your eye as you climb to the good-sized bedrooms with their tribal rugs, sitting corners, new beds and little shower rooms, then on up to the terrace. Two terraces, in fact, with all those plants, a lemonwood table and space above for sunbathing. The staff are as quiet as the house and extremely attentive; it is intimate, appealing, excellent value.

rooms	4: 3 doubles, 1 triples.
price	485Dh.
meals	Lunch or dinner 120Dh, or à la carte. By arrangement. BYO.
closed	Never.
directions	From Place Jemaâ El Fna take Riad Zitoun El Qdim; pass Hôtel Sherazade, 2nd left.

Michel & Nadia Orcel-El Mattane
tel   +212 (0)44 42 66 43/66 59 17 59
e-mail   michelorcel@hotmail.com

Guest house

map 3   entry 71

Angel's Riad

6 Derb Houara, Berrima, Marrakech-Medina

Blue mosaic stars fell from the sky into the harmonious little patio, a troupe of white angel cherubs came too (brought by those storks?) – and it works! The house breathes serenity and simple gaiety and Claudia's calm young smiling presence will convert you instantly. A remarkable woman of Greco-Armenian extraction, she speaks seven languages and has created a haven of relaxation: you can choose just the hammam or a full course of wellbeing treatments with therapist friends. And good, essentially organic Moroccan food: you'll watch your tagine cooking on its traditional earthen brazier on the super terrace. The gentle, welcoming rooms fit this image: big and light for so small a riad, sweetly done with plain walls, heaps of bright little cushions, the occasional star in an iron lamp or a niche in the wall and fabrics that softly echo the colour theme of each room. Bathrooms are superb in their top-quality ivory tadelakt and sober good taste. Claudia came to find a quieter life and, with the help of Hassan and his team, to develop her passion for health and happiness – come and share for a while.

rooms	5: 4 doubles, 1 suite for 4.
price	350Dh-700Dh.
meals	Lunch 80Dh. Dinner 100Dh. By arrangement. BYO.
closed	Never.
directions	Directions given on booking.

Claudia Koranian & Hassan Kebdani

tel	+212 (0)44 38 02 52
fax	+212 (0)44 38 02 52
e-mail	kclaudia7@hotmail.com

Guest house

Dar Ibtissam

Authentic Discoveries, 10 Derb El Ferrane - Riad Laarouss, Marrakech-Medina

Ideal for family rental, Dar Ibtissam has not been overcooked in designer sauce: it is simple, friendly, practical, with glimpses of Marrakchi crafts – dishes, candlesticks, lamps. The patio, cool and comfortable, rising whitely from its checquered floor and lion's head water spout, gives onto the pastel-coloured dining and sitting rooms where there's plenty of space for all to lounge, eat and play. Up the pretty tiled stairs you pass an astonishingly long thin loo/shower room and arrive at the domed bathroom – attractive beige tadelakt and gleaming copper washbasin – that is shared by double room and suite. Here, in the big white/yellow sitting area, a festival of newly-carved stucco lifts your eyes as you pass through the arch to the unwindowed bedroom area with its tall mosquito net and many cupboards. Up again to the generous roof terrace where the warm, fawn bedroom has its own little terrace salon in front and domed throned bathroom across the roof. Fabrics are pleasingly natural, bedcovers are harmonious sabra stripes with matching cushions, materials are wood, wicker, linen and string. Excellent value.

rooms	3: 1 double; 1 twin/double, 1 suite sharing bath.
price	600Dh-900Dh. Sole occupancy for 6: 1,800Dh per day.
meals	By arrangement.
closed	Never.
directions	Directions given on booking.

	Alain Bonnassieux
tel	+212 (0)44 37 60 55
fax	+212 (0)44 37 60 54
e-mail	bonnassieuxalain@hotmail.com
web	www.riadmania.com

Catered house

map 3   entry 73

Riad Maizie

95 Derb Al Qadi, Azbest, Marrekech-Medina

Fruit and veg stalls line the streets, the alley is narrow, the old door is beautiful: you know you are living in real Moroccan Marrakech and the English owners of this old Moroccan family house have kept it genuine while installing good lighting and bathrooms (not en-suite to save the shapes). Finishes are fine tadelakt, delicate zellige and warm bejmat, colours are stimulating, furniture is mosaic-topped or hand-painted, beds as wide as possible in those narrow riad rooms over the citrus patio – so fabrics glow with the reflected light of Morocco. There's a really good kitchen off the dining room, a fireplace in the sitting room, an amazing pink salon upstairs, a stunning painted ceiling, a nomad tent and a splendid dome to greet you as you emerge onto the plant-filled roof terrace to sing with the fountain and salute the distant Atlas mountains. The douiria, a tiny adjoining house with bedroom, bathroom and salon for a couple wanting a bit of independence, joins the big house by the roof. Nourdine manages brilliantly and will even shop for you. A lovely traditional family house for you, your family and friends.

rooms	4: 3 doubles, 1 twin sharing 3 baths.
price	18,000Dh per week, including breakfast.
meals	Cook available. BYO.
closed	Never.
directions	Directions given on booking.

	Miranda Innes & Nourdine Fartmizi
tel	+212 (0)44 38 59 28/68 67 48 33/ +34 952 034 321
e-mail	miranda_innes@hotmail.com
web	www.marocandalucia.co.uk

Catered house

Dar Rhizlane

Avenue Jnane El Harti, Marrakech-Hivernage

Within buzzing distance of the medina, this is a world apart. Behind high walls, light dapples through muslin, lattice and claustra, finds its way past fronds and rich draperies, bounces off the lily pond onto fabulous great urns from the deep south – these gardens are sumptuous and the renovation and extension of the blocky declarative 1940s house are imposing. Sunburnt hues plus Moroccan blue shading into mauve, pink and crimson flow over brick and tadelakt, silk and brocade and, above all, the architect's astounding coloured floor pictures. Salons are rich in ceramics from Fès, remarkable Syrian furniture, intricate brass lanterns, soft deep sofas, hand-picked carpets. It is elegant enough to deserve the 'guest palace' label. Bedrooms and suites are all up to the standard – you will live, sleep, bath and eat like princes in this house. The food is renowned in all Marrakech, the dining room, luscious in its coloured clothes and all those touch-tempting textures, stands wide to the garden: the light, yet again, gleams in silver and porcelain and staff are, of course, princely polite and ever-attentive.

rooms	19: 5 doubles, 4 suites, 2 apartments for 4, 2 apts for 6.	
price	2,300Dh-4,000Dh including afternoon tea.	
meals	Lunch or dinner 150Dh-350Dh.	
closed	Never.	
directions	From medina, Ave Mohamed V for Guéliz; 1st r'bout left on Ave M'y El Hassan; pass El Harti stadium, 1st left (Jnane El Harti/Pt Kennedy), house 250m on right.	

	Ahmed Sadki & Myrvette Dkaki
tel	+212 (0)44 42 13 03
fax	+212 (0)44 44 79 00
e-mail	rhizlane@iam.net.ma
web	www.dar-rhizlane.com

Small hotel

map 3   entry 75

The Red House

Avenue El Yarmouk, Marrakech-Hivernage

Longing for real old-style luxury? This is the place to indulge. Built in 1940 under the French Protectorate, now transformed by its Moroccan owners and standing in a rich old garden of superb design, the colonnaded multi-lobed house, a harmonious mix of Andalucian and Moorish architecture, has a classic French-style salon in royal-rustic Louis XIII, Napoleonic Empire, slim-legged Louis Philippe: surprising, yet remarkably fitting, and Moroccan salons in red and gold; all details and materials are high-class noble stuff. Bedrooms, with private terraces over the garden or the floodlit ramparts, look utterly French in their canopied brass beds, brocaded wall fabrics and 19th-century furniture and, although beautifully turned-out grooms and rose petals on the bed at night reinforce the dated atmosphere, no mod cons, DVDs or strong boxes are forgotten. There's an island in the nicely secluded pool where two lovely palm trees grow. Equally stylish and refined, the restaurant is one of the best in Marrakech – round carpets, round white-clothed tables, impeccable and stylish service, fabulous French and Moroccan food.

rooms	8: 4 doubles, 3 suites for 2, 1 suite for 4.
price	2,500Dh-7,500Dh including airport transfers & soft drinks.
meals	Lunch or dinner in house restaurant from 350Dh.
closed	Never.
directions	In front of the ramparts at Bab Jdid.

Yasmine Jabri Bichara,
Samira Cherkaoui, Fouad Naciri
tel +212 (0)44 43 70 40
fax +212 (0)44 43 70 41
e-mail contact@theredhouse-marrakech.com
web www.theredhouse-marrakech.com

Small hotel

Villa Dar Zina

4 Jnane Brika, Marrakech-Targa

Out in the peace of the Targa palm grove, Didier Vidal, a colourful, cultured and talkative character who loves the good things in life, creates a brilliantly easy, interesting atmosphere. His staff – 16 people for 8 rooms, they include masseur and beautician – are like a big family, utterly devoted to Didier and his guests. The house is big too, columns and cupola, palm trees and citrus all in proper Marrakchi style, the vast pool and cotton parasols less so; or there's the Berber pisé pavilion with its Saharaoui furnishings for greater authenticity. Under arches and vaults, wide rooms have high ceilings, shades of orange-ochre and always magnificent flowers: it is smart, luxurious, cared for, not too overdone – and the antique Venetian mirror is a marvel. The big bedrooms, full of Moroccan craftsmanship and *zouaké* furniture, invite you to quiet privacy: a balcony, a writing table, a sitting area, possibly a fireplace, all among fine soft fabrics and some lovely old objects, make each one a special place and the raspberry-red tadelakt bathrooms are so tempting. A welcoming house of peace and Marrakchi luxury.

rooms	8: 4 twins, 4 suites.
price	1,980Dh-3,480Dh.
meals	Lunch 250Dh. Dinner 350Dh. By arrangement.
closed	Never.
directions	15 minutes drive from centre but first time telephone for escort from Hilton pastry shop on Targa road (extension of Ave Mohammed V).

	Didier Vidal
tel	+212 (0)44 34 66 45
fax	+212 (0)44 49 56 55
e-mail	info@villadarzina.com
web	www.villadarzina.com

Guest house

map 3   entry 77

Riad Musk

Route d'Ouarzazate - km12, Lotissement Tichka, Marrakech

Your hosts, who used to live in Casablanca, are thrilled with their vast Marrakchi house, an old, traditional, non-medina riad. Their daughter has done the gardens with consummate talent: you arrive along a corridor of multi-coloured rose bushes, all the trees and shrubs of Morocco are present, the little kiosk is the best place ever to retire with a book and the pool hides behind the ferns as the Atlas mountains peek over the wall. Riad Musk is a showcase for all forms of oriental arch, coloured tadelakt (there's a smashing black bathroom) and variegated carpets. The white-pillared marble-fountained central patio is so devastatingly big that it's divided into four sitting areas, there are five other salons (Moroccan, snug, bar, telly, billiards)… and a tea room. Bedrooms have kept the rusticities of old beams, ochre and brick-red washes, alcoves and corners; bathrooms are stocked with traditional soaps and scrubs for the hammam. Chadia and Ahmed love mixing with people from other cultures, exchanging ideas and experiences, possibly over a game of *boules* in the garden – you will feel very welcome here.

rooms	8: 7 doubles, 1 suite for 4.
price	1,000Dh-1,500Dh.
meals	Lunch 160Dh. Dinner 220Dh. Picnic 80Dh-100Dh. By arrangement.
closed	20 July-20 August.
directions	From Marrakech centre for Ouarzazate 12km. Signposted on left just after American School.

	Chadia & Ahmed Bouazzaoui
tel	+212 (0)44 32 94 62/61 31 03 20
fax	+212 (0)44 32 94 62
e-mail	riadmusk@lycos.fr
web	www.riadmusk.com

Guest house

Villa Hélène

89 boulevard Moulay Rachid, Marrakech-Guéliz

Bruno is a stickler for detail yet his house has a touch of poetry, Amama cooks brilliantly and Zora manages her team (and guests) with joyous authority – an ideal combination for one of the great 1930s villas of Guéliz. The original architecture is clear and pleasing – an S-shaped colonnade round the front, a wonderful Bauhaus-style staircase up to the first floor, coloured mosaic floors that are impossible to find nowadays. Bruno and Hélène have matched it with simple Art Deco furniture made by skilled and knowledgeable local craftsmen, lots of iron and glass, pure white walls, Tataoui ceilings over big angular steel windows, Berber rugs on those super old floors, some perfect light fittings – and books and music in a quiet corner. There's one suite on the ground floor, one in a garden pavilion and the big apartment upstairs – privacy and space for all. The terraces are generous, too, and the beautiful great garden demands proper attention: you can find practically every Moroccan plant as you walk its gravel paths and there's a pergola by the secluded pool. It's hard to believe you are in the heart of busy Guéliz.

rooms	3 apartments: 2 for 4, 1 for 2.
price	950Dh-1,055Dh.
meals	Lunch or dinner 150Dh-215Dh. Picnic possible. By arrangement.
closed	Never.
directions	Behind main Guéliz post office, opposite Trésor Public building.

Bruno & Hélène Richez

tel	+212 (0)44 43 16 81/61 24 55 27
fax	+212 (0)44 43 16 81
e-mail	bruno.richez@wanadoo.fr
web	www.villa-helene.com

Guest house

 map 3   entry 79

The Garden Room

20 Quartier La Zahia-Majorelle, (Seed), Marrakech-Guéliz

What wonders cannot be done with light and little colour? What better place to seek quiet, cool refuge from the medina chaos than Jennifer's delicious Scandinavian-Moroccan garden room in the old French town? After years in Norway, she found her sunspot in a tidy little street behind the Majorelle Gardens (owned by Yves Saint Laurent, used for nesting by booted eagles). Artist and designer, she has brought all her strands together in this beautiful conversion of house and garden room: bejmat floors, pale sandy walls, curvaceou tadelakt bathrooms, sculpted spaces. Furniture is a few well-loved pieces in old wood, natural wicker, hand-wrought iron, each proud in its proper place: in your Garden Room, that wonderful bed is from Cyprus, the desk is Norwegian, baskets and ornaments are Marrakchi, all bathing in light and air from the flourishing little garden. Jennifer's house is just across the way – she's English and a fascinating person, embedded in the local design scene where her mix of northern minimalism and Moroccan tradition are much admired, yet she remains laughingly independent and relaxed.

rooms	1 double in garden pavilion.
price	600Dh.
meals	Lunch 75Dh. By arrangement.
closed	Rarely.
directions	At crossroads of Ave Y. El Mansour & Bd Safi, left behind Shell garage; 4th house on left, sign "SEED".

	Jennifer Lloyd
tel	+212 (0)44 33 16 10/62 29 78 38
fax	+212 (0)44 33 16 10
e-mail	lloyd_project@hotmail.com
web	www.houseofwonders.com

Guest house

Le Bus Antique

Rue Budgette, Marrakech-Secret

Perfect for a busman's holiday this, within camel-hurling distance of Marrakech. An old Moroccan bus that once trawled the streets of London for a different clientele, has been given a third lease of life in the featureless scrubland that you see here. Step up and through the natty concertina doors and under the eagle eye of the owner, deposit your luggage in the handy rack then find your room where you can. Top deck facilities are reached via an authentically treachorous spiral staircase but uninterrupted views of sky and scrub make the climb worthwhile. Most guests sleep sitting up – you may find yourself in close proximity to others but on no account make contact as it's not the done thing. Bathroom facilities are minimal, that is there aren't any: this is a genuine nature experience. Your brass-buttoned host is usually more than keen to collect your money upfront – in fact he will probably come round every ten minutes or so. Nights can be something magical here when fellow guests gather in the aisle to sing, wishfully, 'the wheels on the bus go round and round' because, of course, they don't. Exceptional.

rooms	1 long communal space comfortably provided with padded benches.
price	Fares please.
meals	Second-hand chewing gum and the odd apple core. BYO.
closed	During owner/busman's holidays.
directions	There and back again.

	Charente & Pineau Lepauvre
tel	Number 34
e-mail	stop@the-stopped-bus-stop.svp
web	www.busted.bus.biz

map 0   entry 81

Villa Chems

63 Lotissement El Hamra - Amerchich, Quartier El Ksour, Marrakech

Chems, a simple new place with no pretensions to designer chic, is a real guest house, occupied and animated by Jean-Pierre, filled with his lively tales of discovering Morocco and his knowledge of history. He is an excellent host, the heart and soul of the house that he also keeps in perfect order. In the small flowered garden, windows and balconies stand open and welcoming – you know instantly that you'll be happy here. Jean-Pierre's love of all things Moroccan is such that his salons and dining room are done in the purest tradition: lots of space, arches dripping with intricate stucco work, shoulder-height zellige, an elaborately-tiled keyhole-arch wall fountain as centrepiece for the Moroccan salon and yards of rich blue carpets. Bedrooms are pretty and comfortable in their practical simplicity: more rugs, a Moroccan sitting corner and a piece of balcony each, sabra or haïk bedcovers matching the curtains, good, well-equipped bathrooms. Finally, Jean-Pierre's origins in gastronomic Roanne mean that food is particularly good here and his dinners are memorable for both the food and the talk.

rooms	6: 1 double, 1 triple, 1 suite for 4; 1 double, 2 twins sharing bath.
price	300Dh-700Dh.
meals	Lunch or dinner from 100Dh. By arrangement. BYO.
closed	Never.
directions	From Marjane (Casablanca road on edge of Marrakech) on Avenue Al Fassi, 1st left, 2nd left, 3rd impasse left, 2nd house on left.

	Jean-Pierre Barral
tel	+212 (0)44 33 14 67
e-mail	barral_villachems@hotmail.com
web	www.villa-chems.com

Guest house

Mektoub

48 Akiod, Marrakech-Semlalia

Philippe and Isabelle feel that this house is their destiny (*mektoub*). In an utterly calm neighbourhood not far from the centre, it is semi-detached with a tiny front garden and a wide-open space inside. You'll simply love the kitchen in greengage tadelakt with its plum-coloured frieze. It has all the right bits of equipment and gives onto the dining room which leads in turn to the sitting area where the vast low table, made from a lovely old door, is attended by colourful traditional benches and cushions. There's a mass of greenery on either side of the spreading windows here and a little pool in the garden. Out of the hall winds an open staircase to the bedrooms. They are done with simple good taste: pale walls, misty mosquito nets to protect the beds, haïks to cover them in softly harmonious colours. The blue tadelakt bathroom has a real bath with a shower fitting in it. The cleaner comes in every day but if you really want to have that amazing kitchen to yourself you'll have to invite the cook to go and enjoy herself. This pretty, peaceful house and garden are ideal for an independent stay in Marrakech.

rooms	3: 2 doubles, 1 twin, sharing bath.
price	Sole occupancy for 6 inc. cook & cleaner: 1,400Dh per day, with breakfast; 7,000Dh per week inc. airport transfers.
meals	Cook available, you provide the ingredients. BYO.
closed	Never.
directions	In Semlalia park by Café du Diamant Vert and ring for escort.

Isabelle Niclot
& Philippe Arrossagaray
tel +212 (0)65 16 81 31
e-mail mektoubmarrakech@yahoo.fr

Catered house

map 3   entry 83

Jnane Tamsna

Douar Abiad, Circuit de la Palmeraie, Marrakech-Palmeraie

The garden flowering in the oasis gives organic veg for excellent meals. There is space, light, air (and a clay tennis court) beneath the palms and arching colonnades, the Atlas beyond the roof terrace, splendid rooms. Meryanne, erstwhile barrister and a vibrant, accomplished designer with Caribbean-Senegalese roots, mixes Morocco, Africa and Europe in her highly original furniture – exotic woods, peasant iron – and luscious layered fabrics. Here are columns of bone bracelets from Senegal, 'Syrian' antiques, echoes of the three Mediterranean religions, good pictures and prints so artfully hung that you just have to pay attention. These rooms, earthy or fiery or coolly limpid, are a delight. Set back beside its own pool, the Travellers' House takes you from west to east, Africa to India, in five rooms of Islam-inspired design. Gary, an ethno-botanist, works passionately for bio-diversity and village development; take one of his interesting and valuable conservation-centred tours and contribute to Moroccan development. Remarkable people in a very special house. *15 mins from town. See Dar Tamsna, entry 94, for catered villas.*

rooms	15: 10 doubles in main house, 5 in garden house.
price	2,000Dh-4,500Dh inc. airport transfer & dinner on arrival. Seasonal terms.
meals	Lunch 140Dh-280Dh. Dinner 300Dh-450Dh. By arrangement.
closed	Never.
directions	From Marrakech for Fès onto Circuit de la Palmeraie for Douar Abiad; pass Hôtel des Deux Tours; house 500m beyond, left through arch.

	Meryanne Loum-Martin & Gary Martin
tel	+212 (0)44 32 94 23/61 24 27 17
fax	+212 (0)44 32 98 84
e-mail	info@tamsna.com
web	www.tamsna.com

Small hotel

Topkapi
Rue Al Atlas, Route de Fès - km4, Marrakech-Palmeraie

Such an easy, willing young couple, all they want is to make your stay perfect. Outside, set in the semi-desert where date palms wave those skinny fronds, their 'Sultan's Palace at Istanbul' looks like a cross between an emir's oasis palace and a small fortress: big, bold, ochre, it is Modern Marrakech in traditional materials set in swathes of lawned garden by a fine dark pool. In the low wing of calmly luxurious orange-ochre living rooms, the stars are Space, adorned with books, frescoes and elegant carved furniture, and Light, falling on Persian rugs and bright cushions. In the two-storey guest-room riad, a brilliantly clear, peaceful patio in softer hues points the way to light, colourful bedrooms with gauzy Indian hangings, sabra throws on excellent beds, original wall hangings, louvres and muslins to filter the light and heat, two-toned tadelakt bathrooms whose every detail pleases. You can be as solitary or as gregarious as you like in all this space and cannot fail to enjoy your delightful yet very professional hosts, their super food and lovely hammam, a mere seven minutes from the Koutoubia.

rooms	10: 7 doubles, 3 twins.
price	1,700Dh inc. airport transfers.
meals	Lunch or dinner 200Dh. Picnic possible.
closed	July.
directions	From Marrakech for Fès 4km; left at Al Majal sign 300m, house on left.

	Dimitri & Lætitia Jalon
tel	+212 (0)44 32 98 89
fax	+212 (0)44 32 98 90
e-mail	topkapi_marrakech@hotmail.com
web	www.topkapi-marrakech.com

Small hotel

map 3   entry 85

Dar Liqama
Douar Abiad, Marrakech-Palmeraie

There's more to Mike and Terri's gourmet mansion than the eight gleaming cookers round teacher's table – but it's a promising start. You have already come up the palm-lined drive, met the lovely ponds leading to the warm-earth 'House of Green Mint' with its columns, pediment and Berber-star brick friezes – a Greco-Moroccan temple? – and dreamed of relaxing on its ample first-floor terraces. Now inside, you lift your eyes past the patio fountain and up the splendid spiral staircase. But wait! What about the big white, buff and brown salon, so quiet and sober? and the joyously baroque purple dining room dominated by two giant iron chandeliers and… fabulous food (the cellar is one of the country's best)? Or there's Dar Louisa, smaller, cosier: lots of little salons, alcoves, that brick patio (below) and larger bedrooms, some over the scented herb garden. All rooms are different – maybe a canopied bed, your own fireplace, a private terrace -each with a fine bathroom and a chess set (Mike's passion). Two swimming pools, a big walled garden, superbly stylish staff serving memorable meals – and cookery lessons.

rooms	13: 9 doubles, 4 twins/doubles in 2 villas.
price	1,750Dh-4,250Dh including airport transfers.
meals	Lunch 200Dh. Dinner 300Dh. Picnic possible. By arrangement.
closed	Never.
directions	From Marrakech for Fès onto Circuit de la Palmeraie for Douar Abiad; pass Hôtel Les Deux Tours & Dar Maha sign; left to enter estate, 4th house along.

Michael William, Terri Rhode, Khalil Guerraoui

tel +212 (0)44 33 16 97/98
fax +212 (0)44 32 95 45
e-mail darliqama@iam.net.ma

Small hotel

Dar Ayniwen

Tafrata, Marrakech-Palmeraie

This house has a soul, the vibrations of a genuine family home and the Abtans still live nearby. The image of the soberly grand Moorish mansion shivers down a series of formal ponds and the sublime gardens have matured into a corner of paradise, ancient palms telling their celebrity tales to giant olive trees over secluded benches. Beyond the majestic old door with its mane of bougainvillea and the oversized atrium with its stunning lattice balconies, the scale becomes human again. Jacques Abtan, who loves Morocco and its 1920s antiques with a passion, has filled the house with wonders and an endearingly dated feel: at any minute, Hercule Poirot might step in to solve a mystery. It is orientally, luxuriously, overly decorated and we love it for its authenticity – brocades, brasses, kilims and all. With, of course, wide new beds and all things IT in the splendid bedrooms, amazing marble and tadelakt bathrooms, a fine marble hammam with full spa treatments on the spot, divine food and first-class staff under the caring, professional eye of son Stéphane, who trained in America then returned to his beloved childhood home.

rooms	7 twins/doubles.
price	2,200DH-5,400Dh including airport & city transfers, hammam, sauna.
meals	Lunch or dinner 350Dh. By arrangement. BYO.
closed	Never.
directions	From Marrakech for Fès onto Circuit de la Palmeraie for Douar Abiad; after palm in middle of track, first track right and straight on to great wooden door.

	Jacques & Stéphane Abtan
tel	+212 (0)44 32 96 84/85
fax	+212 (0)44 32 96 86
e-mail	infos@dar-ayniwen.com
web	www.dar-ayniwen.com

Small hotel

map 3   entry 87

Dar Zemora

72 rue El Andalib, Marrakech-Palmeraie

One of the Palmeraie's calmest, most human-scale houses, Dar Zemora is designed with perfect proportions and top-quality materials for serene, elegant living. Light and taste are masters here. Cupolas add interest, the salons adapt to all seasons, the peaceful ivory tadelakt finish is in wonderful harmony with the stained woodwork and natural bejmat floors. Furniture, an attractive, personal mixture of contemporary and antique plus high-class Moroccan craftsmanship, is set off by plain purple High Atlas carpets and one handsome old mirror. Only the red dining room differs in its superb G'naoua pictures backed by almond green and ochre curtains. You'll love your big, light-filled bedroom – it may have a four-poster bed, an antique chest, a sitting area or a private terrace, and they all have perfect pastel-coloured tadelakt bathrooms. The owners are English and their new garden is already blooming with white oleander and bougainvillea round the pool and fine palm and olive trees that rise to decorate the eternally blue sky. Valérie manages her excellent staff with charm and smiles and puts everyone at ease.

rooms	6: 5 doubles, 1 pavilion.
price	2,000Dh–3,500Dh.
meals	Snack lunch from 80Dh. Lunch 150Dh. Dinner 250Dh. By arrangement.
closed	Never.
directions	From Marrakech towards Fès, pass Circuit de la Palmeraie. After 40km sign, 1st left, 1st right; bear left and follow to Dar Zemora.

Paul & Lindsay Kentish & Valérie

tel	+212 (0)44 32 82 00/61 08 07 61
fax	+212 (0)44 32 82 01
e-mail	darzemora@menara.ma
web	www.darzemora.com

Guest house

Dar Ifilkou
Douar Abiad, Marrakech-Palmeraie

Everyone's a VIP here – a drink when you arrive, fresh fruit and pastries in your room – but the best value in this luxurious place is the separate lodge for four with its own pool. Ifilkou (Berber for flower) has the beauty of clean lines and clear design, the quiet, confident architecture lets in just enough light to illuminate but not dazzle, rooms are big but not daunting, nothing is artificially oriental but antique doors speak of true Morocco and tadelakt finishes soften the surfaces. Resolutely contemporary décor and furniture play with dark and light: chocolate sabra cushions and unbleached cotton draperies, dark moucharabieh armchairs on richly sombre Tazenaght carpets, a fireplace in the sitting area of each bedroom – every detail fits the theme of simple rich comfort. Outside, wide terraces survey the magnificent garden, the pool and the dining tent stand apart among palms and olive trees, fruit and vegetables grow quietly for table and jam pot – you can ask for a cookery lesson in the fine kitchen. Lara runs the place with the smooth care of one who learned her art in places of high luxury.

rooms	7 suites: 2 doubles, 2 twins in house; 2 twins with private pool in pavilion; 1 twin in lodge.
price	2,500Dh including hammam, putting green, soft drinks.
meals	Lunch 200Dh. Dinner 300Dh. Picnic possible. By arrangement. BYO.
closed	Never.
directions	From Marrakech for Fès onto Circuit de la Palmeraie towards Douar Abiad; beyond village, track to right, left into estate, 3rd house on left.

Ruth Marczewski & Lara Cleminson

tel	+212 (0)44 32 95 19
fax	+212 (0)44 32 95 44
e-mail	darifilkou@menara.ma
web	www.darifilkou.com

Guest house

map 3   entry 89

Villa Maha

Douar Abiad, Marrakech-Palmeraie

The house, the garden, the palm trees are all new and young and growing beautifully, white flowers bloom all year among meditative ponds, pebbles and papyrus before a vast green lawn. With its squat roundnesses and tall arches, the soft earth-coloured house sits in peace, its pool sheltered by the reception wings that flash glimpses of refinements inside. A superb plum-tadelakt living room is the showcase for inlaid Syrian armchairs, French period pieces, antique carpets, deep scarlet sofas and a magnificent great dining table. All over the house, sleek unadorned walls — just a couple of slim windows, a carved mirror — leave breathing space for embroidered cushions, superb sabra fabrics, carved doors and Olivia's dazzling collection of Chinese objects. Her family, oriental antique collectors, also run an excellent restaurant in town: Villa Maha's art, food and wine cellar prove it. Bedrooms, three in the main house (the best value), two in the lodge, the smallest in a little garden house, are pretty elegant too, and restful. Olivia loves this place, puts all her energy into it and is a peerless hostess.

rooms	6: 2 doubles, 1 twin, 3 suites.
price	1,500Dh-3,950Dh. Sole occupancy 13,100Dh-19,150Dh per day.
meals	Lunch 250Dh. Dinner 350Dh. Picnic possible. By arrangement. BYO.
closed	Never.
directions	From Marrakech for Fès onto Circuit de la Palmeraie for Douar Abiad; pass Hôtel des Deux Tours, first track on left, last house on left.

	Olivia Grigaux
tel	+212 (0)44 32 95 78
fax	+212 (0)44 32 95 72
web	www.villa-maha.com

Guest house & catered house

Dar El Sadaka

Sidi Saïd Ghot, Ouled Hassone, Marrakech-Palmeraie

This extraordinary house looks like a typical pisé village, all angles and levels round its patio. Inside are the luxury of modern wealth and the zaniness of Jean-François' artistic invention, with brilliant light effects. Beyond the tented hall and tunnel you discover the salon, by artist Sandra Ancelot: a vast, pink room of classic design with a raised amphitheatre at one end, a fireplace beneath it, superb contemporary paintings, fuschia pink and vermilion felt furniture and fuschia organza curtains – and it works! Jean-François' daringly original sense of form and texture takes your breath away; traces of his 'creative weeks for artist friends' surprise and enchant. Outside: a large orange and yellow dining tent, a wisteria-draped conservatory, a giant nanny-goat sculpture by the mosaic pool and live oasis animals – camels, donkeys, sheep – in the great garden; inside: super restful bedrooms in brick, palm-wood and tadelakt, the prices varying with their size (the 'presidential' bed has a roll-back roof for star-gazing), water gurgling everywhere and wonderful staff under Anne's smiling and enthusiastic guidance.

rooms	9: 6 doubles, 3 suites.
price	2,000Dh-5,000Dh.
meals	Lunch or dinner 250Dh; wine extra. By arrangement.
closed	Never.
directions	From Marrakech for Fès on Bab Atlas road; cross Pont Talmet then left at sign.

Jean-François Fourtout & Anne Herouet

tel	+212 (0)44 32 91 10/
	+34 916 508 758
fax	+212 (0)44 32 91 11
e-mail	darelsadaka@iam.net.ma
web	www.darelsadaka.com

Guest house

map 3   entry 91

Villa des Palmiers

Dar Faracha, Jnane Abiad, Marrakech-Palmeraie

Well named is this sober, elegant house: it has the calm symmetry of a Renaissance villa – in local pisé and brick – and the perfect perspectives of an impeccable classical garden – beneath the palm trees. Séverine, a refined, relaxed hostess, and Bernard, a deeply knowledgeable Morocco-lover and trek-organiser, live on the estate and built this guest house in order to share their passion for their country with like-minded visitors. Vast windows look down the garden to the Atlas, their light dapples the treasures inside: the gentle Marrakchi décor of pure arcades and smooth ivory tadelakt, a few carefully-chosen prints, paintings and 1920s posters, just the right amount of furniture – all making for restful, uncluttered elegance and unostentatious comfort. Bedrooms are, of course, big and in the same spirit with rich chocolate and caramel bedcovers, a sitting area each, a super bathroom and, above all, a wide balcony: you are encouraged to look outwards to the garden, the mountains and the call to relaxation. Exceptional value for the *Palmeraie* and such intelligent, interesting people.

rooms	6: 2 doubles, 4 twins.
price	1,100Dh-1,900Dh including airport transfers.
meals	Lunch 150Dh. Dinner 250Dh. By arrangement.
closed	Never.
directions	From Marrakech for Fès; left for hotel Lookéa Issil; where road turns right after hotel, continue straight on track to end of telephone line.

	Séverine Fabry
tel	+212 (0)44 31 39 01/03
fax	+212 (0)44 31 39 05
e-mail	atlassaharatrek@iam.net.ma
web	www.villadespalmiers.com

Guest house

Dar Kerma

Rue Soussan, Marrakech-Palmeraie

Dar Kerma, the Rousseaus' home, has grown organically over their forty years in Morocco. Handsome trees, including the great fig (*kerma*), stand beside plots of wheat and barley, the olives produce superb oil: you are close to nature here, with a pretty pink house by a big blue pool and marble fountain, a peaceful scene overlooked by the master-room balcony. Inside are fabulous carved cedar ceilings, painted doors, arches and columns, family antiques. Raymonde is a painter: she designed the lovely pastel-tile floors, chose the warm bright curtains, organised the delightful bedrooms, all different, all highly attractive. She and Michel, the easiest, friendliest hosts you could imagine, stay in the garden pavilion when they are not in Rabat; otherwise it's a super budget option. Their love of people, beautiful things and authentic Morocco is visible in every corner. Mehdi and his marvellous family are always here to help and advise – more than staff, they are real, caring friends. With Mehdi at the helm and his wife in the galley – she's an excellent cook – you are sure of a great cruise on the Kerma.

rooms	5: 2 doubles, 1 suite for 2, 1 suite for 4, 1 pavilion for 2 with kitchenette.
price	1,200Dh–1,800Dh, pavilion 500Dh. Whole house for 14 inc. breakfast 6,000Dh–6,500Dh per day, 38,000Dh–42,000Dh per week.
meals	Lunch or dinner 150Dh. By arrangement. BYO.
closed	Never.
directions	From Marrakech for Fès onto Circuit de la Palmeraie; past Hôtel Lookéa Issil, 1st right, last house at end.

Raymonde & Michel Rousseau

tel	+212 (0)37 72 03 15
fax	+212 (0)37 20 70 95
e-mail	smadire@elan.net.ma
web	www.darkerma.free.fr

Guest house & catered house

map 3   entry 93

Dar Tamsna

La Palmeraie - Route de Fès, Douar Tamsna, Marrakech-Palmeraie

There is such exotic luxury here you may think you've died and gone to heaven – a 1930s heaven reached by extraordinary spiral staircases, filled with inlaid oriental armoires, deeply embracing blocky furniture, strong fireplaces, shimmering silks and brocades, antique brasses, simple, human Berber pottery, and administered by angels who fulfill your every wish before it surfaces, appearing from behind the carved screen with infinite stylish discretion and iced juice. Chief angel Issa runs this domain with smiling, intelligent impeccability. In its own piece of lush garden with its own pool, each house bathes in this mix of colonial extravagance and contemporary cool; the cottage is a perfect little extra nest. The terraces, balconies and objects of each room, all so different, deserve close contemplation and bathrooms are stunning. Meryanne's designer talents are on brilliant show here, the whole experience is a hymn to her cultural sensitivity and sense of top-notch hospitality, much appreciated by all sorts of celebrities whose notes and drawings in the visitors' book are great fun to read. *Minimum stay 4 nights.*

rooms	3 houses for 6-24: 4 bedrooms, 3 baths; 6 bedrooms, 5 baths; 2 bedrooms, 1 bath.
price	Sole occupancy p.p. per week: B&B 20,000Dh; full board 25,000Dh (inc. driver, minibus, music evening). 6 persons min.
meals	Breakfast, lunch & dinner included.
closed	Never.
directions	From Marrakech for Fès, 3rd left after Circuit de la Palmeraie to Douar Tamsna.

Meryanne Loum-Martin
tel	+212 (0)44 32 94 23/61 24 27 17
fax	+212 (0)44 32 98 84
e-mail	info@tamsna.com
web	www.tamsna.com

Guest house & catered house

Dar Sidi Yahia

Douar Jennate Arst Bouhassoune, Marrakech-Palmeraie

Unusual and highly interesting, both the house and this part of the Palmeraie: near the village with its little houses, its well, its lively working culture, this is the only 'grand' house, sitting very discreetly in two olive-green hectares. Designed by Elie Mouyal, **the** pisé architect, it consists of owner's house, guest wing, hammam and well-concealed pool area, all in traditional materials alternating matt and gloss finishes in soft, warm ochres and earth colours. In vast yet remarkably comfortable spaces, the earth-brick vaults draw gasps, the painted tataoui ceilings are superb, the great salon with its varnished brick fireplace and wall of antique African pots is extraordinary. Each bedroom/salon has books and telly, fireplace and desk, platform beds, gentle brown-striped fabrics and really good carpets – simply beautiful. The master suite is something else: the dreamlike bedroom up under the tower vault – raw linen hangings, moucharabieh – has a devastating view of palm grove and Atlas, below are the children's room and an incredible bathroom. Fabulous garden, super staff, good food – minutes from the centre.

rooms	7: 6 twins/doubles, 1 suite for 4.
price	Sole occupancy for 1-6: 10,000Dh per day; for 7-12: 13,000Dh per day; including meals.
meals	Lunch, dinner, picnic. By arrangement.
closed	Never.
directions	From Marrakech for Fès onto Circuit de la Palmeraie; pass Hôtel Lookéa Issil; 1st track left & continue left to village; house before village.

Karim Soufny
tel +212 (0)44 32 95 20/21
fax +212 (0)44 32 95 22

Catered house

map 3   entry 95

Alan Keohan

Kasbah Agafay

Route de Guemassa - km20, Marrakech

Lively and intelligent, Abel is half English but his is a totally Moroccan idea: top-class suites in tents with antique draperies, ornate bathrooms, even air conditioning; other, big, bedrooms giving onto private patios where fountains fount and décor is as simple-white as fittings and services are sophisticated; all in a genuine old towering hilltop fortress set in an oasis of greenery. Inside one of the country's typically austere pisé kasbahs you can live a while wearing one of Kasbah Agafay's plain *foukias* (indoor jellabah) while soaking in the smooth, luscious luxury of natural products in a perfect tadelakt bathroom, the bloody sun setting over the arid hills, water tinkling in both your ears and a spa-fitness centre in case of over-indulgence. You can ask to dine wherever you like, wherever you happen to be – in the scented garden, your own patio, one of the Moroccan salons – and be served with friendly care by delightful staff. There are tables made of antique carved doors, secret terraces, an organic vegetable plot and a yoga room – and those tents climbing the hill to heaven. *Photography Alan Keohan*

rooms	20: 16 doubles in 6 riads, 4 suites in tents.
price	4,000Dh-5,000Dh including Marrakech airport transfers.
meals	Lunch or dinner from 350Dh.
closed	Never.
directions	From Marrakech on airport road 20km for Guemassa; kasbah on hill on left.

	Abel Damoussi & Thierry Costanza
tel	+212 (0)44 36 86 00
e-mail	info@kasbahagafay.com
web	www.kasbahagafay.com

Small hotel

Tigmi Tagadert

Route d'Amizmiz - km24, Douar Tagadert, Marrakech

Tigmi (Berber for house), Max's hilltop retreat, is a cluster of reconstructed village houses between Marrakech and mountains, a three-dimensional metaphor of the Moroccan world view: the best things are hidden within walls of density and intention. You must find your way to the top of the wiggling earth hamlet and ask to enter the heavy door in the high blank wall to discover the pretty pool garden; then trust your guide. From the next patio, flower-draped with a very striking high triple-arched portico, you are led onwards and upwards through endless courts and corridors, arches, alcoves and corners where light and dark play games with your eyes and level-changes confuse your geography. The peace of the place can now take over. Materials and forms are organic: irregular walls of stone and lime-washed plaster, ceilings of eucalyptus wood and woven oleander leaves, bathrooms of pale skin-sheen tadelakt, quietly, unobtrusively furnished bedrooms where you will find rest and refreshment. And the monastic serenity does not preclude gentle yet high-class hotel service from attentive, caring staff.

rooms	9 suites for 2-4.
price	Half-board 1,760Dh for two.
meals	Lunch 100Dh-250Dh.
	jBy arrangement.
closed	Never.
directions	From Marrakech for Amizmiz 24km; left at sign; 2km track through village: Tigmi is high earth-coloured building at top of village.

	Max Lawrence
tel	+212 (0)61 25 83 47/49
e-mail	maxlawrence@menara.ma
web	www.tigmi.com

Guest house

map 3 entry 97

La Ferme
Route d'Amizmiz - km39, Takerkoust, Marrakech

At the end of an impressive avenue of ancient olive trees, surrounded by a splendid garden, the fine old pisé farmhouse holds its flowering courtyard in the traditional U-shaped embrace. Patrick found his refuge from city life and renovated it for perfect country comfort without spoiling any of its authenticity. In the guest wing, the big bedrooms are appealingly Designer Rustic, all in softness and earthy, sandy tones, traditional materials and pretty country furniture – with the odd giant urn to hold the twisty sticks, a short 'hay-loft' ladder to remind you where you are and superb new beds. Very urbane bathrooms are in good contrast. Outside eating and sitting areas are shaded with straw and furnished with cotton-on-wood. It is restful, harmonious and there's something Tuscan about the tall cypresses, stocky olive trees and yards of overhead vines creating shady walks. The English-speaking staff contribute hugely to the pleasing relaxed atmosphere of The Farm, Moumia's cooking is simply exquisite and Patrick, a gentleman farmer who serves superb wines by candlelight, is a man of experience and much interest.
Photography TREAL / Ruiz

rooms	7: 4 doubles, 2 twins, 1 triple.
price	600Dh. Half-board 840Dh for two.
meals	Lunch or dinner 120Dh. Picnic possible. By arrangement.
closed	Mid-July–mid-August.
directions	From Marrakech for Amizmiz 39km then follow signs.

Patrick Morand
tel	+212 (0)44 48 41 26/65 43 65 88
e-mail	champlat@yahoo.fr
web	www.lafermemarrakech.com

Guest house

Villa du Lac

Villa Karine, Quartier Amzough El Kabil, Lalla Takerkoust, Marrakech

In his piece of paradise beside the lake beneath the olive and eucalyptus trees, your host will introduce you to his enthusiasms and passions: real contact between visitors and Moroccans (he was the first to organise countrywide tours staying only in guest houses), real family cooking prepared before your eyes with home-grown and local produce (super-light breakfast crêpes and local *khobs* – little loaves cooked in the village bread oven), the serenity of the traditional patio-centred architecture brightened by the trilling of budgies and canaries. Floors are beautiful in their speckling of glazed brick and zellige, a profusion of colourful cushions and Berber carpets scatters the rooms, the salon has a scented eucalyptus-log fire, board games, billiards and books for cooler days. Bedrooms are all different: a canopied bed, a zebra bed, an oriental fantasia, a Souiri blue and white theme... with perfect tadelakt and mosaic bathrooms. And outside in the big green garden are the flowers, the nomad dining tent, the pool that seems to take you straight into the lake and up the mountains. A place to breathe deeply.

rooms	6: 5 doubles, 1 suite.
price	Half-board (lunch) 800Dh–1,700Dh for two, inc. airport transfer.
meals	Dinner 300Dh.
closed	Never.
directions	From Marrakech for Amizmiz 25km. Signposted.

Rafik Loufki
tel   +212 (0)44 31 12 05/48 49 56
fax   +212 (0)44 31 12 16
e-mail villa.du.lac@wanadoo.fr
web   www.villadulac-marrakech.com

Guest house

map 3   entry 99

Le Relais du Lac

Route d'Amizmiz, 42200 Lalla Takerkoust, Al Haouz

Blue and tranquil beneath the white-tipped Atlas, the lake is out of this world and its Relais is great for families. It's got the lot: kayaks for exploring, a Cleopatra-type barge for showing off your tan, pedal-boats for... pedalling, shooting and archery, donkeys and quad bikes – and oodles of space, so the open-air restaurant, or two well-furnished tents in winter, where groups congregate, the great central hearth that cooks their pounds of flesh and the camp with immense nomad tents where they sleep, are well apart from the charming little stone and brick inn. Set in the garden near the swimming pool, it has lawns, roses, wrought-iron chairs on its sheltered terrace and a simple yet elegant eggshell dining room full of light and well-designed iron furniture. Also the peaceful group of guest rooms. These pleasant, plainly furnished spaces are impeccably clean, have good bedding, a private outside area each, pretty tadelakt bathrooms and a clutch of candles for when the generator stops at 10pm. Some even have fireplaces. This is a fun place where you will be well cared for by smiling professionals.

rooms	8: 6 doubles, 1 suite for 4 (double & twin), 1 apartment for 4.
price	Half-board 400Dh p.p.
meals	Lunch & dinner included. Other meals 130Dh.
closed	Never.
directions	From Marrakech R203 for Asni 5km; fork right for Amizmiz 28km to barrage; 1st left after barrage 3km; signposted.

	Daniel Thebaud & Jean-Charles Puech
tel	+212 (0)61 18 74 72/61 24 24 54
fax	+212 (0)44 43 81 41
e-mail	contact@hotel-relaisdulac-marrakech.com
web	hotel-relaisdulac-marrakech.com

Inn – Bivouac

Auberge de Tameslohte

Douar Laaouina, 40013 Tameslohte

Intelligent and full of the simple joys of life, Jérôme and Michèle – and darling little Clémence – communicate their love of their adopted country, its rugged spaces and healthy food, as naturally as they welcome you to their delightful farmhouse inn. You sleep in one of the en-suite rooms in an outbuilding constructed, brick by clay brick, by Jérôme himself – big ochre-tinted blue-doored rooms with beams and wicker furniture, warm Berber blankets and good kilims – or in charming bedouin style in your own space in the garden: a top-class brown camel- and goats-hair tent stretched over metre-high walls and furnished with good beds, pretty rugs, lanterns and a chest for your things. Life at the Tameslohte centres on the attractive pool area: underneath the straw huts at the bar, in the tents with their pretty embroidered tablecloths, or round the barbecue. It all has the warm easy atmosphere of a simple country inn and your relaxed, laughing hosts, fans of 4x4 cross-country treks, can also arrange shooting expeditions (within official conservation limits). A real country holiday 15 minutes from the Koutoubia.

rooms	9: 4 twins, 2 triples; 3 twin-bedded tents sharing 3 showers, basins, wcs.
price	300Dh-600Dh. Half-board 480Dh-780Dh for two.
meals	Lunch or dinner 130Dh. Picnic by arrangement.
closed	Never.
directions	From Marrakech for Amizmiz 16km then follow signs.

Michèle & Jérôme Royer

tel	+212 (0)44 48 48 40/66 64 45 80
fax	+212 (0)44 48 48 41
e-mail	raid@wanadoo.fr
web	www.auberge-de-tameslohte.com

Country Inn – Trekking base

map 3   entry 101

Caravan Serai

264 Douar Ouled Ben Rahmoun, Marrakech

A *caravanserai*: once an inn for caravaneers on desert treks, here a dream of a refuge for today's wayfarer. Dynamic and young, Max and Mathieu turned a clutch of old clay houses into a romantic hideaway; the mile of rutted track and the village, as authentic as can be, are part of the experience, grounding this new inn in the age-old reality of alleys, palm groves, fields. Trumpets might flourish you through the mighty arch into the serenity of the pool courtyard where light and shade, air and water play with space, any newness is roughed out and your discovery of the maze of patios, salons and terraces begins. The naturally rustic beige finish is broken by the odd rich blue wall; arches, columns and doorways, some with wonderful old doors, punctuate the labyrinthine layout; it is all warmly organic. Rooms, some really big, some with their own garden, fireplace or pool, have simply crafted furniture, good rugs, fabrics in unpretentious colours, bathrooms that look like sculptures. Wonderful food by the French-trained Algerian-Danish chef – and a handsome hammam in the purest tradition. *Free shuttle to town 3 times daily.*

rooms	17: 4 doubles, 1 single, 12 suites (2 with private pool)
price	700Dh-4,000Dh. Advance booking essential.
meals	Lunch 200Dh. Dinner 180Dh-260Dh.
closed	Rarely.
directions	From Marrakech-Guéliz for Casablanca 8km; cross bridge, right for Ouled Ben Rahmoun, fork right, 600m, right by aerial, white markers into village; right, next left: high building on left.

	Max Lawrence & Mathieu Boccara
tel	+212 (0)44 30 03 02/(0)61 13 44 22
fax	+212 (0)44 30 02 62
e-mail	caravanserai@menara.ma
web	www.caravanserai.com

Small hotel

Maison Boughdira

Route d'Amizmiz - km9, Marrakech

Both architects – Youssef is one of Morocco's specialists in earth architecture – your hosts built this fascinating house as a glowing example of old techniques in a modern context. In the big olive grove, they have added a cottage for guests where you have independence, space and comfort in a simple, stripey, Berber-style interior with lots of wood and wool, the suite has a little kitchen, each room has its own terrace and there's a barbecue. Outside you can swim in the blue mosaic pool, play on the clay tennis court, watch the olive press at work or the variegated fowl paddling in their pond: the house has its own water source, there are horses and most of the food is organic or home-grown. You will be invited into the main house if you choose to dine here – done with superb, natural taste, it has a quiet human atmosphere that will gather you up and Michèle, your wonderfully sparkling, smiling hostess will take great care of you. She did her last design just before opening her house to guests and loves her new activity. Boughdira is a place of peace and beauty, made for real contact over time – you should stay a week.

rooms	2: 1 double/triple, 1 suite for 4. Book ahead.
price	750Dh–1,100Dh.
meals	Lunch or dinner 150Dh. By arrangement.
closed	Never.
directions	From Marrakech for Amizmiz 9km. Signs.

Michèle & Youssef Gharnit
tel   +212 (0)61 17 36 23
fax   +212 (0)44 33 09 99

Full rental

map 3   entry 103

Dar Zarraba

Douar Akarra, Tassoultant, Marrakech

Michel conceived an early, devouring passion for Morocco's traditional earth architecture, spent years studying it and at last bought his own olive grove to build a wholly earth house with the help of the best craftsmen in the land. The cluster of kasbah-like buildings – little towers with terraces looking over the orchard to the Atlas – has the most charming effect, the great salon with its majestic fireplace, lovely tataoui ceiling and elegant polished-earth walls (a technique unearthed in an obscure village near Skoura) is its hub: library, world music, simple floor-level Saharoui furniture on lovely carpets and occasional G'naoua or Berber folklore musical evenings. In the shade of the olive trees lies the fine pool, decorated with Berber emblems. Michel, a man of gentleness and light, receives with simple generosity, bedrooms are as lovely and authentic as the rest, plus copper Arabic letters set in the floors, magnificently simple walnut and metal furniture and warm-hued bathrooms. Michel employs delightful villagers and is active in projects to develop the local economy. *Real French-approved disabled facilities.*

rooms	9 twins/doubles.
price	490Dh.
meals	Breakfast 35Dh. Lunch, dinner, picnic by arrangement.
closed	July.
directions	From Marrakech take Ourika Valley road 13km; cross canal, 1st left; left over 2nd bridge over canal; 1st track right 500m to house.

Michel Lachaud

tel	+212 (0)68 99 92 35
e-mail	dar.zarraba@laposte.net
web	www.zarraba.com

Guest house

Le Bled

Douar Coucou Taseltant, Route de l'Ourika - km5, Marrakech

After 14 years in Switzerland, Moha returned to Marrakech with his young family to open an elegant restaurant and become one of the city's leading lights, his warm enthusiasm and superb cooking endearing him to all. You can now taste rural Morocco at his delightfully informal farm five kilometres from town where you sleep in country peace, harvest your own veg from the organic *potager*, enjoy the huge orchard with wonderful Brahim who knows all about gardens, or flop onto the cushions beneath the pergola after a swim in the superb pool. The three older rooms round the gentle courtyard have a lived-in family feel, the four splendid new rooms have glass walls onto the pool, a terrace each, 'designer Moroccan' furniture and fine tadelakt bathrooms over the lily pond. Fresh, healthy, delicious meals are served in a Berber tent in summer, by the conservatory fire in winter. You can explore the three flourishing hectares to your heart's content – a refreshing convivial place filled with Moha's exuberance just 15 minutes from the medina. He supports an AIDS centre with fabulous charity barbecues for jet-setters here.

rooms	7 doubles/triples.
price	Half-board 600Dh-1,200Dh for two.
meals	Lunch or dinner included. Other meals 150Dh. BYO.
closed	Never.
directions	From Marrakech take Ourika Valley road 4.5km; left at Poteries Berbères sign; at end of road, left: 1st house on right.

	Moha & Alma Fedal
tel	+212 (0)44 38 64 00/(0)61 24 93 11
fax	+212 (0)44 38 69 98
e-mail	darmoha@iam.net.ma
web	www.darmoha.ma

Country Inn – Trekking base

map 3   entry 105

جبال الاطلس

the atlas ranges

Without the Atlas, Morocco would be a desert and one easily forgets that more that half the territory is covered in mountains. The Atlas landscapes are incredibly varied, from the peaceful 'alpine' pastures of the Middle Atlas to the majestically high narrow valleys of the High Atlas which have protected and preserved to this day an astoundingly authentic Berber pastoral culture (there are umpteen opportunities for hikes and mule treks here) to, finally, the thrilling gorges of the Anti Atlas, the last barrier before the great Sahara.

Throughout the Atlas, the visitor may find places to stay that are simple, even basic, but touchingly typical. This is where the Amazerien (Berber) culture finds its most genuine expression.

To make the most of these regions, to explore the still virgin areas of unspeakable beauty, it is best to travel in a 4x4 vehicle.

Fès, the former capital of the Cherifien empire and the intellectual, cultural and religious centre of the kingdom, stands apart. This is the city whose medina hides the greatest palaces of Morocco, the historical base of the real aristocracy. The buildings are bigger, higher, richer and... far more expensive to renovate and maintain (some patios are 15 metres high) and the renewal of the glories of Fès comes at a price, a price that is partly covered by the visitor to fabulous guest house and fashionable restaurants. If the cost per night is higher than average, the magnificence and refinement of these old palaces really justifies it. If your budget is limited, stay 45 minutes away in quiet, reasonable Meknès and make the trip to Fès each day.

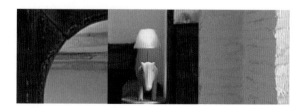

Photography by Caravan Serai, entry 102

Hôtel Transatlantique
Zankat El Meriniyne, Meknès

Wonderful people, who really do seem to enjoy their work, welcome and serve you at this big old/new hotel built in the thirties, during the French Protectorate, on the edge of the 'medina of 100 minarets'. The original Moroccan side of the Transatlantique has more character than the more modern, international wing (it's quite a hike from one side to the other) and its refurbished rooms have a pleasing feel: looking over the small rose garden, they are furnished with renovated 1940s pieces that are part of the history of this once-grand place. The comfortable rooms carry the marks of passing time as well as televisions, old panelling as well as wall fabric, copies of Moroccan paintings and prints, huge beds and decent bathrooms with thinnish towels and masses of extras. The nostalgia of faded nobility and old colonial society is dispelled by the live international music played in the bandstand out by the bar but there are lots of garden corners to sit in and look out over the medina, two swimming pools, three tennis courts and excellent food. A very decent stopover in the old imperial city.

rooms	120: 118 doubles & twins, 2 suites.
price	750Dh–1,720Dh.
meals	Buffet breakfast 55Dh. Lunch 50Dh–150Dh. Dinner 170Dh.
closed	Never.
directions	From Rabat motorway exit Meknès Ouest; entering town, follow signs to hotel.

	Ali Kournaf
tel	+212 (0)55 52 50 50 to 55
fax	+212 (0)55 52 00 57
e-mail	transat@iam.net.ma
web	www.transatmeknes.com

Hotel

Palais Didi

30 avenue Moulay Ismaïl, Meknès

The rough-looking outside has little to do with the delights hiding inside. This 18th-century medina palace has been in Ismaïli's family since it was built by a descendent of Sultan Moulay Ismaïl. The magnificent patio means lots of light and great elegance, ground-floor rooms have proper grand proportions (this is where the suites are, of course), the harmonious blue and cream colour scheme is peaceful though upper-floor rooms have smaller windows and therefore rather less light. Within this framework, Ismaïli's renovation aims for typical Moroccan palace style with quantities of stucco, kilims, carpets, lamps and hubble-bubbles that struggle to match their aristocratic surroundings. But the Didi is in a stunning position, right next to the Alaouite mausoleum, while up on the terrace you discover the wonderful Meknès roofscape and... the royal golf course, quite a surprise in a medina. Bedrooms have great new style, all bathrooms are thoroughly, newly tiled and equipped and the first-floor restaurant is warmly done in painted wafer brick while the little second-floor pool is most tempting. And lovely staff.

rooms	13: 3 doubles, 2 twins. 3 singles, 5 suites.
price	950Dh-1,200Dh.
meals	Dinner 150Dh-200Dh.
closed	Never.
directions	From Rabat on motorway, exit Meknès Ouest for Centre Ville; hotel behind Moulay Ismaïl mausoleum (Dar El Kibera car park).

	Ismaïli Raouf & Alaoui Zaki
tel	+212 (0)55 55 85 90
fax	+212 (0)55 55 86 53
e-mail	reservation@palaisdidi.com
web	www.palaisdidi.com

Small hotel

map 2   entry 107

Ryad Dar Lakbira

79 Ksar Chaâcha, Dar Lakbira, Meknès

Brilliantly central and snug against the old medina ramparts built in the 17th century by Moulay Ismaïl, now floodlit at night – no number of tourists can dilute this authenticity –, Ismaïli's is a mansion with real personality and all the ingredients of the wedding-cake Moroccan style. He is young, charming and enthusiastic – a very good sort. His patio restaurant is the inner sanctum of the big house: quiet, intimate, lots of rambling greenery, mosaic tables, old geometric-carved doors and the compulsory fountain, only ruffled when tour groups invade for lunch. There is also a vast and very Moroccan salon, a hall with dazzling tiles and an unexpected collection of old radios at the end of one dark corridor which sets the tone of the décor. The big bedrooms show the same exuberance of stucco, lattice screens, patterned tiles and brass things. They are all different in their contrasting colours and ideas, draperies and ornamental objects – we liked the blue room best. Family-run, the Lakbira brings the friendly welcome of genuine Moroccan staff who make it a special place to stay.

rooms	6: 4 doubles, 2 twins.
price	750Dh.
meals	Lunch or dinner 110Dh-160Dh.
closed	Never.
directions	From Rabat on motorway, exit Meknès Ouest for Centre Ville; riad near Bab El Mansour gate (Sidi Amar car park).

Ismaïli Mohamed Raouf

tel	+212 (0)55 53 05 42
fax	+212 (0)55 53 13 20
e-mail	riad@iam.net.ma
web	www.maisondhotes.fr.fm

Guest house

Gîte Dayet Aoua

Route d'Immouzer à Ifrane - km7, Ifrane, Fès

Abdelhamid Ghandi is an interior decorator whose eye for clean sober lines and use of space may well have been inspired by the mountains and lakes of the Atlas that he so loves. Down by the cedar-ringed lake (*dayet*), in this area of outstanding beauty, he first cultivated an apple orchard; then he built his comfortable chalet-like inn where visitors can taste the Berber sense of spontaneous hospitality; then he became one of the leading lights of country tourism in the province – as well as writing a book on wrought-ironwork: a charming, compelling host. His gîte is run by a team of warm and courteous villagers who also cook the simple delicious food. Apart from water fun they have horses, donkeys, guides and advice on hiking, biking and bivouacs as well as the cultural things. It's carefully rustic with beams, Berber blankets, some super decorative plates on white walls and good solid furniture. Bedrooms are clean, simple and pretty, suites are one double room and one Moroccan salon with bench beds. In the relaxed atmosphere, people have great fun here, far from the pressures of the city.

rooms	5 suites for 4.
price	400Dh.
meals	Lunch or dinner 100Dh-150Dh. By arrangement.
closed	Never.
directions	From Immouzer for Ifrane 7km; left for Dayet Aoua following lake round on right. Signposted.

Abdelhamid & Fouzia Ghandi

tel	+212 (0)55 60 48 80
fax	+212 (0)55 60 48 52
e-mail	aouagite@yahoo.com
web	www.legite-dayetaoua.com

Inn – Bivouac

map 2   entry 109

Gîte Ras El Ma

Route Nationale 8 - km8, 53000 Ifrane

So new that when we visited in high hot summer the little stone house in the prairie was open – to guests and to the elements; the arms of the charming young owners too. It's all wrapped up and cosy now but the welcome will always be as genuine. Aziza was born here, educated away and returned to her beloved cedar forested valley to apply her flair and intelligence to farming and tourism – you can visit her fish tanks and walk with her sheep. She and Mehdi have made a delightful inn here with local materials and good taste: pretty little bedrooms and communal washrooms, a fine fireplace in the tadelakt salon, quiet gardens. The delicious food is, fully local and chemical-free, the hiking circuits, based on Aziza's deep local knowledge, take you to all the riches of the area: the forests and their monkeys, the wild bees and their honey, the lakes, waterfalls and hidden valleys. And they are, above all, a kind and gentle couple who respect their land and other people and know serenely where they are going. Once you see it, you have to stop; once you stop, you have to stay.

rooms	3: 1 double, 1 triple, 1 dormitory for 6, sharing 3 showers & 3 wcs.
price	200Dh p.p.
meals	Lunch or dinner 80Dh. BYO.
closed	Never.
directions	From Fès for Azrou 70km; 8km after Ifrane, signs for Ras El Maa lakes.

	Aziza & Mehdi Naceur
tel	+212 (0)55 56 00 08/64 16 36 98/99
e-mail	giteraselma@yahoo.fr
web	www.giteraselma.ifrance.com

Country Inn – Trekking base

Villa des Oliviers

Ferme Reda, Sidi Al Makhfi - Sidi Addi, Par Azrou

When your hosts first found this little valley, far from frenzied Casablanca, where they could walk straight into the mountains and contemplate the glory of the setting sun on their return, they instantly plumped for the fabulous site where their house and farm now stand. From accountant to gentleman farmer, from city lady to yoga and meditation adept, their journeys are worth hearing about. At the end of four kilometres of good track, standing firm above that sweeping arid landscape, the house conceals a luscious green garden, big windows over gentle terraces, a sparkling pool shaded by tall cypresses and heaps of conviviality. The food is all organic, lots of it from Monsieur's own kitchen garden and fields, there is a meditation room and the peace is palpable. Without any flash designer's touch, it's a simple, comfortable guest house where, if you share the Redas' taste for walking and quiet country pursuits, you will feel instantly at home. Bedrooms are big and light, the European-style salon has the perfect fireplace, the food is genuinely, creatively vegetarian.

rooms	2: 1 double, 1 suite.
price	600Dh-1200Dh.
meals	Lunch or dinner 100Dh.
closed	Never.
directions	From Azrou for Khenifra, just after Sidi Al Makhfi, turn off following signs.

Monsieur & Madame Reda-Fathmi

tel	+212 (0)61 21 66 24/06 77 88
fax	+212 (0)22 22 34 09
e-mail	francoise-reda-fathmi@hotmail.com

Guest house

 map 2   entry 111

Kasbah Asmaâ Hôtel

Route d'Er Rachidia, Midelt

Standing proud above the great red plateau yet dwarfed by the wakening power of the first hills of the Atlas, it's a modern kasbah hotel and, as warmly welcoming as Berber tradition would have a kasbah be – one of the Alaoui family's smallest and most convivial. The delightful garden with its palms, roses, pots and other authenticities is the place to sit around or swim. Inside, the covered patio has an imposing fountain built of local rock as its focus whence you have a choice of three dining-room décors, blue, red or green velvet brocade, each with a fireplace, all typically Moroccan – as is the excellent food served there. The staff are quietly charming, all smiles and easy friendliness, the big bedrooms are decorated in a simple modern style warmed by spangled Berber blankets and the odd mural but the heart and soul of the place is Rachid himself. With a consuming passion for his place of birth he organises extraordinary excursions into the Atlas for those who really want the authentic experience: several days of nomadic life in genuine nomad tents. An ideal spot between the imperial cities and the deep south.

rooms	35 doubles & twins.
price	Half-board 600Dh for two.
meals	Lunch or dinner 125Dh.
closed	Never.
directions	Signposted on road out of Midelt towards Er Rachidia.

	Rachid Alaoui
tel	+212 (0)55 58 04 08
fax	+212 (0)55 58 04 08/04 05

Small hotel

Auberge Jaafar Kasbaa Itto

Route du Cirque Jaafar & Imilchil km6.5, Berrem, Midelt

What an amazing place, this organic farm hidden in its greenery high up on the arid Midelt plateau. Your host was born here, spent 30 years drilling holes all over the world and came home to grow chickpeas in peace. But being a gregarious sort, he decided to turn his farm into a haven for committed walkers and nature-lovers. The great 40-day Atlas crossing starts here, just 15km from the Jaafar cirque, its first stunning halt. The inn is deliciously old-fashioned, like an 1890s river-side café: you can eat, drink, laugh and even dance here, when the occasion is right – people come for weddings, birthdays, family reunions; the landlord's bonhomie keeps the atmosphere jovial and welcoming for guests, campers and locals who come for the super food, either in one of the Moroccan salons or out under the brown Berber tent – they can spit-roast 40 sheep for really big events. Terraces and gardens have great views to the Atlas peaks, bedrooms are simple and spotless. A gateway to an unknown region that's really worth exploring and is so wild and untouched that you can only see it on foot or in a 4x4 vehicle.

rooms	33: 14 doubles, 3 suites; 16 doubles in towers sharing showers & wcs.
price	Half-board 500Dh for two.
meals	Lunch à la carte.
closed	Never.
directions	From Er Rachidia through Midelt; after bridge over oued, left onto poor road 5km.

	Saïd Rahdou
tel	+212 (0)55 36 02 02
fax	+212 (0)55 58 34 15

Inn – Bivouac

map 5   entry 113

Auberge des Artistes

Route d'Imilchil - km50, Beni Mellal

No telly, no tinned food, no noise here, just an unassuming and solidly real little *auberge-camping* sitting small in that gigantic landscape. Prepare to be overawed – then rejoice in the warmth of human kindness that you'll find inside. François and Patricia are the sweetest French couple, happy as larks in their little heaven, cooking succulent kebabs and advising all their guests, campers and house-guests alike, on the innumerable lovely walks and trips to do in the area. The pergola is a great spot to gorge yourself on their generous country breakfast before setting out into the hills, or there's the cheerful dining room in cooler weather. Very simply done, the bedrooms are small and neat in little stone bungalows that stand in a pretty garden dotted with local terracotta urns. And at the end of the day, before that miracle called the mountain-desert sunset, you will understand why some people can never leave this country. The perfect place for lovers of the wilderness, artists, poets and all those who are looking for real life experiences rather than sophisticated luxury. And a pretty village, too.

rooms	3 doubles.
price	290 Dh. Enquire about camping.
meals	Breakfast 40Dh. Lunch or dinner 40Dh-120Dh à la carte.
closed	Never.
directions	From Beni Mellal approx 50km; right for Imilchil; after El Ksiba bend, follow signs to inn.

	Patricia & François Gattano
tel	+212 (0)23 41 54 90/62 11 94 05
fax	+212 (0)23 41 54 90

Country Inn – Trekking base

Sofitel Palais Jamaï

Bab Guissa, Fès

In this living legend, a Sultan's palace for 50 years, the spa is superbly venerable and the King has his quarters. An hotel since 1930, it dominates magical Fès, its exceptional gardens a version of the Andalucian dream of earthly paradise; the lobby may dwarf you with its vast magnificence but the beauty and detail of the original rooms are a knockout. The Grand Vizier commissioned the very best craftsmen to make pictures with the finest zellige, carve intricacies on ceilings and doors, turn plaster into lace, and his suite is a must for celebrity honeymoons. The big 1970s wing obviously can't have these ancient splendours but the good-sized rooms, all alike in their Moroccanised European comfort, have plush Fassi-decorated furniture. Only a few (the cheaper ones) lack a view of the sensual gardens where orange and lemon trees scent the air and fountains make the music. The Jamaï is a special member of the Sofitel group in being allowed better fittings and staff ratios – you will find them helpful and efficient – while respecting their good environmental rules. And the Moroccan restaurant is really excellent.

rooms	142: 123 doubles & twins, 19 suites.
price	2,660Dh–3,160Dh.
meals	Lunch or dinner 250Dh–430Dh. Picnics available.
closed	Never.
directions	On northern side of city, against medina wall: signposted from all directions.

Jean Le Priellec

tel	+212 (0)55 63 43 31
fax	+212 (0)55 63 50 96
e-mail	H2141@accor-hotels.com

Landmark hotel

map 2   entry 115

Riad Fès

5 Derb Ben Slimane, Zerbtana, Fès El Bali

Your host: gracious and charming, a fount of history and architecture, a refined gourmet; his reflexion: this noble old palace. The Moors brought design ideas from Andalucia after the reconquest, the Fassis brought others after discovering Europe 130 years ago and Chakir Sefrioui, a renowned architect, gives present meaning to this age-old alliance. Riad Fès is exceptional in beauty and riches, the perfect place to stay and learn. Islamic carvings, antique doors, myriad mosaics, fountains and palm trees, a grand piano beneath a truly impressive Fassi lamp in the lace-arched patio, Moroccan velvet divans and 1930s armchairs – all create a dazzling atmosphere. Each big room is a showcase for eastern and European furnishings: dark cedar beams and Edwardian antiques, keyhole arches and fabulous floors, handmade Fassi quilts and Venetian mirrors; each bathroom is a copper-tinted work of art. The green-pool patio is in sleek contrast and the terrace dominates the whole medina: up here, two smaller rooms have private terraces and the incomparable view. The gastronomic restaurant is the final, remarkable, flourish.

rooms	15: 7 doubles, 8 suites.
price	1,700Dh-3,000Dh; Royal Suite 6,000Dh.
meals	Lunch or dinner 260Dh-380Dh (residents); 420Dh-500Dh (non-residents).
closed	Never.
directions	From Place Sidi el Khayat, Batha district, telephone for escort to house.

	Chakir Sefrioui
tel	+212 (0)55 74 12 06/74 10 12
fax	+212 (0)55 74 11 43
e-mail	riad.fes@iam.net.ma
web	www.riadfes.com

Small hotel

Dar El Ghalia

13/15 Ross Rhi, Fès-Medina

All the graciousness of a long-standing Fassi family, their art, culture and traditions, are met in this 17th-century palace – and, moreover, so is Dar Tajine, one of Morocco's most famous restaurants and Omar Lebbar's first idea for his family house; now you can sleep here too. The dark narrow hall, rich in mosaics and promise, projects you into the light of a magnificent colonnaded patio where antique rugs lie on a brilliantly intricate floor and luxurious salons open their hand-painted doors to show off more cushions, carvings and finely-worked brass. In bedrooms and suites, beneath generous arches and satiny hangings or rich Moroccan quilts, are a splendid mix of 19th-century European beds, carved armoires, elegant daybeds and Moroccan paintings – rooms fit for royalty. You may find a fireplace or a mezzanine, a jacuzzi or a four-poster and always a beautiful tiled bathroom. In surroundings of such authentic splendour, a shining example of the harmony of symmetrical riad volumes and traditional Moroccan decorative arts, the poised and helpful staff are perfect and your host's attention to detail unfailing.

rooms	13: 4 doubles, 8 suites, 1 Suite Royale for 6.
price	1,300Dh-2,800Dh.
meals	Lunch or dinner 250Dh-500Dh. By arrangement.
closed	Never.
directions	In medina (Fès el Bali), follow signs from Bab Jdid (south-west gate).

	Monsieur Omar Lebbar
tel	+212 (0)55 63 41 67/74 15 74
fax	+212 (0)55 63 63 93
e-mail	darelghalia@hotmail.com
web	www.maisonshotes.co.ma

Guest house

map 2   entry 117

Riyad Shéhérazade

23 Arsat Bennis, Douth, Fès-Medina

Shéhérazade, the noblest of the riad hotels, is the triumph of one of the city's leading couples. With his love of Fassi culture, Adbelhaï launched the famous Festival of Sacred Music and works to preserve the Fassi heritage; with her elegance and dynamism, Najiba organises incomparable receptions; their hotel – a small palace where 500 can have the party of a lifetime – is a summit of luxury and beauty. Its generous spaces hold perfect examples of all Moorish architectural and decorative themes, the patio alone is a masterpiece, the restoration was done by the best craftsmen in town, lace-fringed arcades and pure white tablecloths shimmer beside graceful palms in the azure pool – and then the musicians strike up from the 1900s 'bandstand': it's fairyland. Inside, in salons and bedrooms, carved cedar breathes warmth onto sculpted plaster, ornate mirrors reflect brocade cushions, fabulous moucharabieh play with the light while antiques confirm the richness of the place, bathrooms are solid marble. Upstairs, you dine by lanternlight beneath sublime pergolas with the medina at your feet. Out of this world.

rooms	14: 3 doubles, 11 suites.
price	1,200Dh–5,000Dh.
meals	Lunch or dinner 280Dh–400Dh. By arrangement.
closed	Never.
directions	In Place de l'Istiqlal, telephone for escort.

Abdelhaï & Najiba Ben Ghazi

tel	+212 (0)55 74 16 42/61 18 98 60
fax	+212 (0)55 74 16 45
e-mail	sheheraz@iam.net.ma
web	www.sheheraz.com

Small hotel

Dar Ziryab

2 rue Ibn Badis, Fès-Ville Nouvelle

Here in the quiet air of the new town is a genuine guest house inhabited by an exceptional man of letters and passions and his mother who cooks with such refined subtlety that your idea of Moroccan food will be transformed. So will you, if you spend enough time for Jalil to convey his fabulous knowledge and love of Fès (he was an official national guide and speaks five languages) and of Arab-Andalucian music (Ziryab the Wise brought musical culture from Baghdad in the 9th century); his slide show talks are as renowned as Madame El Hayar's spiced vegetables. In the same spirit, he chose the best ma'allems to decorate the interior of his big new house in beautiful style with the best materials, including a splendid Moroccan salon for all the gourmets wanting to dine here. Colours are soft and careful of the many fabulous antiques and works of art; bedrooms have a touch of drama, be it a carved or painted bedhead, draperies or cushions, niches or fireplace; bathrooms are masterpieces of shape, colour and decoration. With Jalil as your guide, you will enter a new universe of wonders – and his wife can teach you cookery.

rooms	8: 3 doubles, 2 twins, 2 suites, 1 apartment for 4.
price	900Dh–2,800Dh.
meals	Gastronomic lunch or dinner 350Dh. By arrangement.
closed	Never.
directions	In new town, behind Sheraton Hotel.

Jalil El Hayar

tel	+212 (0)55 62 15 61/61 17 39 97
fax	+212 (0)55 62 31 67
e-mail	darziryab@wanadoo.net.ma
web	www.darziryab.com

Guest house

map 2   entry 119

Riad Norma

16 Derb Sornas - Ziat, Fès-Medina

A very fine house, a lively, sparkling owner who lives on the spot with her cat, exceptional breakfasts – Riad Norma is quite a find. Built in the thirties, it has the look, style and refinement of a classic old Fassi house with the dimensions of a modern one: wider rooms and bigger windows onto the lovely tiled patio. Unusually, the embroidered arches let you out through a high gate into a pretty, intelligently designed garden with shady trees, lots of flowers and a plunge pool – so welcome in summer. Monique fell in love with this place and moved from Paris to throw all her energy into it. Very French, she is formal yet dynamic with a subtle flair for décor: hers is magazine style with good colour mixes against pale walls but nothing ostentatious, lots of Moroccan fabrics and crafts but no clutter, the latest fittings in spotless bathrooms. Harmony and comfort are her aims. The two smaller (and cheaper) rooms in the little douiria are just as good as the biggest L-shaped suite with its warm wooden furniture and sheeny sabra fabrics. Great attention is paid to food too: exquisite dinners and glorious breakfasts.

rooms	7: 2 doubles, 3 twins/doubles, 2 suites.
price	650Dh-2,500Dh.
meals	Lunch or dinner 260Dh. By arrangement.
closed	Never.
directions	Park at Bab Ziat and ring for escort.

	Monique Devaux
tel	+212 (0)55 63 47 81
fax	+212 (0)55 63 47 48
e-mail	monique@riadnorma.com
web	www.riadnorma.com

Guest house

Ryad Mabrouka
25 Derb El Miter, Talaâ K'bira, Fès-Medina

High up in the medina, this aristocratically elegant house is exceptional in having a real garden where an emerald pool reflects the old citrus trees and Michel's gargantuan breakfast can be enjoyed in birdsung peace. The house is typical of 18th-century Fès in its central pillared patio, mosaic-floored galleries with their antique cedarwood doors, shoulder-height zellige, intricate stucco above and carved ceilings to cap it all. But go up to the luminous great veranda for tea at sunset and watch the medina catch fire – unforgettable. More views are to be had from the terraces where soft divans in low-slung tents invite you to laze the day away. Michel's love and knowledge of Morocco inform the whole house, his books and advice are ever available, the mixture of antiques from both countries gives it a style and charm all its own and his taste in bedroom décor shows such rich, subtle variety that you'll want to come back to sleep in them all. His long experience of running hotels, his charm and easy manner make this one of the most restful places to stay in the country and his staff are, naturally, perfect.

rooms	8: 2 doubles, 5 suites for two, 1 suite for 3.
price	900Dh-2,100Dh.
meals	Lunch 150Dh. Dinner 200Dh. By arrangement.
closed	Never.
directions	Ring from Bab Boujloud for escort to Ain Azliten car park and riad.

	Michel Trezzy
tel	+212 (0)55 63 63 45
fax	+212 (0)55 63 63 10
e-mail	ryadmabrouka@iam.net.ma
web	www.ryadmabrouka.com

Guest house

map 2   entry 121

Riad Zamane

12 Derb Skallia Douh, Batha, Fès-Medina

The architecture gives the harmony, the owner brings the vibration – who could resist Sakina's smile? She is attentive and aware, she listens and understands, she's a marvellous hostess who insists there be cheese for breakfast. Having lived for years in France, she came back to her native Fès and this lovely 1860s house where the blue mosaic zellige shimmer across floors and up walls, the little fountain sparkles and simplicity is truth. With intelligent, creative frugality, Sakina uses misty organzas and cottons against white walls, good wooden furniture – a little desk in each room, a carved table here, a padded stool there – and excellent beds to concoct rooms where you instantly think you'll. The little double is adorable, the suites are pretty big. Her caringness reaches out: solar heating, flowers at all times, traditional Fassi cooking of last-minute marvels rather than long-stewing tagines, an uncluttered dining area. All this and deeply incised stucco alcoves, embracing arches and rich tadelakt bathrooms as well. Finally, the terrace sweeps you from the enfolded medina out to the rugged hills.

rooms	5: 1 double, 3 double suites, 1 twin suite.
price	1,200Dh-1,500Dh.
meals	Dinner 200Dh.
closed	Never.
directions	From Place Istiqlal-Batha, park at entrance to medina and ring for escort.

	Sakina Belcadi
tel	+212 (0)55 74 04 40/61 10 04 41
fax	+212 (0)55 74 04 41
e-mail	contact@riadzamane.com
web	www.riadzamane.com

Guest house

Riad Al Bartal

21 rue Sournas, Ziat, Fès-Medina

The birds (*bartal*) that sing in this ineffable patio were the sole tenants when your exceptionally charming, intelligent hosts, after months exploring the backroads of Africa, found the haven they were looking for on a dusty backstreet of Fès. Neglected it was but great riches of stucco, woodwork and zellige, as well as original doors five metres high, had survived to live in glory again. Prepare your Moroccan trip here: they have absolutely all the books; read them on the roof terrace while the sun sets over ancient Fès, or in your room where eastern magic brings dreams of the Morocco that was, or under the sensual arches of the cool tiled patio where creepers and craftsmanship drip peace – impossible that the anarchy of the medina's ancient souks should be so close. Carved furniture, Mauretanian wall hangings, more glittering tiles, tadelakt bathrooms with plate-sized bronze shower heads, giant copper tanning vats for baths – it's superb and the suites are ideal for families. Modernity also lives here in the shape of a permanent exhibition of excellent local artists. A perfect balance and utterly caring hosts.

rooms	7: 2 doubles, 5 suites (twin/double beds).
price	750Dh–1,250Dh inc. use of garage.
meals	Dinner 170Dh. By arrangement.
closed	Never.
directions	Enter at Bab Ziat heading north; first left Rue Sournas, house on left.

Mireille & Christian Laroche

tel	+212 (0)55 63 70 53
fax	+212 (0)55 63 70 53
e-mail	riadalbartal@iam.net.ma
web	www.riadalbartal.com

Guest house

map 2   entry 123

Riad Louna

21 Derb Serraj - Talâa Sghira, Bab Boujloud, 30200 Fès-Medina

In this ideally positioned old house, the base is genuine traditional Fès: the mosaic and 'planetary' tile patterns, the terracotta, the majestically high carved wooden doors with their brass fittings and, of course, the fine riad architecture centred on an ever-musical fountain, lit by lanterns at night that throw the deep-chiselled plasterwork into impressive relief. Within this frame, your friendly and amusing Belgian hosts (Belgians are noted for their quirky, self-deprecating sense of humour) have done their guest house in simple, modern style: good divan beds, comfortable armchairs, the occasional four-poster draped in gauzy white; with nods to Moroccan decorative ideas: long benches with damasky-brocade cushions, local ceramic stoves for those cool winter evenings, some fine great vases. White walls are the perfect foil to modern paintings and Moroccan prints – there's lots of interest here. Two terraces onto the patio, one glazed, one open, give ample space for daytime sunning or evening tea-drinking when the lanterns are lit. Jean-Pierre runs his house and his remarkable staff with a masterly touch.

rooms	6: 2 doubles, 1 twin, 3 suites.
price	650Dh-950Dh. Sole occupancy 4,200Dh.
meals	Lunch or dinner 150Dh. By arrangement.
closed	Never.
directions	By Batha post office, telephone for escort.

	Jean-Pierre Parent
tel	+212 (0)55 74 19 85
fax	+212 (0)55 74 19 85
e-mail	riadlouna@iam.net.ma
web	www.riadlouna.com

Guest house & catered house

Résidence La Roseraie

Route de Taroudannt - km60, Val d'Ouirgane

This place has it all. Riding? Take a sturdy, willing Berber Arab pony into the mountain splendour. Hiking? It's two hours to a refreshing plunge into the Ouirgane waterfall, three hours along a breathtaking valley to mint tea in a remote Berber village. Health? Indulgence? Three pools, a lovely '1920s' spa centre, massages, beauty treatments and delicious organic food. 25 hectares of paradise gardens surround the bedroom cottages, pergolas drip with roses, palms filter the light, the cliff plunges down to the river bed. Each room is a suite, smaller or bigger, with sitting corner and private terrace, the older in rustic wrought-iron and florals, the newer in smart padded hotel manner – you feel welcomed into your own space. With traditional Moroccan décor married to European comforts – fine Berber rugs and thick curtains, moucharabieh furniture and good lighting, typical tiling or a bath in an alcove – you get the best of both worlds. The music room is astonishing with its great zellige-faced Renaissance fireplace. In such an atmosphere, staff are relaxed and smiling. Stay for days and discover some of hidden Morocco.

rooms	45: 8 doubles, 12 twins, 20 suites for 2, 5 suites for 4.
price	2,200Dh-3,000Dh.
meals	Lunch 100Dh-250Dh. Dinner 300Dh.
closed	Never.
directions	From Marrakech for Taroudannt 60km. Signposted.

Abdelkader & Nabil Fenjiro

tel	+212 (0)44 43 91 28/48 56 93
fax	+212 (0)44 43 91 30
e-mail	roseraie@cybernet.net.ma
web	www.cybernet.net.ma/roseraie

Small hotel

map 3   entry 125

Au Sanglier Qui Fume

Route de Taroudannt - km61, Vallée d'Ouirgane, Ouirgane

This simple village inn tells the story of France in Morocco: first a canteen for bridge-building legionnaires in the 1920s, then a hunting lodge (*sanglier*: wild boar) until, in the pioneering days before tarmac or electricity, Annick's parents created a much-loved staging post for travellers over the pass and, at 1000 metres, a refuge from Marrakchi heatwaves. They gave their all to create pretty rooms and stunning gardens and happily did not see it destroyed by floods in 1995. Annick, now the Sanglier's quietly sensitive and excellent manager, and her jovial, expansive inn-keeper husband Richard, left their life in France to save the inn and the livelihood of the Berber families who'd shared the work for generations. They have done wonders: from pre-flood-old to brand new, their rooms are charming in their pretty, rustic simplicity (some are very smart – great value) with fireplaces, warm colours, decent little bathrooms, good beds. Father's gardens are reviving to beauty: superb rockeries, wisteria dripping, storks nesting. Excellent food, relaxed and friendly atmosphere, generous hospitality in a ring of mountains.

rooms	23: 13 doubles & triples, 10 suites.
price	385Dh–585Dh. Half-board 585Dh–785Dh for two.
meals	Lunch 110Dh or dinner 120Dh. Picnic possible.
closed	Never.
directions	From Marrakech for Taroudannt 61km; in village of Ouirgane, on left.

	Richard & Annick Pousset
tel	+212 (0)22 12 12 08/44 48 57 07
fax	+212 (0)44 48 57 09
e-mail	contact@ausanglierquifume.com
web	www.ausanglierquifume.com

Inn – Bivouac

La Bergerie

Marigha, Route de Taroudannt - km59 par Marrakech, Asni

From the south, come over the spectacular Tizi n'Test pass then down the little track to the old sheepfold: it's unforgettable. From majestic Morocco you arrive, amazingly, at hillsides of rosemary and juniper, gardens of mimosa serenaded by bees, sheep and donkeys, and... a Provençal inn with stone walls, beams, gingham cloths and copper kettles. This is Françoise and Christian's five-year-old baby, their refuge from the consumer culture – and yours too, for a spell. Several low buildings cling to the slopes, respecting the shape of the land and guests' privacy; stone is local, earth walls traditional, furniture gleaned at auction or made by nearby craftsmen, ingredients for the excellent food sourced locally (one old chap brings frogs' legs and wild asparagus down from the hills and streams by Tizi n'Test). The sober bedrooms and fine suites, soft-coloured and attractive, have pretty fabrics and Moroccan rugs, earthenware lights and, oh luxury, a private garden each. Your lively attentive hosts cultivate a warmly civilised *auberge* atmosphere and will point you to walks in the Royal Reserve where gazelles and moufflons roam.

rooms	16: 10 doubles, 3 suites, 3 bungalows.
price	Half-board 880Dh-1,250Dh for two.
meals	Lunch or dinner 150Dh. By arrangement.
closed	Never.
directions	From Marrakech for Taroudannt 59km; at sign 'Marigha', right to inn.

	Françoise & Christian
tel	+212 (0)44 48 57 16/17
fax	+212 (0)44 48 57 18
e-mail	labergerie13@hotmail.com
web	www.passionmaroc.com

Small hotel

map 3   entry 127

Chez Momo

Route de Taroudannt - km61, Ouirgane

The sweetest little Moroccan country inn you could hope for, Momo's place is infused with his natural gaiety and dynamism and, since he was born in the village, all his helpers are members of the family – a genuine Berber atmosphere nourished by centuries of simple mountain hospitality. The snug rammed-earth house has all the shape and style of High Atlas country architecture, the food is made to real Berber recipes – how about dill-flavoured chicken baked in olive purée? – and the bread, real Berber *tanourt* cooked in a handmade earth oven, arrives hot at your table; it's all excellent and served in the pink dining room or outside under the nomad tent or on the terrace. Momo has decorated his house with simple rustic taste: there's lots of ironwork, some lovely old doors have found new uses, rugs and bedcovers, lamps and ornaments come from local craftsmen, the bedrooms are charming. Outside, the generous terraces look over the olive grove growing by the Ouirgane river and the great Atlas peaks seem to protect the whole place. Peaceful, pretty and remarkable value.

rooms	7: 6 doubles, 1 twin.
price	Half-board 500Dh-680Dh for two.
meals	Lunch or dinner included. Other meals 100Dh.
closed	Never.
directions	After Ouirgane village, on right near 61km mark.

	Mohamed Idlmoudn
tel	+212 (0)44 48 57 04/61 58 22 95
fax	+212 (0)44 48 57 27
e-mail	chezmomo@iam.net.ma
web	www.aubergemomo.com

Inn – Bivouac

Dar Al Abir - Espace Al Arkam

Douar Asni, Asni, Marrakech

In the house of the passer-by (*abir*), European and Berber meet and understand. Jean-Jacques left success and consumerism to find truer roots in the High Atlas with his Berber wife. Their earth village house of almost monastic simplicity is adorable in its rose-hung, rug-strewn patio, convivial in its big salon warmed by dark local wood furniture, restful in its rough-beamed Berber bedrooms. And the food is exceptional, a creative mix of Arab and Berber using local ingredients and inspiration: these people care about real uncanned pleasures. And... 1.5 hours' walk away is Al Arkam (this friend of the Prophet's built his house with local materials), their mountain retreat where water comes daily by mule to be heated by the sun, you sleep in nomad tents woven from local goats-hair, buildings are made of local materials by villagers and you can walk for a day or a week deep into the Atlas to visit remote Berbers and briefly share their lives. A fine centre for eco-cooperation and personal development, there's no other place like it – you may discover hidden meaning in yourself and your life. *Outdoor smoking only.*

rooms	4: 1 double, 1 single, 2 triples, sharing 4 showers, 2 wcs. Al Arkam: tents and communal wash houses for up to 35.
price	Half-board 360Dh for two. Book ahead for Al Arkam.
meals	Lunch or dinner included. Other meals 75Dh. BYO.
closed	Never.
directions	From Marrakech for Taroudannt to Asni; continue for Imlil 2km; right following signs.

Jean-Jacques Gérard & Saïda Aït Sakel

tel	+212 (0)44 48 47 57
e-mail	alarkam2000@yahoo.fr
web	www.al-abir.com

Inn – Bivouac

map 3   entry 129

Kasbah du Toubkal

BP 31, Imlil, Asni

Below North Africa's highest peak the valley soars away on wings of fertile terraces and red villages. This exceptional mountain retreat is an imaginative Berber-European union born of the desire to share Jbel Toubkal's splendours with like-minded visitors without destroying them. Painstakingly rebuilt by tireless Haj Maurice, run by his wife Arkia, the feudal stronghold provides two-budget sleeping: Berber salons (red-cushioned sitting/sleeping benches round double-height rooms), fine double rooms with bathrooms and one superb cliff-hanging apartment. Hospitality is a Berber talent: big open smiles, intelligent local knowledge, deep respect for people and animals. Get fascinating glimpses of their culture while walking and mule-trekking; arrange an unforgettable seminar. Only 90 minutes from Marrakech, it's a world away in atmosphere; day trips are easy. The Kasbah supports the local valley community in education and health, rubbish collection, ambulance; five per cent is added to your bill to help fund these projects. "Leave the world more beautiful than you find it" is their motto. *Day trips from Marrakech.*

rooms	15: 11 doubles; 1 apartment for 6; 2 Berber salons for 3-7; 1 Berber dormitory for 10 sharing baths.
price	1,320Dh-1,870Dh; salons 990Dh-1,320DH for 3; dorm 220Dh p.p. (w'out sheets). Whole house avail.
meals	Lunch or dinner 165Dh. Full board 330Dh p.p. BYO.
closed	Rarely.
directions	From Marrakech for Asni then Imlil (65km). Park in village (guard); 500-metre walk or mule ride.

	Mike McHugo & Omar Maurice Aït Bahmed
tel	+212 (0)44 48 56 11
fax	+212 (0)44 48 56 36
e-mail	kasbah@discover.ltd.uk
web	www.kasbahdutoubkal.com

Country Inn – Trekking place

Chalet du Club Alpin Français (CAF)

Oukaïmeden

Only one hour from broiling Marrakech, the climb up is as exciting and majestic as a mountain road can be. Up there, on the edge of the Toubkal National Park, in Morocco's leading ski resort, 'the meeting place of the four winds', the chalet sits firm on its ledge 2600 metres above the Haouz plain. The welcome is so warm and generous you may want to stay a month. Passionate hikers and mountain-lovers, Jean and Michèle are deeply knowledgeable about hiking and skiing in the area, which is spectacular in all seasons. They took over the pre-war chalet 15 years ago and have created an Alpine echo in the Atlas. The stone and wood building looks thoroughly French, the simple pine-panelled dining room is immensely convivial with its big wooden tables and benches, the food is European and the bar serves draught beer. Furniture is, of course, all made of wood, including the storage lockers in the dormitories; there's a bridge room, a telly room and a well-stocked library; the communal washing facilities are impeccably maintained, the showers in proper little cabins. *Smoking allowed in common room only.*

rooms	158 beds in mountain refuge: 82 in dormitories, 76 in 4-8-bed rooms.
price	139Dh p.p.; linen for hire 20Dh per bed. Book ahead and join the CAF.
meals	Lunch or dinner 91Dh. Sandwiches possible. By arrangement. BYO.
closed	Never.
directions	On right as you enter Oukaïmeden ski resort.

**Michèle & Jean Minet
& Henri Boyé**

tel	+212 (0)44 31 90 36/61 18 34 54
fax	+212 (0)44 31 90 20
e-mail	ouka@cafmaroc.co.ma
web	www.cafmaroc.co.ma

Country Inn – Trekking place

map 4 entry 131

Auberge Le Maquis

Vallée de l'Ourika - km45, Aghbalou

Jean-Pierre fell in love with Morocco, its hill-walking – and Saïda. She, with her stunning smile and sense of hospitality, willingly followed him to this former hunting lodge turned inn. The dining room has typical tiles on the pillars and very unusual fireplaces, masses of red carpets and bright blue cloths, guns on the walls (hunting is traditional) and coloured glass in the arched windows – all quite surprising when you come in from the looming hills and flourishing vegetation outside. The gardens and the views from the terrace are marvellous. Outside also contains games for children, bikes, a potter's wheel, plastic furniture, table tennis, a hammam…. and Jean-Pierre can organise trips to the famous Yagour plateau and its prehistoric stone carvings. The bedrooms are set apart among the greenery, the new block of four white rooms being the nicest, with fashionable tadelakt bathrooms; others are canary yellow or sponged pastel; all have good-looking pine furniture, floral print fabrics, embroidered towels and sheepskin rugs – a comforting mountain refuge feel. With the superb food, this is unbeatable value.

rooms	8: 3 doubles, 2 triples, 1 quadruple, 1 suite for 2, 1 single.
price	Half-board 300Dh p.p.
meals	Lunch or dinner included. Other meals 120Dh.
closed	Never.
directions	From Marrakech take Ourika Valley road; at 45km mark, right along river bed.

Jean-Pierre & Saïda Blanc

tel	+212 (0)44 48 45 31/61 34 78 41
fax	+212 (0)44 48 45 61
e-mail	contact@le-maquis.com
web	www.le-maquis.com

Inn – Bivouac

Tigmi Atlas

Douar Ansa, CR Tighrouine, Par Aït Ourir

You have to come and see: the wild beauty of this spot deep in the valley of the Oued Zate, one of the loveliest in the High Atlas, is beyond words. Built entirely of local materials by local hands, the gîte looks as if it has stood on its 2000-metre cliff for ever, part of the deliciously genuine Berber village of Ansa (600 inhabitants, 60 families). The track from the road takes you from village to village, through pastures speckled with little mills and rich in walnut trees. Walk it if you can, it's the best introduction to the glorious hikes to be taken from Tigmi. Having worked with the villagers on sustainable development in the valley, Alain has now opened this small walking centre, planned and run in harmony with the culture and resources of the area: careful use of water, local food, masses of wood and stone, respect for the wonders outside. The big salon has a generous fireplace for winter warmth, a solid wooden dining table up on a platform, Berber rugs and blankets, loads of atmosphere; the snug dorms are all wood, including their storage alcoves; food is fresh and wonderful and guests may use the kitchen. *Photography Jacques Paul*

rooms	2 dormitories with bunks for 6 sharing 3 washrooms.
price	Half-board 190Dh per person.
meals	Lunch 75Dh. By arrangement. BYO.
closed	Rarely.
directions	From Marrakech for Ouarzazate 47km; right for Tighrouine; last stretch 4x4 only or 5 hours walk.

Alain Bonnassieux

tel	+212 (0)61 24 52 38
fax	+212 (0)44 37 60 54
e-mail	bonnassieuxalain@hotmail.com
web	www.riadmania.com

Guest house

map 4   entry 133

Riad Cascades d'Ouzoud
Ouzoud, Tanant-Azilal

Patrick's careful renovation of this gentle old building in its incomparable position on the waterfall is a perfect match for the style of the region: walls are of local earth, architectural ornamentation is authentically simple, the quiet, centred riad atmosphere is well preserved. His light touch is felt in every room where white walls, ochre-washed floors, rugs and hangings, a fireplace each and some furniture from Marrakech are all you need to fall for the charm of the place. The one decorative flourish that brings it out of the 'charmingly plain' bracket of woven woollen blankets, mosaic tables and Berber cushions is his set of wonderful doors fantastically painted with Islamic designs. Otherwise there are red-ochre tadelakt bathrooms with burnished copper basins, clay pots and plants everywhere, views to watch for hours from the terrace, an orange tree to sit under in the cool patio while you contemplate the swallows at their nests. Patrick has time for his house and time for his guests – an interesting, unusual host in a calm, well-loved and harmonious house serving good honest food.

rooms	6: 3 doubles, 2 twins, 1 triple.
price	680Dh. Half-board 900Dh for two.
meals	Lunch or dinner 130Dh-150Dh. By arrangement.
closed	Never.
directions	From Marrakech P24 for Beni Mallal 175km; right for Azilal, right for Ouzoud. Hotel at end of tiny village.

	Patrick Lamerie
tel	+212 (0)23 45 96 58/07
fax	+212 (0)23 45 88 60
e-mail	riad@ouzoud.com
web	www.ouzoud.com

Guest house

Dar Itrane

Douar Imelghas, Vallée des Aït Bougmez, Azilal

Take time, breathe: the twisty four-hour drive brings you through splendour and dazzle to a secret valley of such unspoilt beauty and an inn so genuine that you'd scarce believe. Bernard Fabry, ever the pioneer, knows the secrets of the Atlas 'like his pocket' and opened this remote spot for real seekers 15 years ago. Brahim, the head man, helped build the three traditional levels, earth walls against earth terraces, cooks exquisite soups with mountain spices, makes a unique herb tea, knows all the muleteers and some astounding walks. His whole team are smiling and ready to help. The great Berber living room, its walls white as the snow on the M'Goun peak and adorned only with geometric patterns and Koranic verses, niches for candles and cedar door frames, has gorgeousness in its Aït Bougmez painted ceiling, bright handmade cushions and big fireplace; bedrooms are all-white, monastic cell-like and deeply comfortable; bathrooms are little gems. A natural, friendly inn where, in luminous simplicity, a Euro-Berber partnership really works. The riches of this exceptional place and its people deserve at least two nights.

rooms	11: 7 doubles, 4 family.
price	Half-board 500Dh for two.
meals	Dinner included. BYO.
closed	Never.
directions	From Azilal 50km south on twisting mountain road; fork right into Aït Bougmez valley, through Agouti to Imelghas; inn on hillside on left.

	Bernard Fabry
tel	+212 (0)44 31 39 01
fax	+212 (0)44 31 39 05
e-mail	atlassaharacom@iam.net.ma
web	www.atlas-sahara-trek.com

Country Inn – Trekking base

map 4　entry 135

La Gazelle d'Or
Route d'Amezgrou, Taroudannt

Known the world over as a very special place to start or end a visit to the fabulous southern Moroccan valleys – oases and kasbahs, camels and dunes to your heart's content – the Gazelle d'Or has an atmosphere all its own made of luxuriating gardens, turtling doves, salons that coddle the weary guest and a club-like group of cottages that make it feel oh-so-select. For 20 years, Rita Bennis has laboured with love to renovate and extend the old place, first opened in 1961, and rekindle its former spirit of convivial comfort and discreet service. So when you can tear yourself away from your smart garden house, you have to choose between library or cards room, tennis court or croquet lawn, riding or the driving range, the excellent restaurant or the poolside buffet – or simply a long exploration of those acres of really fabulous gardens. There's an hotel farm too, which grows all their fruit, vegetables, herbs and dairy produce organically – not a chemical touches these heavenly surrounding, you find health, comfort and huge attention to detail at every turn. Expensive perhaps, special definitely.

rooms	30 cottages: 8 doubles, 21 suites, 1 house.
price	Half-board 4,600Dh–5,100Dh for two.
meals	Other meals available. Picnic possible. By arrangement.
closed	Mid–July–mid–September.
directions	From Taroudannt centre for Amezgrou 2km; well signposted.

	Madame Rita Bennis
tel	+212 (0)48 85 20 39/48
fax	+212 (0)48 85 27 37
e-mail	reservations@gazelledor.com
web	www.gazelledor.com

Landmark hotel

Riad Hida

Ouled Berhil, Taroudannt

The fine kasbah clay walls shout "come in, it's cool inside" across the rough lane: the exuberant gardens are indeed splendiferous, the stately riad like a cross between Luxor and Alhambra, a Brighton Pavilion where Ali Baba and his famous forty might lurk. Magnificent, exotic, historic, nostalgic – they all fit. Morocco meets Europe in colonial antiques while slightly faded furnishings have all the class of the 19th century pasha who built the place but are never stiff or contrived. It's grand yet inviting, rich without being haughty, and the master suite, furnished for the Danish millionaire who bought it from the pasha, is the stuff of fairytales, right down to its fabulous old-style bathroom. Other bathrooms are less striking, bedrooms more modern but all are different and attractive with pretty rugs, woollen Moroccan blankets, good light from doors or windows onto the garden. Dining and drawing rooms have exceptional painted doors and cedar ceilings, light dapples the terraces, the upstairs views reach across the garden canopy into the High Atlas. Add a friendly efficient welcome and you have amazing value.

rooms	14: 11 doubles, 3 suites.
price	550Dh-750Dh. Half-board 750Dh-950Dh for two.
meals	Lunch or dinner 100Dh. By arrangement.
closed	Never.
directions	From Taroudannt for Talouine & Ouarzazate 45km; take RP 32 and follow signs. Airport transfer possible.

Mohamed Laäfissi & El Haj Aziz

tel	+212 (0)48 53 10 44
fax	+212 (0)48 53 10 44
web	www.riadhida.com

Guest house

map 3   entry 137

Riad Maryam

Avenue Mohamed V/Derb Maalen Mohamed, 140 Bab Targhount, Taroudannt

Wind through the maze of small streets and under the arches of the "prettiest old town in the south", push the door and enter the rug-strewn fine-tiled garden where birds sing in the lemon trees. Over 100 years old, this family house has the traditional thick earth walls and cool garden courtyard; off the patio are five simple rooms where zany bright colours contrast with soft old tiling. Not in the least luxurious, it's wonderfully cheerful, Habib and his family can't do enough to help their guests and the wild kitschy décor of mixed colours, shapes and patterns is congenial and fitting. You are always aware of opening onto the calm of the garden, the cool and pleasant salon has restful couches for quiet reading and one bedroom clutches a finely lacquered and carved set of wardrobe doors. The kitchen is available for guests to use, too – an exceptional privilege: in this entirely family-run guest house, there are no staff to stake territorial claims. The whole simple place is spotlessly clean, the family's sense of hospitality is generous and genuine and dinner beneath the greenery a real treat after a long hot day.

rooms	5: 1 double; 1 double, 2 twins, 1 quadruple, sharing two baths.
price	350Dh–800Dh.
meals	Dinner about 150Dh. By arrangement.
closed	Never.
directions	Instructions given on booking.

	Habib Moultazim
tel	+212 (0)66 12 72 85/65 48 54 52
e-mail	ryadmaryamtaroudannt@yahoo.fr
web	www.riadmaryam.fr.fm

Guest house

Centre Culturel & Environnemental

Derb Afferdou, Taroudannt

An hour from Agadir, these people will help you wriggle under the skin of fascinating 'Real' Morocco. From an immaculately clean Taroudannt townhouse, they organise enlightened, sustainable tourism and cultural contact. Modern pine beds and padded Moroccan divans for simple comfort; tiling and high windows for cool, shady rooms; the roof to take in the sun over the distant Atlas and a chaotic roofscape – satellite dishes and all. Founder Jane Bayley met her staff and devised this project while researching wildlife conservation in Morocco. With Kamal, Fatima and 'little' Latifa, her committed, charming and intelligent manager Latifa Assefar and tour leader Saïd Ahmoune tailor itineraries to suit small groups, families or individuals. Activities include trekking between Berber villages, bird-watching, botany, geology, cultural experiences; there's a library, a 'museum' of finds, photos and more. The food is so good that visitors' clamour has led to cookery courses, too: fresh daily from the local market, meals include meat, vegetarian and vegan options. Care and knowledge combine here to bring you genuine insights.

rooms	2 3-room apartments i.e. 9 double or twin rooms, most with Moroccan divans for 2-3 extra people, 4 full baths, 4 showers, 4 wcs.
price	£215 p.p. one week B&B, 5 full meals, 3 day excursions, 3 cultural experiences, airport transfers. Advance on-line booking essential.
meals	Included. BYO. Access to self-catering facilities.
closed	Never.
directions	Directions given on booking.

	Jane Bayley
tel	+44 (0)709 234 3879
fax	+44 (0)709 237 9725
e-mail	info@naturallymorocco.co.uk
web	www.naturallymorocco.co.uk

Country Inn – Trekking place

map 3   entry 139

Hôtel des Cascades

80300 Imouzzèr Ida Outanane, Agadir

Wind 1,200 metres up from the coast through vast palm groves and plunging gorges to this gracious, relaxing place wrapped in well-tended gardens. Birdsong and the sound of water flood in; long views of the Atlas foothills – and to the distant sea on a clear day – unwind you further. Monsieur Atbir couldn't be more charming. He has been gradually expanding his hotel with its three-storey bedroom wing; rooms get smarter and more individual as you go up but all are large, comfortable, open to the view. Upstairs there are balconies, on the ground floor you're straight onto the garden to wander down to the pools (there's one for children) without running the corridor gauntlet. Eat at wooden tables on the terrace or in the rather formal dining room with cool marble mosaic floors, slatted screens, elegant arches and central canopied fireplace. There are plans for a roof terrace, too. Helpful staff can arrange donkey-riding, trekking, mountain biking, you name it. The famous waterfall is generally a winter phenomenon but the welcome and the views make it worth a visit all year round.

rooms	27: 14 doubles, 13 twins.
price	570Dh. Half-board from 820Dh for two.
meals	Lunch or dinner 100Dh-200Dh.
closed	Never.
directions	From Agadir for Essaouira 12km; at Tamraght right approx 50km for Cascades. Signposted. Airport transfer possible.

Jamal Eddine Atbir

tel	+212 (0)48 82 60 23/60 16 05 05
fax	+212 (0)48 82 60 24
web	www.cascades-hotel.com

Small hotel

Hôtel Riad des Golfs

Route des Golfs, Aghrod Ben Sergao, Agadir

Designed remarkably by Bernard Brilhaut himself, the shell of this luxurious neo-Moroccan oasis has the best of local tradition: strong geometric forms, arches and colonnades, sunken mosaic fountain, cool interiors with high high ceilings, endless angles and perspectives. Round the lofty light-filtered atrium, the big rooms are decorated in a hot-house version of high-class French style mixing softness and clarity in a symphony of ivory, indigo and magenta. The lines are clean, the finish velvety, the details all there. Your hosts indulge in extravaganzas of fresh flowers repeated by multitudinous mirrors: once you've entered the gates, all living happens within the walls, the patio and the fine pool area are your garden – it feels intimate and safe. Bedrooms are just as cool, calm and sophisticated with tempting big beds, lots of space, a terrace or balcony each and outstanding bathrooms. Bernard and Paule's attitude is that guests are friends they have not yet made and they yearn to share their passion for food. You will eat and sleep extremely well here, in a stylish mixture of modern and classical Moroccan moods.

rooms	8 suites for 2-3.
price	1,500Dh-2,400Dh.
meals	Lunch 160Dh. Dinner 270Dh. By arrangement.
closed	Never.
directions	From Agadir airport for Agadir Centre 12km, left for Golf des Dunes & Golf du Soleil on Souss Estuary road 50m; right for Hotel Pyramid, riad 100m beyond Pyramid on right.

	Bernard & Paule Brilhault
tel	+212 (0)48 33 70 33
fax	+212 (0)48 33 54 55
e-mail	riadgolf@menara.ma
web	www.riaddesgolfs.com

Guest house

map 3   entry 141

Ksar Massa

Complexe balnéaire de Sidi R'bat, Commune Rurale de Sidi Wassay, Chtouka Aït Baha, Agadir

On six hectares of national park, come watch the rare and wonderful birds that hang out on this stretch of coast – flamingoes, cranes, ibis; then it's your turn, at the squiggly-chaired sea-view bar in this picture of a brand-new ksar – or is it a mud hut of vast proportions with high-pressure hot water from dinner-plate shower heads, superb towels and refined cooking? In any case, with its rich, sombre atmosphere, it is a very special place for lovers of space, peace and real comfort. All earthy red and yellow ochre tones with rich blue arches, excellent old or modern rugs and artefacts to pick up the colours, it is deep Morocco. The impressively designed bedrooms – wrought-iron screens, carved furniture, original mirrors, more lovely rugs – look out to sea or onto the enclosed garden where newly-planted mature palms wave. Bathrooms are brilliant: moulded, deep-coloured, intended to look old but with immaculate modern fittings. Unostentatious and outstanding, it has a friendly, efficient and philanthropic owner who works with the local community, organises sports days and loves his sandcastle guest house.

rooms	10: 2 doubles, 8 suites.
price	1,300Dh; half-board 1,600Dh (lunch) or 1,900Dh (dinner); full board 2,200Dh.
meals	See above.
closed	Never.
directions	From Agadir for Tiznit about 50km; after Had Belfa (aka Aït Bella), right to Massa; there, follow signs: 5km of track.

	Nasser Laraki
tel	+212 (0)61 28 03 19/62 80 24 85
fax	+212 (0)22 47 13 72/48 25 57 72
e-mail	ksarmassa@ksarmassa.com
web	www.ksarmassa.com

Small hotel

Hôtel Kerdous

Col du Kerdous, Route de Tiznit à Tafraoute - km54, Kerdous

In a country where stunning views are the norm, this one beggars description. At the top of a craggy ridge, dominating the land for miles like a romantic castle, the Kerdous is castellated and towered, the wind howls at the gate, the feel is Hollywood Gothic. In fact, interior of the old kasbah is more Ouarzazate Moorish in its ornately painted ceilings, bedheads, tables, doors – the lot. But everywhere, that awesome landscape takes over. The dining room is like a glass ship sailing 1000 metres above the surface – look outwards to the majesty of North African nature and the tiny self-coloured villages huddled against her flanks rather than inwards to the modern pink tiles. The terrace, another eye-stretching spot, holds the fine keyhole-arch pool and some less fine plastic chairs. Bedrooms, large and comfortable with good beds, are furnished in Moroccan style with rugs and painted furniture on good-looking terracotta tiles and many look out to The View – ask for one of these. Bathrooms may look a bit worn but renovations continue and the slight traffic noise should let up at night.

rooms	35: 2 doubles, 33 twins.
price	580Dh. Children under two free.
meals	Lunch or dinner 120Dh.
closed	Never.
directions	From Tiznit R104 for Tafraoute 54km; hotel at top of pass.

Abderraman Belkahia

tel	+212 (0)48 86 20 63/60 03 12
fax	+212 (0)48 60 03 15

Small hotel

 map 3   entry 143

Maison d'Hôtes Les 3 Chameaux
Mirleft, Tiznit

Between desert and ocean, the house of the three camels is a converted colonial fort – the commander's stunning view down the valley, over the village and out to sea can now be yours; from the other side, he surveyed the mountains – amazing. The ruins of a former kasbah add a powerful romantic touch; a rusty old army car at the entrance reminds you of the place's more recent past. The renovation has been done with deep respect for the colours and shapes of the area: strong low arches, colours of sand, earth and sea foam, nothing gaudy or over-decorated, simply a few lovely carpets on chequered floors, natural tatoui ceilings, locally-crafted urns and whitewood furniture and lots of old doors – the whole atmosphere is earthy and warm and leaves space for the inspiring landscape. This subtle refinement is a reflection of the owner's taste, his staff are another with their smiles and discretion. For meals, you can choose between the smart dining room with its white cloths, the relaxed and open Moroccan salon and the convivial nomad tent; the food in all three is delicious. And the treks are full of discovery.

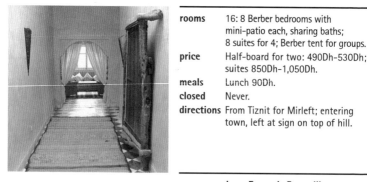

rooms	16: 8 Berber bedrooms with mini-patio each, sharing baths; 8 suites for 4; Berber tent for groups.
price	Half-board for two: 490Dh-530Dh; suites 850Dh-1,050Dh.
meals	Lunch 90Dh.
closed	Never.
directions	From Tiznit for Mirleft; entering town, left at sign on top of hill.

	Jean-François Bouguillon
tel	+212 (0)48 71 91 87/66 54 85 79
e-mail	3chameaux@online.fr
web	www.3chameaux.com

Guest house

Dar Infiane
Douar Infiane, Tata

Come to unsung Tata! Fascinating in its desert-edge austerity, its 20,000-strong palm grove the finest in the south, it has given its name to those sensual ceilings of woven palm and oleander. Dar Infiane, a superb old stone kasbah, appears suddenly on a rocky outcrop among the palms. Pass the great old door, duck through others (small openings let in less heat) to discover four leafy patios, painted tataoui ceilings, lofty spaces, and up to the panoramic terrace for a heart-stopping view. This house is naturally integrated in its environment, modern in its services: besides the soberly respectful Berber salon with its painted plaster ceiling, there is an ethnography museum and a telly room, a cyber café and a library corner, a small pub (yes) and big comfortable bedrooms where you are greeted by lovely stripey Rif fabrics against earthy walls, antique tataoui chests, excellent beds and shower rooms. Patrick Simon works tirelessly for the rehabilitation of the southern palm groves, the only viable basis for life in these desert regions; Latifa keeps an impeccable, smiling house and cooks utterly memorable meals.

rooms	6: 4 doubles, 2 twins.
price	900Dh.
meals	Lunch or dinner 200Dh. Picnic possible. By arrangement.
closed	August.
directions	Leave Tata south for Akka; after town gate, 50m on right after 'cycle track' sign. Taxiplane from Marrakech: 1,000Dh for 5 max.

	Patrick Simon & Latifa Maali
tel	+212 (0)44 30 06 58/95 55
fax	+212 (0)44 30 10 11
e-mail	maintaero@wanadoo.nct.ma

Guest house

map 3   entry 145

الجنوب

the south

Between the High Atlas and the great western Erg of the Sahara that edges into Morocco, lies a vast territory dotted with oases and imposing rammed- earth kasbahs, a buffer between the more urbanised north and the desert, a fascinating land where people live with little (especially water) yet share what they have with the traveller - originally the caravaneer, then the colonial, now the tourist. One is happy to swap luxury for their conviviality, charm and authenticity.

Between the river-fed palm groves of the Dra, Todra, Dadès and Ziz valleys lie swathes of arid stoniness sculpted into a terrifying rugged beauty. This has always been a land of farmers and traders - signs point off the road, apparently into the barrenness, actually towards little farms round tiny water holes - and these Berber families are multi-skilled. Some are nomads driving caravans of laden camels to market, others grow cereals and dates in the oases, still others, semi-nomads in the mountains, herd sheep and goats from pasture to pasture with their thick tents, the women and children staying in the villages to spin and weave. Between oases and mountain villages were the traders' resting places. One such is N'Koob, the village of the 50 proud kasbahs.

In the towns, you will be offered desert and mountain treks almost as often as carpets. At desert inns, you will be given bottles of iced water when leaving to confront the dusty track.

The new road from Zagora to Erfoud via the oases of Alnif, Tazzarine and N'koob now makes it possible to complete the Ouarzazate-Zagora-Erfoud triangle. Zagora is a lively place, its modern centre a creation of surpassing ugliness, its palmeraie a delightful shady maze of walled alleys, gardens and houses. Erfoud or the desert market town of Rissani are essential if you want to visit the dunes at Merzouga, the first reaches of the Sahara's 3000km. The famous sunrise-viewing spot can be reached with any standard car: 4 x 4 is not essential, but a guide is – avoid the false ones if possible and don't go during a sandstorm.

Photography by Alain Bonnassieux

Auberge Kasbah Derkaoua - The Desert Inn
Route de Rissani-Merzouga - km21, Erfoud

After the daunting, fascinating desert, the kasbah entrance arch in a seemingly endless red wall announces civilisation, the trees peeping over it promise refreshment, the oasis inside is cause for rejoicing. Oasis it is, with all that the word implies of gentle hospitality. A wiry enthusiast, Michel is a remarkable man: desert-struck since childhood, he has lived his life within reach of the Sahara. He resuscitated Derkaoua, a ruined Sufi *zaouia* founded in the 1800s by holy man Kaoua, and it is now a virtually self-sufficient inn with two wells, a tanker lorry for the two giant generators, a vegetable garden, an orchard, a farm full of goats, hens, sheep and… Dutch cows. Horses and camels stand by for desert treks; the big pool lies apart from the fabulous shady gardens with their lounging and eating spaces (expect really good Moroccan food); big attractive bedrooms in soft desert colours with Berber blankets and hangings have excellent bathrooms. A dry, dusty, deserty inn whose extraordinary atmosphere of sand-filtered peace brings you back to essentials, a sense of adventure and, perhaps, monastic contemplation.

rooms	21: 11 doubles, 5 bungalows, 3 apartments, 2 tents.
price	Half-board 450Dh p.p.
meals	Lunch or dinner included. Other meals 165Dh.
closed	January & June-August.
directions	From Rissani for Merzouga 16km; left at sign, follow excellent track 5km (green & white markers).

	Michel Auzat
tel	+212 (0)55 57 71 40/61 34 36 77
fax	+212 (0)55 57 71 40
e-mail	aubergederkaoua@hotmail.com
web	aubergederkaoua.com02.com

Guest house

Kasbah Mohayut

Ksar Hassi Labiad, Merzouga

From your bedroom window, beyond the garden, are the first sand dunes of the Sahara – Erg Chebbi rises before you, the only part of Morocco that qualifies as sand desert. All that dryness out there – and two garden courtyards with greenery and fountains inside, a cool, life-saving contrast that can fill you with gratitude. The owner took a degree in English then, realising that tourism had become the only source of livelihood for his friends and relatives here, returned to his family house to build it up into a delightful desert-edge guest house. He loves contact with others and puts all his energy into making each guest's stay a special one. The old rammed earth building technique is the basis of this wide rambling single-storey complex where palm and eucalyptus beams hold the roof, old Berber doors are carved with traditional symbols, walls are encrusted with lettering and the whole family works together with welcoming smiles and caring attention. Bedrooms are properly simple and sober, shower rooms perfectly adequate, wrought iron furniture stands on Berber carpets everywhere. Lovely people, great value.

rooms	10: 4 doubles, 2 twins, 2 triples, 1 quadruple, 1 family for 5.
price	Half-board 300Dh for two.
meals	Lunch or dinner 50Dh-100Dh. Picnic 40Dh. By arrangement. BYO.
closed	Never.
directions	From Rissani for Merzouga, left at sign then 2.5km of track.

	Mohammed Oubadi
tel	+212 (0)66 03 91 85
fax	+212 (0)55 57 84 28
e-mail	mohamezan@yahoo.fr

Country Inn – Trekking base

map 5   entry 147

Auberge Tombouctou
Hassalbeid, Merzouga

An unbeatable combination of a new pisé kasbah at the foot of the Erg Chebbi dunes and a private oasis two hours camel-ride away for sensational overnight bivouacs. Coming from a long line of caravaneers who plied the Merzouga-Timbuctoo route, the Ettayeks still know all the camel-drivers in the area and organise treks across the dunes to their super little oasis where you arrive to watch the sun go down, eat entirely Berber food cooked in the glowing embers while the drums keep time and songs go up, sleep in nomad tents and, if you're lucky, watch the moon rise over the same dune. They then guide you back to Merzouga and a wonderful breakfast at the inn. It is a simple, charming place with peace in its arcaded patio, space in its utterly plain bedrooms, spotless little bathrooms (except when the inescapable sand blows in) The Ettayek family are a vibrant example of the Berber genius for hospitality: under the influence of Baba's innate sense of comedy and public relations, you will be completely at home within 30 minutes of arriving, even singing his songs as if to the language born. Glorious.

rooms	11 rooms for 2-4 at inn (tents also available); tents at oasis.
price	Half-board 250Dh p.p. inc. dinner, breakfast and camel ride to overnight bivouac; 150Dh p.p. without oasis trip.
meals	Lunch 70D.
closed	Never.
directions	From Rissani to Merzouga; 3km before Merzouga, Tomboctou sign on roof on left.

	Frères Ettayek
tel	+212 (0)55 57 70 91
fax	+212 (0)55 57 84 49

Country Inn – Trekking base

Kasbah Hôtel Riad du Sud

Tamsahalte, Tazzarine

A delightful kasbah hotel, the Riad du Sud will entice visitors to a fascinating corner of the vast Moroccan wilderness and thereby contribute to the development of Tansahalt: the people of the village are very much involved and create a relaxed, happy atmosphere. Part-owner of the kasbah, Lahsen also owns the camels. Young, dynamic and ambitious for his luminous project to succeed, he will organise camel treks for you to remote spots that other tourists can't reach. Edi, the Swiss owner of the Tomboctou in Tinghir, was his tenant here for years. They now share the running of the hotel and one or other is always present to welcome guests with wit and knowledge and guide them on their explorations. The décor is utterly faithful to local tradition, the old pisé architecture has been carefully preserved – upstairs, the original doorways are so low that you may have to duck – but space has been found for proper little shower rooms, the wrought-iron beds are big and new, bedrooms have views to the garden, the palm grove and the mountains beyond. Simply superb. And moreover… Mohamed's tagines are excellent.

rooms	9: 2 doubles, 4 triples, 1 family, 1 apartment.
price	470Dh. 15% reduction for cash.
meals	Lunch or dinner 95Dh, Picnic 50Dh. BYO.
closed	Never.
directions	Directions given on booking.

	Eduard Kunz & Lahsen
tel	+212 (0)44 83 49 34
fax	+212 (0)44 83 22 23
e-mail	hotelsudriad@iam.net.ma
web	www.hotelriaddusud.com

Small hotel

map 4   entry 149

Ksar Jenna
Aït Ouzzine, N'Koob, Zagora

There may still be fifty old kasbahs in this amazing village where southern traditions are fiercely upheld, but the Ksar Jenna is brand new. Its deeply committed couple of owners, Youssef a son of the south, Stella who came from Italy and couldn't bear to leave, have created a big modern restaurant where they serve convivial meals beneath a splendid great carved and painted dome and, separately, five excellent guest rooms done with simple taste and all the best in traditional décor. This means high beamed ceilings, smooth tadelakt walls, Berber carpets on soft natural bejmat floors and, in recognition of modern habits, good big beds: building a new kasah has made it possible to have wider rooms than the old norm. By the same token, shower rooms are big, light, simply good and equipped with decent towels. Outside, the big leafy garden greets you with arcades, all sorts of southern trees and swathes of lawn. Youssef and Stella want you to remember your stay for ever: they arrange excursions that reproduces the caravan trek along the old Dra Valley route and luxury bivouacs at M'Hamid or Merzouga. Wonderful people.

rooms	5: 3 doubles, 2 triples.
price	800Dh–2,000Dh.
meals	Lunch 150Dh. Dinner 200Dh. Picnic 60Dh–100Dh.
closed	Never.
directions	From Ouarzazate for Erfoud via Adgz 136km; through N'Koob for Erfoud; ksar signposted just outside village.

Youssef Amiri & Stella Mischiatti

tel	+212 (0)44 83 84 90/67 96 32 48
fax	+212 (0)44 83 84 91
e-mail	info@ksarjenna.com
web	www.ksarjenna.com

Guest house

Kasbah Baha Baha

N'Koob, Zagora

In the village of 50 kasbahs, halfway between Dra valley and mountain pasture, Brahim has renovated his kasbah in the purest tradition for a remarkable eco-development project. For example, the treated waste water feeds humidity-generating trees around his kasbah, creating a beneficial micro-climate; by the tented camp, professional weavers make the long dark goats-hair strips used for nomad tents; there's a small eco-museum in the courtyard; and much more, all fascinatingly authentic. The kasbah, tall and strong, offers like-minded visitors an experience of the enduring Berber lifestyle: sleep in a home-woven tent or a most attractive traditional kasbah suite of two rooms with woven palm-leaf furniture, a 'Berber washbasin' (earthenware pitcher and bowl) and communal tadelakt bathroom, eat delicious home-grown organic food and, possibly, join in a genuine wedding of members of the Aït Atta tribe. The two ground-floor en-suite rooms are tempting, too. Superb natural hospitality, vast terrace view, desert and mountain excursions, unforgettable. *Please do not bring alcohol into the kasbah.*

rooms	36: 2 doubles; 9 sharing bath & wc; Berber tents: 15 doubles for 2, 10 for 6, sharing 6 showers & wcs.
price	Double 450Dh; double sharing bath 350Dh; double tent 200Dh.
meals	Lunch 25Dh–75Dh. Dinner 50Dh–150Dh. No alcoholic drinks.
closed	Never.
directions	From Ouarzazate for Erfoud via Adgz 136km; in N'Koob, left at sign, follow small street to end (signs).

	Brahim Elouarzazi
tel	+212 (0)44 83 97 63
fax	+212 (0)44 83 97 64/30 69 65
e-mail	bahabaha@mailcity.com
web	www.bahabaha.com

Guest house

map 4   entry 151

Villa Zagora
La Palmeraie d'Amzrou, Zagora

Behind the trekking shops and camels, this house has instant presence. Walking into the airy open-plan living room, you breathe in the welcoming atmosphere of a personal creation. Michèle Arnaud's version of the Moroccan house, it has the proper four-pillar central focus, tataoui ceilings, lots of space, more windows than is orthodox, and definitely more bathrooms. Your eye quickly finds the two super modern paintings, just the thing for a week's contemplation, the fabulous brown, green and white Zagora tiles all the way up the staircase and the door into the big kitchen. Here, the windows are a series of small openings in the wall, the layout intelligent, the crockery a luscious deep green. Bedrooms are simply perfect with loads of storage, mosquito nets, interesting things on the walls, soft colours and textures. The roof terrace onto the palm grove is ideal for evening lazing (spare loo and shower too) – or the shady little garden with its small pool. You will find the right spot whatever the time of day. An excellent place for families and groups of friends, with so much to do and see in the area.

rooms	4: 1 double, 2 twins; 1 twin with separate bath. Tent for 7.
price	400Dh–500Dh B&B; tent 150Dh B&B; full rental 8,000Dh–11,000Dh per week.
meals	Lunch or dinner 120Dh.
closed	Never.
directions	From Zagora centre, cross River Dra, pass Kasbah Asmaâ, house signposted on left behind Caravane du Sud shop.

Michèle Arnaud
tel +212 (0)44 84 60 93
e-mail michelearnaud@easynet.fr
web www.mavillaausahara.com

Guest house & catered house

Dar Raha

Hay Amzrou, 45900 Zagora

Here are the real riches of Morocco: a thoughtful, creative, committed trio of owners have made Dar Raha (*raha* means rest) into a place for encounters. Under their guidance, you discover local history, architecture and culture, meet craftsmen and families, glimpse their gentle, traditional lifestyle, take mountain, valley or desert treks with seriously knowledgeable guides all in partnership with a local association. In the heart of dusty red Amzrou where the flourishing palm grove of the Dra valley keeps the desert at bay, their big old family house sits proud and cool beneath a protecting kasbah. Its long mysterious corridor leads past the dining platform to a dramatic patio whose four huge pillars rise pale and unadorned to the light above. Sober pisé architecture, minimal decoration, simple comforts. Rooms have their own or shared terraces, colourful Moroccan fabrics to match their spice labels, ingenious 'clothes ladders', shared washrooms. From the terrace, way up above, you can watch 5,000 years of history melting into the palm grove as earth bricks give way to cement. Your interest will help save some of it.

rooms	5: 4 doubles, 1 triple sharing 4 showers & 4 wcs.
price	350Dh–500Dh.
meals	Lunch or dinner 100Dh–150Dh. By arrangement. BYO.
closed	Mid-July–mid-August.
directions	From Zagora centre for M'Hamid; over bridge; 500m enter Amzrou; right at Maison Toudra; follow signs.

	Josiane Morillon, Antoine Bouillon, Salah Aït Baba Aroub
tel	+212 (0)44 84 69 93
fax	+212 (0)44 84 69 93
e-mail	darraha_zagora@yahoo.fr

Guest house

map 4   entry 153

I Roccha
Tisseldei, Ouarzazate

The welcome is as wonderful as you'd expect from a happy, harmonious couple doing what they love. Smiling and diplomatic, Ahmed brought his bright, artistic Catherine from France to the tiny mountainside village where he was born. They built a traditional stone and earth house then opened it to guests, also providing valuable jobs for a few local people. With a courtyard garden at its heart, the house faces spectacularly south across a picture of a sweeping landscape – you could sit for hours on the shady terrace, noticing a new detail at every moment. Rooms, simple but not basic in their sandy rough-plastered frames, are done with solid wooden furniture, unusual bits of art, variegated fabrics and neat little shower rooms. The big Berber-style sitting/dining room has generous windows to those views, laughter in the air and a fine tataoui ceiling. In the little salon is Catherine's brilliant modern version of a painted ceiling – geometric shapes in strong dark colours like a child's building bricks. Good honest food, too. *A no-smoking house. Unlit track to house: better to arrive in daylight the first time.*

rooms	5 doubles.
price	Half-board 300Dh–350Dh p.p.
meals	Lunch 100Dh by arrangement. Dinner included.
closed	Never.
directions	From Marrakech for Fès 9km; right for Ouarzazate 150km to Tisseldei; sign in village on left, follow track round to right (50km from Ouarzazate).

Ahmed Agouni & Catherine Rophé
tel   +212 (0)67 73 70 02
e-mail   asifatlas@hotmail.com
web   www.terremaroc.com

Guest house

Dar Daïf

Douar Talmasla, Ouarzazate

Rebuilt from ruins, the house rises from the holy man's tomb by the front gate to the village street above, gathering its galleries and a clutch of terraces round the central well of the original kasbah. Inside, there are salons and spaces, tables, chairs and rugs galore, pots, kettles and dishes. Up and up it goes on handmade tiles, past little bedrooms with masses of charm, neat bathrooms and just the right amount of authenticity, to the big top terrace, level with the crazy storks' nests, where your eye disappears over the plain into the snowy Atlas peaks. Your fascinating, knowledgeable hosts, he Basque, she Berber, have made something of a cultural centre here. Steeped in Morocco, they can show you Berber culture from the inside. Zineb takes groups of women for week-long visits to High Atlas villages to spin, weave, cook and... converse with Berber women. Jean-Pierre and his team run brilliant desert and mountain treks of three days to three months (you can get on and off on the way), on foot, dromedary or four-wheel drive; he even has an English-speaking driver-guide. Just meeting these people is a privilege.

rooms	11: 9 triples, 2 suites for 3.
price	600Dh–1,080Dh for two or three.
meals	Lunch 140Dh. Picnic 90Dh. By arrangement. Dinner, compulsory except late arrivals, 170Dh; children 100Dh. BYO.
closed	Never.
directions	From Ouarzazate for Zagora; cross bridge; pass Hôtel La Vallée; left at sign for Dar Daïf; follow signs through village (3km track).

Jean–Pierre & Zenib Datcharry

tel	+212 (0)44 85 49 47
fax	+212 (0)44 85 49 48
e-mail	desert@iam.net.ma
web	www.dardaif.ma

Guest house

map 4   entry 155

Kasbah Aït Ben Moro

Skoura, Ouarzazate

Old buildings and genuine materials, simple comforts and traditional hospitality, quiet contemporary design and subtle local craftsmanship – from Juan's passions comes the soft, light feel of this superb pisé kasbah that he brought back from ruin without an ounce of concrete. The Ben Moro clan had left to find modernity, the place was a crumbling grain store with 50 owners. Juan, from Andalucia, now works with descendants of the Ben Moros who built the fortress in the 18th century on their return from... Spain. Their young, natural attitude and intelligent presence fit the kasbah's history and plain, simple décor. Its dungeon-like heart still feels ancient and strong, four great pillars pushing lightwards to sustain the building and catch just enough sky. Floors are local stone, rugs are thick Berber, bedcovers bright yellow or natural sand, ceilings tataoui, Moroccan lanterns carry candles: the electricity goes off at night. From generous triple to wonderfully monastic terrace room sharing shower and loo downstairs, each has a dim, gentle presence and the Mediterranean garden is a fine place for delicious meals.

rooms	16: 8 doubles, 5 triples; 3 doubles sharing bath.
price	650Dh-750Dh. Half-board 500Dh-550Dh p.p.
meals	Breakfast 40Dh. Lunch or dinner 150Dh. BYO.
closed	Never.
directions	From Ouarzazate for Er Rachidia 38km; kasbah on left, before centre of Skoura.

Juan Romero de Dios

tel	+212 (0)44 85 21 16/(0)66 25 11 38
fax	+212 (0)44 85 20 26
e-mail	hotelbenmoro@yahoo.fr
web	www.passionmaroc.com

Small hotel

Kasbah Itran

Route de Tourbiste, El Kelaâ N'Gouna, Ouarzazate

Lots of sharing, lots of humanity, the genuine welcoming simplicity of a Berber family. The Kasbah of the Star (*itran*) is run by the dynamic brothers Ahmed and Lahcen; others living in the luxuriant valley willingly receive foreign families for the day, children, women, men, each with their own: you might gather roses for rosewater, steam in the village hammam, wander in the fertile gardens. Or you can join an expedition to remoter Berber desert or mountain villages. Rooms here are as friendly and simple as the people: ochre-washed cement floors, thick Berber blankets and rugs, minimal handmade furniture, pretty mirrors over Berber washbasins (urn with tap over china bowl, plughole to bucket). Some have stupendous views of valley and sky, some just have internal windows, all have the right feel. Beneath Lahcen's handsome turban is a man of wide-ranging ideas and action: he takes troubled children from France on character-building treks, is planning Berber pottery workshops in mountain villages and is passionate about preserving his people's rich culture. This is a real meeting place of people who care.

rooms	9: 4 doubles; 5 doubles sharing baths.
price	Half-board 350Dh-600Dh for two.
meals	Lunch 90Dh. By arrangement. Dinner included.
closed	Rarely.
directions	From Ouarzazate for Er Rachidia, enter El Kelaâ N'Gouna; left at fork in centre, follow track 4km; kasbah on hill on left.

	Famille Taghda
tel	+212 (0)44 83 71 03
fax	+212 (0)44 83 71 03
web	www.kasbahitran.com

Guest house

map 4   entry 157

Chez Pierre

Douar Aït Oufi, Gorges du Dadès, Boumalne Dadès

Pierre bought a mountainside and built a marvel on it, a vertical poem in brick and stone. From the road, his little inn climbs the slope and tempts you to follow, up the steps, under the arch, out of the tunnel into the light of a leafy terrace-salon. Fabulous food is served on this level: his big white cliff-hanging restaurant, where you sit in low rustic string-backed chairs, is one of the best in southern Morocco. Above, there are terraces of apple blossom, rosemary among the dry-stone walls, vines, creepers and succulents, the beautiful blue mosaic pool with its pale edging and stripey chaises-longues, and the guest rooms, each with a bit of terrace, all separately dotted among the hanging gardens that look up the magnificent gorge. Rooms are very simple with lots of space, good shapes, arches, restful colouring – white and sand with flashes of rugs and curtains against terracotta floors, fittings of raw, twirly wrought iron, arched hangings and shelf alcoves. Bathrooms are simply lovely, the apartment is palatial, it's all brand new and one feels it has belonged here for ever. Exceptional.

rooms	10: 4 doubles, 2 triples, 3 quadruples; 1 apartment for 8-9.
price	650Dh. Half-board 520Dh p.p.
meals	Breakfast 50Dh. Lunch 35Dh-200Dh. Picnic possible 45Dh. Dinner included in half-board.
closed	10 Nov-20 Dec; 10 Jan-10 Feb; 15 June-15 July.
directions	From Boumalne Dadès, slow potholed track along north bank of Oued Dadès 26km; inn on right.

	Pierre Delaude
tel	+212 (0)44 83 02 67
fax	+212 (0)44 83 02 67
e-mail	chezpierre@menara.ma
web	morocco-travel.com/h/ChezPierre

Country Inn – Trekking base

Le Tomboctou

126 avenue Bir Anzarane, Tinghir

Look from the dust-ridden street into the dark tunnel and see promise at the end: light, a fine pot, a living plant. The promise will be kept. A genuinely friendly young man leads you to the warm-coloured, rough-paved patio where high walls and palms protect you (and the pool) from the town. Here too, excellent food is served in the *caidal* tent or at little tables outside. Within those great walls, the central kasbah well lights the way to carpeted landings and good simple bedrooms. Edi runs desert treks and guides climbers up the Todra gorge. His passion for deep Morocco shows inside too: clay models of local ksars line the hall; named after caravan halts on the route to Timbuctoo, bedrooms have old photographs and descriptions of those desert inns; Berber blankets cover the beds. Rooms are a good size with the simplest of wicker furniture and cotton curtains, red earth walls and floors, shower rooms with all the basics and a window each. And once you have climbed the astonishing long-stride steps to the roof you will be rewarded with a vast panorama of the palm grove and the Saghro and Atlas mountain ranges.

rooms	20: 13 doubles; 3 triples, 1 quadruple; 3 sharing bath.
price	470Dh. Half-board 620Dh for two. 15% reduction for cash payments.
meals	Lunch or dinner generally available.
closed	Never.
directions	Entering Tinghir from west, in town centre, right at sign; down on left.

	Eduard Kunz & Roger Mimó
tel	+212 (0)44 83 46 04/83 51 91
fax	+212 (0)44 83 35 05
e-mail	tomboctu@iam.net.ma
web	www.hoteltomboctou.com

Small hotel

map 5   entry 159

Kasbah Oasis de Feznat

Kasbah Jallal, Oasis de Feznat

After living in Morocco for years and organising desert bivouacs, Hélène was thoroughly smitten – she couldn't leave. Then she had a dream, a dream of that desert purity and dry air that feed the soul – and her dream is coming true. In the pretty village that stands at the end of the little oued, in an oasis of palm trees with great views to the mountains, she has built a group of buildings, part-riad, part-kasbah, in a big green garden. There are terraces for all with private corners, pretty bedroom suites in different colours with comfortable beds, storage alcoves and lots of space, all spread among four or five houses and including a real suite for disabled guests with its own terrace. The décor is subtly exotic, a careful, personal mix of Asian and Moroccan that respects the traditional architecture and the spartan customs of the desert peoples. Abderrazak is a manager with long experience of the inns and bivouacs of the south – he will know exactly what to advise for each guest and how to organise it. This fine new place to stay is just the mixture of comfort and authenticity that Merzouga needed.

rooms	6: 2 doubles, 1 twin, 4 suites (1 disabled).
price	Half-board (dinner) 1,200Dh for two.
meals	Lunch occasionally 150Dh. By arrangement.
closed	Never.
directions	From Erfoud for Jorf, right at sign in palm grove.

	Hélène Viant-Bénard
tel	+212 (0)55 78 95 07/61 08 16 49
fax	+212 (0)55 78 95 18
e-mail	helene.viant-benard@ksarjallal.ma

Guest house

WHAT'S IN THE BACK OF THE BOOK?

GLOSSARY

Aïd	Islamic holy day or feast such as Aïd es Seghir, the end of Ramadan, or Aïd el Kebir, the feast of the sheep which commemorates Abraham's sacrifice of a ram instead of his son Isaac (their Arabic names are Ibrahim and Ismael)
Bab	Gate or door
Bejmat	Unglazed terracotta tiles
Berber/nomad tent	A sweep of woven strips of goat and camel hair sewn together and slung low over two or three poles
Bohou/Bhou	Small salon opening directly onto the patio of a traditional house
Caidal tent	Tall rectangular tent of heavy white canvas with dark purple or black 'kasbah tower' designs sewn on at regular intervals. Interior often lined with wide bands in red and green – the national colours
Dar	Traditional Moroccan house with a patio that has a water feature but not necessarily a garden. Also 'residence of' as in Dar Bacha, the Pasha's residence
Derb	Street or neighbourhood, usually in an old town or medina, with one entry from a main street and any number of dead ends within its own system
Dess	or tadelakt-dess, uses the same materials as tadelakt but with more stone chips. Traditionally used for flooring, it requires many hours of hard regular tamping, done in teams, led by the rhythmic chanting of the ma'allem to which the workers respond in unison with their movements. A labour-intensive craft that is less often used nowadays despite its wonderful effect
Douar	Village
Douiria	Small part of mansion with its own patio where guests or staff were lodged or where the women retired for privacy when strangers were visiting
Fassi	Of Fès
G'naoua	Originally a brotherhood of negro slaves, now used for the music and whirling dances in tribal costume performed by Moroccans of G'naoua descent

GLOSSARY

Gebs/djibs	Plaster; sometimes used as another word for stucco
Haïk	Large cloth wrap made of wool from Essaouira and used by women to cover themselves in public
Hammam	Steam bath
Harira	Traditional soup served at sundown during Ramadam
Kasbah	Citadel or countryside stronghold
Ksar (plural Ksour)	Probably derived from 'Caesar' – a fortified village that may contain a number of kasbahs
Ma'allem	Master builder or craftsman
Maillechort	Moroccan silver
Marabout	Holy man or saint of Islam; by extension, a holy-man's tomb, often domed
Marrakchi	Of Marrakech
Medina	Originally 'town', nowadays the old, often walled quarter of a city where most streets are high narrow lanes without pavements and virtually impassable to motors (the Moroccans are endlessly skilled at getting through despite women with baskets, children playing or running errands, men sharpening knives or building furniture, overloaded donkey carts being urged on with blows and jabs to get through the maelstrom and reach their delivery point
Menzeh	In mansion or palace, a loggia or pavilion where one may eat, generally on a terrace or rooftop with a view
Moroccan salon	or dining room: room lined with upholstered benches along the walls for lounging or sitting at low or lowish tables
Moucharabieh	Wood panels carved in intricate filigree pattern to allow women to see out but no-one to see in. Also name for bay windows fitted with these panels. By extension, any lattice wood carving
Muezzin	Cleric who calls the faithful to prayer from the minaret
Oued	River or, more frequently, dry river bed
Palmeraie	French for palm grove, sometimes translated as palmery

GLOSSARY

Pisé   Earth architecture: a form is erected then filled, layer by layer, with a wet mixture of earth and clay that is rammed and packed before the next layer is started. The structure then bakes dry in the sun. Adobe (from the Arabic *t'bud*, brick) is the sun-dried earthen brick method

Riad   Properly, an enclosed, watered garden, presumed to imitate the earthly paradise; by extension, a mansion house with a patio of at least 100m² and a real garden, arcades on all four sides and galleries above; by further extension, any good-sized house with a central courtyard that is not always very big, is generally arcaded but does not always qualify as a garden

Rabati   Of Rabat

Sabra   Shimmering fabric with wide or narrow coloured stripes properly made of cactus fibre or 'silk', nowadays often synthetic

Saharaoui   Of the western Sahara region (also Sahraoui)

Souiri   Of Essaouira

Tadelakt   A waterproof plaster made of a fine mix of lime, ground stone and pigment, carefully smoothed then polished with black soap for an incomparably silky finish; originally used for hammams, has become a favourite with interior decorators for shower cubicles, bathrooms, even living rooms, in contemporary restorations

Tataoui   Coffered ceiling made of reeds or palm or oleander stems and leaves. Originated in Tata, the southern oasis town on the river Tata

Waha!   Yes!

Zelliges   Geometric mosaic tiling patterns of endless variety made with shapes cut from multi-coloured enamelled tiles and repeated ad infinitum. The style originated in Fès

Zouak   Hand-painting with vegetable pigments on wood (ceilings, doors, furniture)

GLOSSARY

NAMES OF HOUSES

Abir	Passer-by, ferryman, taste
Arsat	Orchard or kitchen garden
Assad	Lion
Assafir	Birds
Ayniwen	Palm trees
Bahar	By the sea
Bartal	Bird
Bled	Countryside, home town or village
Borj	Tower
Cadi	Judge of Muslim law
Caïd	Magistrate, local chieftain or governor
Ifilkou	Flower
Itran(e)	Star
Jnane	Garden (of paradise)
Kerma	Fig tree
Hida	Peacock
Liqama	Green mint
Malik(a)	Sovereign
Mehdi	Rightly guided
Nour	Light
Ouarda	or Warda: roses
Qdima	or Qedim or Kdim or Kedim : old
Raha	Rest
Soukaina	A Berber tribe
Tchaikana	The house where one drinks tea
Tigmi	House
Zarraba	Canal

AND MOREOVER

Spaces

Room widths are determined by the length of the beams that span them. Palm beams cannot stay unsupported over more than 2m50 or they bend and flex – so the normal Moroccan room is long and rather thin.

Colours

The four essential colours of Moroccan crafts are saffron, indigo, mint and madder (crimson), all drawn for centuries from pure vegetable dyes. The national colours, as seen on the Moroccan flag, are red and green. That dazzling cobalt colour that is sometimes called Moroccan Blue was in fact painter Louis Majorelle's answer to the light of Marrakech where, in the 1930s, he laid out the gardens that bear his name. They stand today in all their green and blue glory, now owned by Yves Saint Laurent and open to the public. *With thanks to Ros Grimshaw.*

Black and white There is great pride among the carpet and fabric weavers about real wool taken from black and white sheep, spun, indeed 'home spun', then left or coloured with these pleasing natural dyes before being woven into traditional patterns and motifs – always with a personal creative touch to make each object different. A distinction is also made between 'live' wool, from sheared sheep that live to tell the tale, and 'dead' wool, from slaughtered animals: live wool is more hard-wearing than dead wool.

CONSERVATION & DEVELOPMENT

Environmental and ecological conservation reserves

Argan Biosphere Reserve – Essaouira region; to protect, encourage and research further uses of argan oil (cookery, cosmetics, medicinal).

Southern Oasis Biosphere Reserve – between Ouarzazate and Skoura; to protect the fragile pre-Saharan ecology.

Water scarcity and responsible tourism

Born among the desert peoples, Islam celebrates the divine gift of water, putting it at the centre of the earthly paradise; in Moorish gardens, water runs, founts and trickles eternally; the believer must purify himself at the mosque fountain before entering to pray. Morocco, a semi-desert, is a developing country whose people have traditionally conserved their precious water: underground terracotta aqueducts (*khettara*) that reduce evaporation; communal baths (the hammam); cultivation of oasis micro-climates that encourage humidity.

The modern paradox is powerful:

– the population is exploding: half the people of Morocco are under 20 years old and you will often hear it said that every Moroccan family aims to form its own football team, i.e. have 11 children;

– this is the seventh year of desperate drought and the rural exodus is creating horrific pressure on the urban areas and their water supplies (Marrakech had 1 million inhabitants in 1995, in 2003 it had 1.5 million);

– the country is reaching for western technology and standards of living which must be financed with the hard currency brought by exports, tourism being the leading example;

– Morocco basks in a glow of exotic glamour.

The result is a boom in tourism with considerable emphasis on the Saharan-Hollywood type of place that celebrities build for themselves and visitors hope to experience for a night or two. These houses and hotels have a wealth of water-greedy installations – baths big enough for three, vast open-air swimming pools, expanses of lawn worthy of an English country house. Nearby villages will be deprived of their meagre water

CONSERVATION & DEVELOPMENT

supply because these rich neighbours have sunk impossibly deep wells; in the medinas, the original inhabitants living at the end of a *derb* often have to go to the next-door guest house at 7pm to ask them to turn off their high-powered pump (for guests using power showers on the top floor, you understand) so that they can draw water to cook the family dinner with – their tap is dry.

The country needs its tourist trade, vitally, but it also needs ever more intelligent use of water to support development for so many people. So bring your eyes and your ears and your taste buds, experience the mind-boggling differences that Morocco offers   and remember the villagers next door: go easy on their precious water.

Illegal Moroccan wildlife trade

There is a growing list of endangered Moroccan species that it is illegal to capture, buy, sell or export. The Global Diversity Foundation are well under way with their National Geographic-funded wildlife trade survey carried out with the Marrakech Musuem of Natural History. They have made over 1000 collections of plants and animals and interviewed over 100 vendors. The diversity of wildlife in Morocco is still remarkable. To help save a frighteningly dwindling resource, do take note of the banned exports list which includes:

   Tortoises or land turtles

   Snakes

   Chameleons

   Spiny-tailed lizards

   Leopard and other wild-animal skins

   All the indigenous butterflies of the Atlas mountains

   Numbers of indigenous snails
   (mixed with farmed edible snails)

   Hirudo medicinalis leeches

It is also worth pointing out that the thuya tree is becoming an 'endangered species': Moroccan crafstmen have traditionally made their carved, inlaid tables and chests from this strong characterful wood but the trees take years to reach maturity and the developing tourist trade has so increased demand that the forests are being depleted faster than they can replenish.

CONSERVATION & DEVELOPMENT

Heritage sites

The medina of Marrakech has been a UNESCO World Heritage Site since 1985.

Place Jemaâ El Fna was designated the first UNESCO Oral Heritage Site in 2001.

Specific local development projects

• Association des Bassins d'Imlil for the protection and sustainable development of the valley populations around Imlil and the Toubkal National Park. There's a donation box in the hall of Kasbah du Toubkal or donations can be sent to Wafa Bank, Agence Médina, Marrakech.

• ABDBO Education project for Berber village girls to learn contemporary skills alongside cultivation and use of traditional herbal remedies in a mixed environment of weekly boarding school and home village. A year's sponsorship of one student costs only $650. Donations to Association de Bienfaisance et de Développement du Bassin de l'Ourika, BP16, 42350 Ourika.

– preserving the local heritage, recording the memories of the older inhabitants, recruiting and training local youth as tour guides;

– setting up cultural activities designed to help the young to develop and grow in their own district;

– cooperating on communication of the association's aims and activities to all potentially interested groups.

Dar Raha of Amzrou is a founding and active partner of the Akhiam movement.

CONSERVATION &
DEVELOPMENT

General conservation groups (see protected species above)

• Association des Amis du Museum d'Histoire Naturelle de
Marrakech, Université cadi Ayyad, BP 511
e-mail: aamhnm@ucam.ac.ma
Professeur Mohamed Ghamizi

• Global Diversity Foundation
BP 262 Marrakech-Medina
Fax: +212 (0)44 44 85 29 Gary Martin

Greenery and organics

• Maghrebio promotes organic agriculture and healthy cuisine
127 av Mohamed V 1er étage, Marrakech-Guéliz.
Tel: +212 (0)44 43 97 26 Mme Khadija Belkziz

• ARCH Foundation for the Regreening of the Medina.
Lori Anglin, Conservation Director, ARCH, Keltenallee 7,
Anif 5081, Austria
Tel: +43 662 833340   Fax: +43 662 822867
E-mail: lori@arch.co.at

HISTORY OF MOROCCO

Morocco is a land apart, washed by three seas:
the Atlantic, the Mediterranean and the sand-sea of the Sahara.
It is guarded by four great mountain ranges: the Rif stands
watch over the Mediterranean coast, the Middle Atlas halts
easy access from the east while the High and Anti Atlas
mountains stand like a double parapet on the edge of the
Sahara. Innumerable fast-flowing streams and four great rivers
run from these mountains to support pockets of agriculture
in the valleys: verdant necklaces that cut through the vast
pastoral plateau. These geographical determinants are vital
to an appreciation of the distinctive culture of Morocco,
a country naturally riven into dozens of distinctive provinces
but united against the rest of the world.

Prehistory

If East Africa is the original home of mankind, North Africa was
the springboard from which the species spread across the globe.
The world was innocent of man until a million years ago when
Homo Erectus first crossed the Sahara. Evidence of this stone-
and fire-using human ancestor has been found in the sandstone
cliffs just south of Casablanca. By 40,000BC, modern man had
decisively replaced the earlier sub-species, was spread across
the old world and had already divided into separate races.
The retreat of the last Ice Age was complete by 10,000BC
which allowed the Mediterranean to expand into its current
dimensions and separate the otherwise identical populations
of North Africa and Europe.

The Neolithic revolution – the invention of agriculture and
stock-keeping – had reached Morocco by around 3,000BC.
This enormous change was not by conquest but by a slow
cultural dissemination that worked east along the seaboard.
It was an uneven process for there seems to be evidence that
stock-keeping may have first evolved in North Africa anyway,
while it is clear that agricultural techniques were learned –
but then abandoned by some communities. Ultimately, however,
it would transform the drifting groups of hunter-gatherers
into settled communities and vastly increase the population.
The indigenous people of North Africa can henceforth be

described as Berbers, a word of Greek origin, and the earliest historical records speak of their devotion to war, to polygamy, to their chariots and to their herds of sheep and goats.

The Phoenicians and Romans

It was the Phoenician merchants of the coast of Syria who first introduced the higher arts of the civilisations of the Near East to Morocco. They were the fairy godmothers of ancient Morocco, though their motives were entirely mercenary. By 1,000BC they had established a permanent settlement at Tangier, soon followed by other colonies down the Atlantic coast. From these centres the skills of metal-working, stone-carving, weaving, pottery and improved agriculture, with new varieties of crops and trees, were disseminated. Carthage emerged as the leader of all the Phoenician colonies in the Western Mediterranean during the sixth century BC when they all felt threatened by the expansion of Greek colonial settlements. From this period comes a description of the Carthaginian admiral Hanno's voyage of discovery down the coast to West Africa and the techniques of silent barter with the natives for gold.

After the destruction of the city of Carthage in 146BC, Rome assumed the 'protection' of the scattered Phoenician colonies. The interior of North Africa was ruled by native

HISTORY OF MOROCCO

Berber kings whose territories were slowly annexed by Rome over a 200-year period. Juba II, who ruled over northern Morocco from the inland capital of Volubilis (as well as central Algeria), was a noted scholar who had been educated in the household of the Emperor Augustus, where he had met and married the princess Silene, the daughter of Mark Anthony and Cleopatra. (Their son Ptolemy, though he inherited their throne, was murdered on the orders of the Emperor Caligula.) His Moroccan kingdom resisted annexation but was finally conquered in AD44, during the reign of the Emperor Claudius.

This new Roman province of Mauretania Tingitania consisted of just the fertile northwestern coastal plain and was not even connected by road to Roman Algeria. When the Baquates tribe overran the defences at the end of the third century the Empire decided to restrict itself to holding the strategic city ports of Tangier and Ceuta. Later powers like the Vandals and Byzantines followed in their footsteps, and left the fierce Berber tribes of the interior to their own devices.

The spread of Islam and the Arab conquest

This was all to be changed by a theocratic state that had been established in the Arabian peninsula. The Prophet Muhammad died in 632 but the cavalry armies of his successors soon conquered an enormous empire. In 682 Oqba ben Nafi made his legendary raid into Morocco, riding out into the Atlantic surf to prove that there was no land any further west to be conquered for Islam – before returning to his base in Algeria. Musa ben Noussir organised a more thorough conquest of Morocco between 705 and 710. He established garrisons at Tangier and the Tafilalt but it was soon made clear that his real objective had been to conquer Spain and secure the desert trade route. The only value Morocco held for the Arab governors was as a source of slaves and recruits for their army.

HISTORY OF MOROCCO

In 740 the disillusioned Berber soldiers in the Tangier garrison assassinated their Arab governor and revolted. They adopted a rigorous puritanism in order to make a clear distinction between their passionate support of the Muslim religion and their rejection of their Arab overlords.

The Idrissid Monarchy, 789–828

Berber enthusiasm for the new religion was further demonstrated in 789. Moulay Idriss, great-great-grandson of the Prophet Muhammad, had fled to Morocco to escape the vengeance of Harun al Rashid, the great Caliph of Baghdad. He was acclaimed ruler by the Berber tribes around Meknès but was poisoned by an agent of the Caliph two years later. Fortunately his Berber mistress was pregnant and gave birth to a son who later reigned as Idriss II, ruling central Morocco and establishing Fès as a great bastion of Arab and Islamic culture. After his death in 828 his kingdom was divided among nine sons who have attained legendary status as missionary princes who brought the faith to far-flung provinces. Though the power of the Idrissids, the descendants of Idriss II, soon waned, their spiritual prestige remains a strong and continual feature of Moroccan history.

Unity under the Almoravids, 1042–1147

By the 11th century Morocco had deteriorated into a patchwork of petty states and feuding tribes with many of the chief ports and towns under the control of foreign powers – albeit Muslim ones. In the far reaches of the Western Sahara a native scholar, Ibn Yaasin, had returned from Mecca determined to create a true Islamic state. His vision and discipline, allied to the ferocity of the Saharan tribes, created a powerful force of warriors. The *al-murabitun* "the men of the fortress of faith" would become known to Europe as the Almoravids. These warriors emerged out of the desert in 1042 and conquered an enormous desert empire that stretched south to the Niger river and north towards the High Atlas mountains of Morocco. This was to be further extended by Youssef ben Tachfine, an Almoravid general who crossed the mountains and established Marrakech as his base camp in 1071. Within 20

years Youssef had conquered not only Morocco but also the
sophisticated city-states of Muslim Spain. Skilled Andalucian
craftsmen, secretaries and architects were employed by the
Almoravid court and began to introduce the higher civilisation
of Moorish Spain into Morocco.

The Empire of the Almohads, 1147–1248

At the height of the Almoravid Empire, Ibn Tumert, another
native scholar, returned from Mecca full of schemes to establish
an even more rigorous Islamic state. Rejected by the powers
that be, he fled the city and established himself at Tin-Mal in
the High Atlas mountains where he created an obedient army
from the Berber highland tribes. Victory over the Almoravids
was only eventually achieved by his successor, Abdel Moumen,
who established an empire that stretched over Spain, Algeria,
Tunisia and part of Libya. It is the golden period of Moroccan
history, when Almohad fleets dominated the Western
Mediterranean and great philosophers like Averroës received
the full support of the sultan's court. Some of that glory is
still reflected in the magnificent buildings that adorn Rabat
and Marrakech, like the Koutoubia and El Hassan minarets
and the formal gates of Oudaya and Aguenaou. A military
defeat in Spain, at Las Navas de Tolosa in 1213, rocked imperial
authority and the sultans were faced with a series of escalating
revolts. In 1248 the Almohad sultan died while on campaign
on the Algerian border and his leaderless army was massacred
by the powerful Beni Merin tribe as it struggled home. The
tribal chiefs of the Beni Merin established their capital at Fès
but it took another 21 years of war before they could destroy
the last Almohad army that defended Marrakech.

The Merenid dynasty, 1248–1554

The reigns of Sultan Abou Hassan, 1331-51, and his son Abou
Inan, 1351-58, are the zenith of the long centuries of Merenid
rule. In this period, Merenid armies twice occupied Tunis and
seemed at the point of restoring the unity of the Almohad
Empire. The Merenid architecture of the 14th century,
particularly the *medersas* (schools for Koranic studies) that
can be seen in Fès, Meknès and Salé, testify to the exquisite

HISTORY OF MOROCCO

taste of the sultans and their generous patronage of religious learning. The works of Ibn Battuta, 'the Muslim Marco Polo', and Ibn Khaldoun, one of the world's greatest historians, are proof of the lively intellectual life of the period. Wealth poured into the state coffers from the enormously profitable trans-Saharan caravan trade in gold, precious oils and ivory. The period finished in 1358 when Sultan Abou Inan was smothered with a pillow by his vizier as he lay recovering from an illness. This royal murder is a parable for the gradual decline of the state. The sultans became mere figureheads as real power fell into the hands of a corrupt coterie of viziers, financiers and generals. In the 15th century the expansionist Portuguese kingdom began to seize control of a number of Moroccan ports which the Merenids proved powerless to hold. By the mid-16th-century the Portuguese were in almost complete control of the coastline and in 1578 the boy king, Sebastian, attempted outright conquest.

The Saadian Sultans, 1554–1668

The inability of the Merenid rulers to oppose the Portuguese allowed for the rise of a number of local war leaders. The most effective of these were the Saadians, from the oasis valley of the Draâ in southern Morocco, who organised the siege of Agadir in 1510. This Portuguese fort finally fell in 1542, by which time the Saadians were already well established in Marrakech as the rulers of southern Morocco. Seven years later they were strong enough to capture the Merenid capital

of Fès. In 1578 the Saadian dynasty won eternal fame with the crushing defeat of the Portuguese invasion at the battle of Ksar-el-Kebir. Sultan Abdel Malik died in the hour of victory and his brother Ahmed inherited the throne and took the title El Mansour – 'the victorious'. He gained additional fame by the conquest of Timbuctoo whose treasure gave him another epithet – El Dhabbi, 'the golden'. Surviving memorials of Ahmed's reign include the glittering Saadian tombs and the ruins of the palace of El Badia in Marrakech. His sons destroyed their inheritance in a furious war of succession and discredited the dynasty by selling the port of Larache to the Christians in 1610.

Though a number of Saadian princes lived on in splendour at Marrakech, real authority was exercised elsewhere. A three-cornered fight developed between petty dynasties based on the Rif, Anti-Atlas and Middle Atlas mountains.

However, after 40 years of warfare, power fell into the hands of Moulay Rachid, a young prince of holy lineage whose Alaouite family came from the oasis of Tafilalt. Within four years of raising his standard at Taza he had seized complete control of the country. He ruled for just four years and was succeeded by his younger brother, Moulay Ismaïl.

HISTORY OF MOROCCO

Moulay Ismaïl, 1672–1727

Certain monarchs breed legends and the reign of Moulay
Ismaïl has always been in danger of being overwhelmed by
stories of his cruelty and sexual prowess. He was undoubtedly
fertile and tyrannical but his long reign was also a period
of great achievement. He reformed the nation's cult-ridden
religious life, disciplined the Berber mountain tribes,
liberated Tangier from the English and Larache, Asilah and
Mehdiya from the Spanish. The imperial city at Meknès
was built in this period but there are many other testaments
to his energy: the bridges, kasbahs and markets that he built
throughout the country and the numerous mosques, palaces
and walls that he had restored. It was the proud boast of his
reign that the roads were safe enough for a woman or a
Jew to travel across the breadth of the country without being
troubled. This unaccustomed order was only achieved by an
authoritarian regime backed by a standing army of 150,000
Negro slaves. His failure, and it was a great one, was not
to delegate authority to any of his many sons. His death
was followed by a 20-year war as his regiments and heirs
struggled for dominance.

Decline in the 18th and 19th centuries

None of the immediate descendants of Moulay Ismaïl was
to match the great sultan's power. Their authority was in
practice restricted to the coastal plains and river valleys,
the area which was known as the Bled-el-Makhzen, the
land of government, while the mountainous areas of tribal
power were known as the Bled-es-Siba, the land of dissidence.
Sidi Mohammed, who reigned from 1757 to 1790, was one
of the most astute sultans of this period, reforming the
customs service, building new ports and quietly suppressing

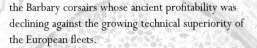

the Barbary corsairs whose ancient profitability was declining against the growing technical superiority of the European fleets.

The 19th century was a period of increasing European Power, graphically demonstrated by the French invasion of Algeria in 1830. After 1856, European merchants in Morocco were running their own law courts while their coinages began to displace the native currency. By the turn of the century the two chief ports of Tangier and Casablanca were effectively under the control of the foreign consuls. Despite the reforms attempted by Sultan Moulay Hassan the country slipped ever more into debt and European influence.

The French Protectorate

The rivalry between the European powers over Morocco was settled by secret negotiations at the 1906 conference of Algeciras. France was given central Morocco and Spain received the poorer areas in the extreme south and north. The next year French troops landed at Casablanca. Several years of confused fighting and diplomacy were resolved in 1912 when the sultan signed away sovereignty through the treaty of Fès. Later that year the tribal army of El Hiba, the Blue Sultan of the desert, was destroyed outside Marrakech. The French immediately began work on the colonial transformation of Le Maroc Utile – 'useful Morocco'. The less rewarding mountain regions were not completely pacified until 1934 while the 1921-1926 Rif rebellion nearly succeeded in expelling the Spanish from the north of the country.

The technical achievements of the 44 years of colonial rule were impressive. A complete road and rail network was established and ports, airfields, dams, irrigation projects and new administrative centres were created. The rewards of this new society – the hotels, hospitals and schools – were reserved for the 300,000 European settlers and the traditional Moroccan ruling class.

HISTORY OF MOROCCO

Independent Morocco

By 1947 the uglier aspects of French colonial rule were
being questioned by Sultan Mohammed V and the Istiqlal,
a small independence party. By 1951, both the Sultan and
the rapidly expanding Istiqlal were working to awaken the
political life of the nation. This was dramatically achieved in
1953 when the French deposed Mohammed V and sent him
into exile in Madagascar. In 1955, the mass demonstrations
for his return had begun to escalate into a guerrilla war.
The French government, which was then faced with a
revolution in Algeria, decided to quit Morocco with grace.
Mohammed V returned and by March 1956 had formally
negotiated independence. He changed his title from sultan
to king while his popularity helped him outmanoeuvre the
party bosses and remain the dominant political figure.

He was succeeded in 1961 by his son Hassan II. In the
following three decades parties, constitutions, crises,
coups and cabinets challenged the system but the king

remained very much in charge. Such key figures as the
Minister of the Interior and the Minister of Defence
always remained the personal appointees of the king.
Successes like the nationalisation of foreign businesses
in 1965 and the Maghrebi Union treaty of 1989 are
eclipsed by the Green March of 1975 which was by far
the most popular achievement of his reign. As General

HISTORY OF MOROCCO

Franco of Spain lay dying, the king led 350,000 unarmed Moroccans across the southern frontier to lay claim to the Spanish-held Western Sahara. This enormous territory is now integrated into Morocco, though the irredentist Saharan nationalist Polisario movement sought independence through a guerrilla war. An armistice has led to a permanent UN presence and an agreement to determine the future of the province in a referendum, though agreement on the qualifications to vote remains a contentious issue.

In July 1999, the old king died and was succeeded by his young son. Mohammad VI dismissed his father's unpopular minister of the interior and has presided over an increasingly democratic and liberal regime. Morocco is a constitutional monarchy with a free press and free and open elections. It also faces great challenges: to feed and find employment for its burgeoning population of 27 million and also to remain a shining example of a Muslim nation – all the more devout because of its tolerance, individual freedoms and intellectual diversity.

Barnaby Rogerson

2003

HISTORY OF ISLAM

لا إله إلا الله محمد رسول الله

ILa ilaha ill'Allah, Muhammad rasul Allah.
(There is no divinity but God, and Muhammad is his Prophet.)

With this short creed, all Muslims profess the basic tenets
of their faith. Islam literally means 'submission' and implies
the offering up to God of total faith and trust. The will of
God was directly passed to the Prophet Muhammad through
the medium of the Archangel Gabriel. Muhammad's principal
task as Prophet was the recitation of this divine message.
It is these recitations of the word of God that are collected
in the Qu'ran, the holy book of Islam.

To Muhammad, Islam was not a new religion, it was
intended to be a reformation of the ancient monotheistic
tradition taught in the Old and New Testaments, the holy
books of Jews and Christians. In both the Qu'ran and
Muhammad's private conversations there are repeated
references to the various prophets who had brought the
message of God to mankind before him. Muhammad was
proud to be numbered in the long line of prophets which
stretched back through Issa (Jesus), Yahya (John the Baptist),
Sulaiman (Solomon), Davud (David), Musa (Moses), Harun
(Aaron), Idris (Enoch), Yakub (Jacob), Yunus (Jonah), Noah
and right back to Abraham and to the first man, Adam.
The Qu'ran was intended to present an opportunity for
the various squabbling Christian and Jewish sects to unite
beneath a new definitive revelation.

However, the task of converting all the Christians and Jews
in central Arabia proved impossible and towards the end of
his life Muhammad realized that Islam must stand alone.
Muslims began to pray facing Mecca rather than Jerusalem
and Friday became the Muslim holy day as opposed to the
Saturday and Sunday celebrations of the Jews and Christians.
Some festivals, such as Achoura (based on the Jewish Day
of Atonement) remained like stranded bridges stretching
between the faiths. The Prophet ordered all Muslims to
respect the 'peoples of the Book', as Christians and Jews
are called. Muhammad's tolerant attitude can be heard in

HISTORY OF ISLAM

his answer to a theological squabble with his neighbours,
'Will you dispute with us about God? When he is our
Lord and your Lord! We have our words and you have
your words but we are sincerely his.'

The Prophet Muhammad

The Prophet Muhammad was born in AD 570. The young
Muhammad was to be thrice orphaned before the age of
eight by the death of father Abdallah (before he was born),
mother Amina and grandfather Abdul Muttalib. He grew up
in the household of his paternal uncle, Abu Talib, who was
the sheikh of one of the most prestigious clans within the

HISTORY OF ISLAM

Quraysh tribe which dominated the oasis city of Mecca. Although of noble blood, Muhammad was not rich and had to earn his keep as a shepherd-boy before being trained to work on the camel caravans that plied the routes that crossed the Arabian desert from Yemen to Syria. As a young man he was known as Amin, 'the trusty one', for his honesty and dignified bearing. This led him to be trusted with the goods of Khadijah, a wealthy widow whom he later married. Mecca was the centre of pagan Arab spiritual life and Mohammed and his wife joined the circle of Hanif who sought enlightenment through some form of monotheism and were familiar with Jewish, Christian and Persian doctrines.

Muhammad received his first revelation in AD 610 when he was 40 years old. The Archangel Gabriel appeared to him in a cave, which he frequently used for prayer and meditation, outside Mecca. Doubtful at first about these revelations but encouraged by his wife, he risked ridicule and shared the word of God. His ardent monotheism and criticism of the pagan worship in Mecca won him some followers but even more enemies. Eventually, the protection of his clan proved inadequate and, to avoid assassination, he moved to the oasis of Yathrib (renamed Medina) where he was welcomed and honoured as the Prophet of God on 15 June AD 622.

This date marks the beginning of the Muslim era known as the Hegira. Muhammad refused any royal or military power and accepted only an official role as mediator. From these modest foundations he established a theocratic state and perfected the daily ritual of prayer and the annual festivals which still dominate the life of a Muslim. He also developed a body of moral and legal codes to cover the practical problems that a Muslim might face. His personal example, his innate modesty, easy approachability and hospitality set an additional example to his followers alongside his teaching. From Medina he waged war on the Meccan caravans and, having survived a number of testing battles and sieges, his authority was gradually accepted by all the surrounding Arab tribes which included those of Jewish and Christian faith alongside the pagan majority. By AD 630, two years before his death, his authority extended over all Arabia and the first Arab cavalry armies had been sent into Syria.

The question of Muhammad's successor, the Caliph, rends the Muslim world to the present day. The first four successors contributed important aspects to the developing body of Muslim faith and are accepted as the 'Rightly Guided' by the majority of Muslims, known as Sunni. Most of North Africa and practically all Tunisians are Sunni. However, an important minority, the Shiites, believe that Ali, who was Mohammed's cousin, his most devoted disciple, son-in-law and spiritual confidant, should have been the first Caliph. Lesser sects like the Ismaiks, Druze and Kharijites are divided by their own interpretations of the rightful succession.

Religious Life

The Qu'ran sets out the five pillars of Islam, the pre-requisites of Muslim life. These are the profession of faith, prayer five times a day, the giving of alms, fasting during Ramadan and pilgrimage to Mecca.

The Muslim profession of faith, "La ilaha ill'Allah, Muhammad rasul Allah" (There is no divinity but God, and Muhammad is his Prophet), is a simple enough matter, though the Prophet himself recognized that there was an enormous difference between submission and real faith. He also recognized that even among that first community of believers in Medina there were hypocrites motivated by fame, wealth and ambition.

The first prayer of the day, known as Moghreb, is held four minutes after sunset, Eshe when it is quite dark, Soobh Fegr at dawn, Dooh at noon (or just after the sun has passed its zenith), and Asr at the end of the siesta but officially calculated as halfway between noon and sunset. At each mosque the muezzin announces prayers by calling "God is great. I testify that there is no God but God. I testify that Muhammed is his prophet. Come to prayer, come to security. God is great." Before the morning prayer an extra inducement, "Prayer is better than sleep," is added. Before prayer all believers ritually purify

themselves by washing with water or, in arid areas, with clean
sand. Facing Mecca, they stand with hands held up and open
to proclaim God's greatness. With hands by their sides they
recite the opening verse of the Qu'ran, the fatiha, before
bowing with hands on knees and then fully prostrating
themselves. Kneeling again, they recite the *chahada*, a prayer
for the prophet. The three positions of prayer, standing, bowing
and prostrate, symbolise the superiority of man's rational
rather than his animal nature, a servant before his master and
submission to the sovereign will of God. Friday is the chief day
of prayer, when the community gathers for noon prayers at the
most important local mosque, followed by a sermon, *khutha*.

Almsgiving was enshrined in the ascetic example of the
Prophet who throughout his life scorned the accumulation of
possessions. It later became a pivotal definition of membership

of the Muslim community which he led from Mecca. All who professed to be Muslim were to offer an annual tithe from their crops and herds to the head of the Muslim community who distributed them to the needy, the deserving poor, widows and orphans as well as feeding travellers, ransoming captives, freeing slaves and relieving debtors. It became enshrined as the *zakat*, the only legitimate tax an orthodox Muslim leader could collect, which was often assessed at a fortieth of wealth. Nowadays tax and alms are usually separate and the practice is purely voluntary.

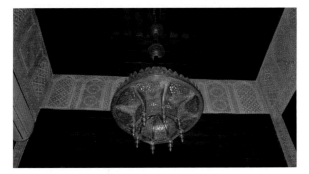

The fast of Ramadan proscribes sex, smoking, drinking and eating during the daylight hours of the ninth month of the Muslim year. Only children, the sick, nursing or pregnant mothers, old people and travellers are exempt. The fast commemorates the month in which Muhammad received his first revelation but is also based on pre-existing Christian and Jewish spiritual practices.

Pilgrimage to the Kaâba at Mecca, revered as the altar of Abraham, takes place between the seventh and tenth days of the last month of the Islamic year (Dhu al-Hajja). It is governed by a strict set of rules and observances involving fasting and long treks between the holy sites in the desert heat. For a poor man it may be the journey of a lifetime, partly paid for by friends who will receive merit by their contribution. He will return to his community with the proud title of 'Haj'. The distance of Mecca from Morocco and the dangers of the

route (from both bedouin tribes and Christian corsairs) made
it especially arduous. This gave rise to the hope that seven visits
to such local pilgrimage centres as Moulay Idris and Moulay
Brahim might equal the journey to Arabia, a pious hope
without any doctrinal backing.

The Qu'ran

Qu'ran means 'recitation', for the Prophet Muhammad
was enjoined by the Archangel Gabriel to recite the word
of God as it was dictated to him. It was orally delivered
by Muhammad to his followers between AD 610 and 632,
memorized and often recited. It was first collected into a
definitive written version 18 years after his death in AD 650.
The Qu'ran is divided into 114 unequal chapters or suras,
arranged in order of length starting with the longest. Each
sura is known by a name, such as the cow, the bee, the ant,
generally believed to have no other significance than as a
memory aid – for Muslims are taught to recite the Qu'ran by
heart. The very beauty of the language of the Qu'ran is taken
as proof of its divine inspiration: "you will never understand...
until you can feel in your heart the poetry and music of
the noble Qu'ran." No passionate Muslim can accept that
a translation from Arabic is adequate as a holy text, though
translations are accepted as a useful commentary for non-Arabs
if placed side by side with the Arabic text.

In content, the Qu'ran divides roughly into four themes:
the worship of Allah, the Day of Judgement, stories of earlier
prophets, and social laws, though it is a feature of the Qu'ran
that each sura can stand alone, like a miniature summary of the
faith. It is also, at times, like receiving only one half of a
dialogue, as if it were a collection of divine answers to
Muhammad's prayers, though these original petitions have been
lost. Although some sura can be identified with a given incident
in the Prophet's life, the Qu'ran cannot be read as a consistent
narrative (like the Gospels) but is rather a series of
exhortations that develop and embroider the same themes of
calling mankind to God. Western critics who talk disparagingly
of repetition have merely 'read' a book that was designed to be
lived.

HISTORY OF ISLAM

Sura 17:22-39 contains a set of commands similar to the Ten Commandments encouraging kindness, charity, sobriety and humility and prohibiting murder, adultery, idolatry and meanness. A secondary source, known as the hadith, is also available to Muslims. This is a collection of the memorized sayings, actions, judgements and traditions of the Prophet Muhammad. It is the Hadith (but never the Qu'ran) which is open to interpretation and to arguments about the validity of the source. A single authoritative edition has never been agreed upon, although Al-Bukhari's multi-volume collection has become the most respected single source.

From the Qu'ran and the Hadith a legal system, known as sharia, was created. Traditional Islamic countries have no civil code and criminal acts as well as spiritual sins are judged according to sharia. In Morocco and a handful of the more progressive states, such as Iraq, Syria, Tunisia and Turkey, civil codes have also been introduced in the 20th century. The difference in legal systems is not as large as may be thought, for most of the so-called secular codes are merely an addition to, not a substitution of, sharia. At the forefront of most fundamentalist campaigns is an official recognition of sharia as the foundation of all law. Although this might seem mere window-dressing, it is acutely relevant as to where sovereignty lies: with a secular assembly, by royal decree or with the scholars of religious law?

Sufism

The spread of Islam was greatly assisted by the Sufi brotherhoods who set up religious centres, known as zaouia, throughout the Muslim world. The term Sufi may derive from 'suf', meaning wool and, by inference, the coarse woollen cloth worn by ascetics. Sufis are not satisfied merely to worship God by obeying Islamic law, they aspire to direct spiritual experience through additional devotions. The Prophet Mohammed's celebrated night journey to Jerusalem serves as the orthodox role model for such aspirations.

In addition, it is believed by many Muslims that, aside from his public declarations on faith, the Prophet Muhammed taught Ali and Fatima various private practices of prayer and meditation which were too confusing and physically demanding for the main body of believers. It is these oral traditions that Ali taught to his own followers, who passed the spiritual heritage on down the generations of believers. Each Sufi brotherhood can trace this spiritual line of descent in the same manner in which the Pope looks back across the centuries to his apostolic succession from St Peter. The various Sufi brotherhoods (who are often compared with Christian monastic orders) each established a set of rituals and prayers to achieve the desired union with God. Most Sufi regimes are simple and ascetic and include outward features such as charity and teaching as well as the inner search for wajd, the ecstatic experience of the divine. They often prescribe a repetitive physical action, such as recitation, music or dancing, as a tool in their quest (for instance, the whirling dervishes). To outsiders, the best-known Sufi trait is indifference to worldly concerns which sometimes led to the practice of self-mutilation to show indifference to pain.

Christianity and Islam

Muslims see their religion as a reformation of Christianity which, with the evidence of the cult of the Virgin, the sacrifice of the Cross, odd doctrines on celibacy and confusing doctrines about the Trinity, they see as a corrupted version of monotheism. Christianity for its part has always found it difficult to venerate

HISTORY OF ISLAM

Muhammad whose long life, many wives and battles seem to be in sharp contrast with the poor, miracle-working Jesus nailed up on a cross aged 33. This contrast is partly about the availability of source material. We know an enormous amount about Muhammad from a number of near-contemporary biographies, as well as thousands and thousands of hadith. For the life of Jesus, the chief sources are the four gospels and the epistles, which were written down 30 years or more after his death, while all rival accounts and the trivial human details of his existence were lost during the Roman suppression of the Judaean revolt followed by the destruction of Jerusalem.

The alarming antagonism between these two religions, however, stems as much from their proximity and continual history of conflict as from actual doctrine. Early struggles in the Middle East between Byzantium and Islam were institutionalized by the Crusades, which continued seamlessly into the Hapsburg-Ottoman War, prolonged by the Corsair Wars of the 16th-18th centuries. In the 19th and 20th centuries, the political dominance of Christian European nations over every Muslim country (except Saudi Arabia and Turkey) has compounded the mutual mistrust. Just when the post-war independence movement and oil discoveries seemed to be establishing a new equality of relationship, the creation of the state of Israel, fostered by the USA, prolongs the tension. Daily, the newspapers carry proof that the age-old ignorance and antagonism that exists between the two faiths continues largely unabated.

HISTORY OF ISLAM

Islamic Celebrations

The main religious event of the Muslim year is the fast of
Ramadan which is still adhered to, in public at least, by the
whole Moroccan population. For the entire month, productivity
drops and a sense of lassitude descends during the day. When
Ramadan falls in the summer, tempers are notoriously frayed,
but everything is forgotten at the setting of the sun, when
cafés fill with hungry customers who traditionally break the
fast with a bowl of steaming soup. Deep into the night towns
reverberate to the sound of revelling as families take to the
streets after their communal meal. Musicians, storytellers and
puppet-shows monopolise the pavements. After a few hours'
sleep and a nourishing breakfast before sunrise, the fast begins
again. The feast of Aïd es Seghir at the end of Ramadan is a
time for new clothes and sumptuous banquets.

Most of the popular rites of passage that are celebrated by
Christians in a church (such as baptism, confirmation and
marriage) do not take place within a mosque in Morocco. The
mosque is just for prayer and the study and recitation of the
Qu'ran and does not act as a ceremonial stage. The Moroccan
equivalent of baptism usually occurs on the seventh day after
birth, when children are named and presented to the family,
adorned with amulets for good luck and to chase away the
'evil eye'. Following the tradition of the Prophet Muhammad,
the name of the child is formally announced by the eldest
male member of family (normally the grandfather) who may
also whisper the call to prayer in the ear of the newborn.
The mother will be the hero of the day and showered with
presents and congratulations from her family and neighbours.

Circumcision is an ancient Semitic rite that predates the
teaching of the Prophet Muhammad by thousands of years. It is
believed to have been instituted by the Prophet Abraham as a
substitite sacrifice after the intended sacrifice of his child
Ishmael (the ancestor of the Arabs and half-brother to Jewish
Isaac) was halted by angels. A popular tale recounts that the
Prophet Abraham was about to use an axe on himself for the
'operation' when once again an angel interceded and suggested
a sharpened razor blade. It is now usually performed between

the ages of five and seven and begins with the young boy's first visit to the mosque accompanied by his male relations. He will be dressed up in the finest traditional robes (including a fez), possibly allowed to ride a horse hired for the day and much will be made of him and his bravery. The surgery is now usually performed by doctors but the local barber still plays his traditional role in country areas. At the moment of circumcision, other older children may break a jar of sweets on the ground, to distract the jinn – the spirits – from entering the child through the wound and to add a distracting element of fun and laughter to drown any moans of pain.

Weddings are often signalled by a cavalcade of hooting, decorated cars or, in the countryside, by a hired lorry or two complete with young drummers. Preparations begin some weeks before with a visit to the lawyer's office where the marriage contract, concerned with dowries and the terms of both marriage and divorce, is drawn up and signed by bride and groom. The old week-long festivities are nowadays often packed into a couple of days. The bride's body hair is all waxed off and the palms of her hands and soles of her feet covered with temporary henna tattoo. Sumptuously dressed, she is shown off to family and friends sitting on a dais, before men and women separate to eat the marriage dinner. Traditionally the bride then walks seven times around her home, bidding farewell, before being taken to her marriage bed. The husband returns from the town with a group of friends who leave him at the door. The last to bless him as he enters the bedroom is

HISTORY OF ISLAM

his mother. Though it is rare for the bloody sheet to be displayed (as graphic proof that the bride came to marriage a virgin) the concept is still a very valid expectation.

Death is greeted with frenzied ululations from female relatives and friends, though men are traditionally supposed to hold back from passionate expressions of grief. In the words of the Prophet, "what comes from the heart and eye – that is from God, what comes from the hand and tongue – that is from Satan". Muslims are buried quickly (normally within a day or two of death, though the requirements of state funerals override these traditions). The body is washed and scented before being wrapped in the simple white clothing of a pilgrim. It is carried to the cemetery on a bier, supported by male friends and relatives and followed by a cortège of male mourners often headed by a man reciting the Qu'ran. There is no solemn funeral march in Islam, in fact, the more religious believe that the dead should be carried at a slow trot to speed them on their way to meet their Maker. The body is often buried on its side facing towards Mecca. For the most pious, the grave should be decorated with no stone memorial though it is common to plant a pair of stones so that the ground is not inadvertently dug up. On the first night two terrifying angels, Munkar and Nakir, are believed to descend into the tomb to question the dead and chastise the wicked. After this severe night, the long sleep of the grave will only be broken by the calling together of the last great Assembly, a time when all mortals shall stand dumbfounded before the divine presence and watch the publishing of the pages of their past life while their very limbs will stand witness against them. They will have to cross the bridge over the fires of Hell to reach the gardens of Paradise, filled with "what the eye hath not seen, nor the ear heard, nor hath ever been thought of by mankind".

Barnaby Rogerson

2003

WHAT IS ALASTAIR SAWDAY PUBLISHING?

Twenty or so of us work in converted barns on a farm near Bristol, close enough to the city for a bicycle ride and far enough for a silence broken only by horses and the occasional passage of a tractor. Some editors work in the countries they write about, e.g. France; others work from the UK but are based outside the office. We enjoy each other's company, celebrate every event possible, and work in an easy-going but committed environment.

These books owe their style and mood to Alastair's miscellaneous career and his interest in the community and the environment

These books owe their style and mood to Alastair's miscellaneous career and his interest in the community and the environment. He has taught overseas, worked with refugees, run development projects abroad, founded a travel company and several environmental organisations. There has been a slightly unconventional streak throughout, not least in his driving of a waste-paper-collection lorry, the manning of stalls at jumble sales and the pursuit of causes long before they were considered sane.

Back to the travel company: trying to take his clients to eat and sleep in places that were not owned by corporations and assorted bandits he found dozens of very special places in France – farms, châteaux etc – a list that grew into the first book, *French Bed and Breakfast*. It was a celebration of 'real' places to stay and the remarkable people who run them.

The publishing company grew from that first and rather whimsical French book. It started as a mild crusade, and there it stays – full of 'attitude', and the more appealing for it. For we still celebrate the unusual, the beautiful, the individual. We are passionate about rejecting the banal, the ugly, the pompous and the indifferent and we are passionate, too, about 'real' food. Alastair is a trustee of the Soil Association and keen to promote organic growing and consuming by owners and visitors.

It is a source of deep pleasure to us to know that there are many thousands of people who share our views. We are by no means alone in trumpeting the virtues of resisting the destruction and uniformity of so much of our culture – and the cultures of other nations, too.

We run a company in which people and values matter. We love to hear of new friendships between those in the book and those using it, and to know that there are many people – among them farmers – who have been enabled to pursue their decent lives thanks to the extra income our books bring them.

WWW.SPECIALPLACESTOSTAY.COM

Britain

France

Ireland

Italy

Portugal

Spain

Morocco

India...

all in one place!

On the unfathomable and often unnavigable sea of online accommodation pages, those who have discovered **www.specialplacestostay.com** have found it to be an island of reliability. Not only will you find a database full of trustworthy, up-to-date information about all the Special Places to Stay across Europe, but also:

- Links to the web sites of all of the places in the series
- Colourful, clickable, interactive maps to help you find the right place
- The opportunity to make most bookings by e-mail – even if you don't have e-mail yourself
- Online purchasing of our books, securely and cheaply
- Regular, exclusive special offers on books
- The latest news about future editions and future titles
- Notices about special offers, late availability and anything else our owners think you'll be interested in.

The site is constantly evolving and is frequently updated with news and special features that won't appear anywhere else but in our window on the worldwide web.

Russell Wilkinson, Web Producer
website@specialplacestostay.com

If you'd like to receive news and updates about our books by e-mail, visit the site and at the bottom of every page you can add yourself to our address book.

THE LITTLE EARTH BOOK

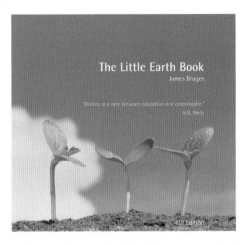

The earth is now desperately vulnerable; so are we. Find out what is going wrong with our planet, and about the greatest challenge of our century – how to save the Earth for us all.

New chapters include:

Climate Change: alarming new findings on the dangers of climate change make this the greatest and most immediate danger facing the world – urgent action is required

Islam: Islam is the fastest growing religion and it is important to understand it. Why is it intrinsically at odds with corporate capitalism?

Civilised Values: the USA is profoundly committed to democracy and freedom – yet pursues unpopular policies abroad. Why do they so readily intervene elsewhere?

The Tyranny of Corporations: the Founding Fathers fled from tyranny. The tyranny of US corporations is now under legal assault from one man. Might he win?

Full Spectrum Dominance: this is official US policy. The US plans, literally, to dominate the world in every sphere – military, economic, etc.

Further chapters cover: water, hydrogen, Kyoto, arms, inequality, debt, antibiotics, farming – and much more.

The Little Earth Book £6.99
4th edition available April 2004

www.fragile-earth.com

THE LITTLE FOOD BOOK

The Little Food Book
An explosive account of the food we eat today

Craig Sams

Our own livelihoods are at risk – from the food we eat. These
are original, stimulating, mini-essays about what is wrong with
our food today, and about the greatest challenge of the new
century: how to produce enough food without further
damaging our health, the environment and vulnerable
countries. Just like *The Little Earth Book*, this is pithy, yet
intellectually credible, wry yet deadly serious.

Extracts from the book:

• In the UK alone 25,000,000 kilos of pesticides are sprayed on
food every year

• In 2001 the WTO fined the EU $120 million for suggesting
that US meat imports should label the presence of hormone
residues

• Aspartame is a neurotoxin that probably causes as much brain
damage as mobile phone use

• 300,000 Americans a year die of obesity

• Research indicates that MSG is a contributing factor in
Alzheimer's disease

• Globally, the market for organic food in 2001 exceeded $20
billion

The Little Food Book £6.99
www.fragile-earth.com

THE LITTLE MONEY BOOK

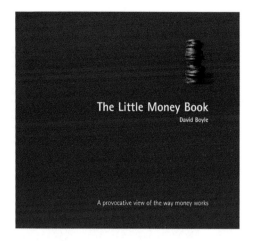

The Little Money Book

David Boyle

A provocative view of the way money works

This pithy, wry little guide will tell you where money comes from, what it means, what it's doing to the planet and what we might be able to do about it. A fascinating read. Money and the complex system that makes it work is a man-made product that we invented and yet, like Frankenstein, it has us all in its grip. From the poorest to the wealthiest we worry about money.

Extracts from the book:

• What is real? Most bank notes when they are withdrawn are now melted down into plastic pellets and used to make garden wheelbarrows

• Every citizen of Alaska gets an annual dividend from the Alaskan Permanent Fund, of about $2,000 a year, paid out from oil revenues

• IMF programmes in Tanzania led to the loss of 40 per cent of their forests between 1980 and 1993

• A group of Nicaraguan workers have been indicted on charges carrying 10 years in jail because they asked for a $0.08 increase per pair of jeans they assemble, which US retailers sell at $30 each

• Green taxes – The recent Irish tax of 10p per plastic carrier bag has cut their use by over 90 per cent

• In 1193 England agreed to pay Germany £66,000 in silver, then a quarter of their GDP, to ransom Richard the Lionheart. It has never been paid in full

The Little Money Book £6.99
www.fragile-earth.com

SIX DAYS

Celebrating the triumph of creativity over adversity

The inspiring and moving story of the making of the stained glass Creation window at Chester Cathedral by a woman battling with Parkinson's disease.

"Within a few seconds, the tears were running down my cheeks. The window was one of the most beautiful things I had ever seen. It is a tour-de-force, playing with light like no other window ..."

Anthropologist Hugh Brody

In 1983, Ros Grimshaw, a distinguished designer, artist and creator of stained-glass windows, was diagnosed with Parkinson's disease. Refusing to allow her illness to prevent her from working, Ros became even more adept at her craft, and in 2000 won the commission to design and make the Creation Stained Glass Window for Chester Cathedral.

Six Days traces the evolution of the window from the first sketches to its final, glorious completion as a rare and wonderful tribute to Life itself: for each of the six 'days' of creation recounted in Genesis, there is a scene below that is relevant to the world of today and tomorrow.

Extracts from Ros's diary capture the personal struggle involved. Superb photography captures the luminescence of the stunning stained glass, while the story weaves together essays, poems, and moving contributions from Ros's partner, Patrick Costeloe.

Available from Alastair Sawday Publishing £12.99

ORDER FORM UK

All these books are available in major bookshops or you may order
them direct. **Post and packaging are FREE within the UK.**

		Price	No. copies
French Bed & Breakfast	Edition 8	£15.99	
French Hotels, Châteaux & Inns	Edition 3	£13.99	
French Holiday Homes (Jan 04)	Edition 2	£11.99	
Paris Hotels	Edition 4	£9.99	
British Bed & Breakfast	Edition 8	£14.99	
British Hotels, Inns & Other Places	Edition 5	£13.99	
Bed & Breakfast for Garden Lovers	Edition 2	£14.99	
British Holiday Homes	Edition 1	£9.99	
London	Edition 1	£9.99	
Ireland	Edition 4	£12.99	
Spain	Edition 5	£13.99	
Portugal	Edition 2	£8.99	
Italy	Edition 3	£12.99	
Europe with courses & activities	Edition 1	£12.99	
India	Edition 1	£10.99	
Morocco	Edition 1	£10.99	
The Little Earth Book	Edition 3	£6.99	
The Little Food Book	Edition 1	£6.99	
The Little Money Book	Edition 1	£6.99	
Six Days		£12.99	

Please make cheques payable to   Total £ _____ _____
Alastair Sawday Publishing

Please send cheques to: Alastair Sawday Publishing,
The Home Farm Stables, Barrow Gurney, Bristol BS48 3RW.
For credit card orders call 01275 464891 or order directly
from our web site **www.specialplacestostay.com**

Title   First name   Surname
Address

Postcode   Tel

If you do not wish to receive mail from other like-minded companies,
please tick here ☐

If you would prefer not to receive information about special offers on our books,
please tick here ☐

MOR1

REPORT FORM

Comments on
existing entries
and new
discoveries

If you have any comments on entries in this guide, please let us
have them. If you have a favourite house, hotel, inn or other
new discovery, please let us know about it.

Existing Entry: Name of property _____
Book title: _____
Entry no: _____ Edition no: _____
Date of visit: _____

New
recommendation: _____
Name of property: _____
Address: _____
_____
Postcode: _____
Tel: _____

Comments: _____
_____
_____
_____

Your name: _____
Address: _____
_____
_____
Postcode: _____
Tel: _____

Please send the completed form to:

Alastair Sawday Publishing,
The Home Farm Stables, Barrow Gurney, Bristol BS48 3RW
or go to www.specialplacestostay.com and click on 'contact'.

MOR1   Thank you.

BOOKING FORM

À l'attention de:
To: _____

Date: _____

Madame, Monsieur
Veuillez faire la réservation suivante au nom de:
Please make the following booking for (name):

_____

Pour	*nuit(s)*	*Arrivée le jour:*	*mois*	*année*
For	night(s)	Arriving: day	month	year
		Départ le jour:	*mois*	*année*
		Leaving: day	month	year

Si possible, nous aimerions   *chambres, disposées comme suit:*
We would like   rooms, arranged as follows

À grand lit	*À lits jumeaux*
Double bed	Twin beds
Pour trois	*À un lit simple*
Triple	Single
Suite	*Appartement*
Suite	Apartment

Nous sommes accompagnés de   *enfant(s) âgé(s) de*   *ans.*
Avez-vous un / des lit(s) supplémentaire(s), un lit bébé; si oui, à quel prix?
We are travelling with   children, aged   years. Please let
us know if you have an extra bed / extra beds / a cot and if so,
at what price.

Nous aimerions également réserver le dîner pour   *personnes.*
We would also like to book dinner for   people.

Veuillez nous envoyer la confirmation à l'adresse ci-dessous:
Please send confirmation to the following address:

Nom: **Name:** _____

Adresse: **Address:** _____

_____

Tel No: _____   E-mail: _____

Fax No: _____

la réservation — Special Places to Stay

AUTHENTIC DISCOVERIES

Researching and selecting the Special Places for this book was mostly done by Authentic Discoveries managed by Alain Bonnassieux, co-editor of the guide.

With six years of solid experience in the field, Alain and his team offer tailor-made itineraries, outside the usual tourist rounds, in direct contact with Moroccan culture. Be it on foot, by mountain bike or on horseback, Authentic Discoveries organises round trips using non-polluting and silent means of transport and communication, so as better to appreciate nature and the inhabitants. Overnight stops are mostly in guest houses, inns and small hotels of character. Comfortable bivouacs can be organised in extremely remote places.

The guides who accompany the visitors come from the areas visited and are eager that the rest of the world learn more about their regions, lifestyles and cultural traditions.

The mission of the agency is to foster discoveries and exchanges within the context of sustainable tourism, far from the consumerist approach that is so rarely respectful of local cultural values and interests.

AUTHENTIC DISCOVERIES

Working closely with MC Voyages of Marrakech, Authentic Discoveries has selected places that abide by an ethical charter that ensures respect for local heritage, ecology and culture. Most of these places have committed to donating a portion of their profits to local development projects (literacy, irrigation, waste processing etc) linked to national NGOs. The details of this charter, the list of places participating in this programme and the itineraries offered by the company can be sent to you upon request to:

Authentic Discoveries
19 Derb el Ferrone
Riad Laarouss
Marrakech Medina

Tel: +(212) 44 376 055 or 61 245 238
Fax: +(212) 44 376 054 or 44 432 461
E-mail: a.discoveries@hotmail.com
Web: www.authenticdiscoveries.com

QUICK REFERENCE INDICES

Hammam, Spa, Well-being

These places offer one or more of the following: hammam, spa, massage and beauty treatments, aromatherapy, relaxation.
Tangier & the Rif • 1 • 3 • 6 • Rabat to Safi • 11 • 13 • 15 • Essaouira-Medina • 20 • 27 • 28 • Essaouira Region • 34 • 35 • 36 • 38 • 40 • Marrakech-Medina • 43 • 44 • 45 • 46 • 47 • 48 • 49 • 50 • 54 • 55 • 56 • 58 • 60 • 63 • 64 • 65 • 66 • 71 • 72 • Marrakech-New Town • 82 • Marrakech-Palmeraie • 85 • 86 • 87 • 89 • 91 • 93 • 94 • 95 • Marrakech-Country • 42 • 78 • 96 • 97 • 102 • 105 • Middle Atlas • 107 • 108 • Fès • 115 • 116 • 117 • 118 • 119 • 120 • 121 • 122 • High Atlas • 125 • 130 • 132 • 135 • Souss Valley & Anti Atlas • 136 • 137 • 139 • 141 • 142 • 143 • 145 • Oasis Valleys • 152 • Kasbah Route • 154 • 155 • 160

Tennis

These places have a tennis court available.
Tangier & the Rif • 1 • Marrakech-Country • 42 • Marrakech-Palmeraie • 84 • 86 • 94 • 95 • Marrakech-Country • 96 • 103 • Middle Atlas • 106 • Fès • 115 • High Atlas • 125 • The Souss Valley & the Anti Atlas • 136 • Oasis Valleys • 146

Meeting Room

These places can cater for mostly small residential meetings.
Tangier & the Rif • 1 • 2 • 3 • 4 • 6 • 7 • 9 • 10 • Rabat to Safi • 11 • 13 • 14 • 15 • 19 • Essaouira-Medina • 23 • 30 • Essaouira Region • 34 • 36 • 40 • Marrakech-Medina • 44 • 45 • 46 • 48 • 49 • 50 • 53 • 54 • 56 • 57 • 58 • 60 • 64 • 68 • Marrakech-New Town • 75 • 82 • Marrakech-Palmeraie • 84 • 86 • 87 • 88 • 90 • 91 • 92 • 93 • Marrakech-Country • 42 • 96 • 97 • 100 • 105 • Middle Atlas • 106 • 111 • 113 • Fès • 115 • 116 • 118 • 119 • 122 • High Atlas • 126 • 129 • 130 • 131 • Souss Valley & Anti Atlas • 136 • 139 • 140 • 141 • 142 • 143 • 145 • Oasis Valleys • 146 • 150 • 151 • 152 • 153 • Kasbah Route • 155 • 158 • 159

500Dh or under for two

These places have a double or twin room for two for 500Dh or under per night. Check when booking.
Tangier & the Rif • 3 • 4 • 5 • 6 • 7 • 8 • 9 • Rabat to Safi • 17 • 18 • Essaouira-Medina • 20 • 21 • 22 • 23 • Essaouira Region • 33 •

QUICK REFERENCE INDICES

Lessons, Courses, Demonstrations

Cookery

Arts & Crafts

Painting & Pottery

Olive oil & Argan oil (seasonal): orchard, press, sale

Excursions & Treks

Walking

QUICK REFERENCE INDICES

INDEX - PROPERTY NAME

INDEX - PROPERTY NAME

INDEX - PROPERTY NAME

INDEX - TOWN

INDEX - TOWN

HOW TO USE THIS BOOK

explanations

❶ rooms

Assume all rooms are 'en suite' unless we say otherwise.

If a room is not 'en suite' we say **with separate,** or **with shared bath:** the former you will have to yourself, the latter may be shared with other guests or family members.

❷ room price

The price shown is for one night for two sharing a room. A price range incorporates room/seasonal differences.

❸ meals

Prices are per person. BYO: you may bring your own wine.

❹ closed

When given in months, this means for the whole of the named months and the time in between.

❺ directions

Use as a guide; the owner can give more details.

❻ map & entry numbers

Map page number; entry number.

❼ symbols

See inside back cover for fuller explanation.

sample entry

MARRAKECH–MEDINA

Ryad El Borj
63 Derb Moulay Abdelkader, Derb Dabachi, Marrakech-Medina

Borj means tower. 150 years ago, when Pasha Glaoui owned the whole quarter, one of the liveliest in Marrakech, he built a lookout here to oversee the area. Still the highest view of the whole city, it is magic at any hour, sublime at sunset. The typical dark entrance takes you down five steps then on to the blue patio, whence up to the green first floor then the red terrace – all properly dramatic. When renovating the ryad three years ago, your host was careful to preserve the original décor and almost all the very comfortably furnished rooms have painted or carved ceilings while the great glass-vaulted suite is remarkable value with its big bedroom, sitting room, excellent bathroom and an extra salon that gives onto the patio via a superb moucharabieh screen. Colours are pale and sober, materials are noble cedarwood and finely wrought ironwork, doors are antique, floors are strewn with carpets and leather cushions from the Saharaoui south giving the wonderful exotic feel of being in a *khaima*, a nomad tent; breakfast is superbly generous. Pool, drinks and meals available just 20 metres away.

rooms	5: 4 doubles, 1 suite.
price	600Dh-1,200Dh. Sole occupancy for 8: 17,0000Dh-23,000Dh per week.
meals	Lunch or dinner by arrangement. BYO.
closed	Never.
directions	From Place Jemaâ El Fna take Derb Dabachi (behind Café de France); pass mosque on right then first left; house 30m along on right.

❶
❷
❸
❹
❺

Daniel Ghio
tel +212 (0)44 39 12 23/61 67 59 42
fax +212 (0)44 39 12 23
e-mail ryadelborj@wanadoo.net.ma
web www.ryadelborj.com

Guest house & catered house

❻ entry 68 map 3

❼ ✐ ♿ ♥ 🐾

Also recommended but impossible to re-visit for this guide:

Fort Bou-Jerif, a remote converted fort on the coast about 25km west of Guelmin
Guy Drumont, contactable by fax : +212 (0)48 87 30 39